Frogtown

Frogtown

Photographs and Conversations in an Urban Neighborhood

Wing Young Huie

MINNESOTA HISTORICAL SOCIETY PRESS • ST. PAUL

The Minnesota Historical Society gratefully acknowledges the following donors for their generous support of *Frogtown*:

Major sponsor

The St. Paul Companies

Sponsors

City Pages

Mr. and Mrs. Wing Ying Huie

Target Stores

Minnesota Historical Society Press
St. Paul

Designed and typeset by Patrick Dooley

Composed in Helvetica typefaces with Helvetica Compressed display type on QuarkXPress 3.3 for Macintosh

Waterless offset printing, duotone producton, and film output by Litho, Inc., St. Paul

Text printed on l00 lb Vintage Velvet Enamel paper

Bound by Midwest Editions, St. Paul

Manufactured in the United States of America
10 9 8 7 6 5 4 3 2 1

International Standard Book Number 0-87351-335-5 (cloth)
0-87351-336-3 (paper)

∞ The paper used in this publication meets the minimum requirements of the American National Standard for Information Sciences—Permanence for Printed Library Materials, ANSI 739.48-1984.

Library of Congress Cataloging-in-Publication Data

Huie, Wing Young, 1955–
Frogtown: photographs and conversations in an urban neighborhood / Wing Young Huie.
p. cm.
ISBN 0-87351-335-5. — ISBN 0-87351-336-3 (pbk.)
1. Frogtown (Saint Paul, Minn.)—Social life and customs—Pictorial works. 2. Saint Paul (Minn.)—Social life and customs—Pictorial works. 3. Ethnology—Minnesota—Saint Paul—Pictorial works. I. Title.
F614.S4.H85 1996
977.6'581053'0222—dc20 96-8838
CIP

Contents

A Frogtown Introduction

Frogtown is a neighborhood of roughly one square mile that is situated just northwest of the Minnesota State Capitol in St. Paul. Local lore suggests that its name was inspired more than a century ago by the indigenous population of frogs in its swampy land. Some, however, believe that the name was an ethnic slur aimed at the French-Canadians, early residents among the German, Irish, Polish, and Scandinavian immigrants who arrived during the second half of the nineteenth century.

In the 1970s the population began changing from mainly white and middle class to ethnically diverse and sometimes very poor, as older residents either died or moved away, making way for an influx of minorities who were drawn to the area by its aging but affordable housing stock.

For years most of what I knew about Frogtown came from newspaper headlines about the latest homicide/crack house raid/prostitution sweep. Those cautionary stories, though, did not deter me from my weekly outings to any of the numerous Asian restaurants on the southern edge of the neighborhood, along University Avenue, just minutes from my downtown studio.

This mile-long strip of Southeast Asian noodle houses and markets—interspersed with businesses such as the Ebony Lady Hair Studio and Butch's Custom MC, a Harley-Davidson supply shop—was like a second home to me after my move to St. Paul in 1982. Much of my life has been spent either working or eating in restaurants like the ones on University Avenue. My father and two oldest brothers owned Chinese restaurants, and there was a time when I believed I would, too.

I have always been curious about places where Asians gather. When in a new city, my first impulse is to find out where the local "Chinatown" is, so I can be ensured of a comforting meal. But it's not just the appeal of the food. I went to Hong Kong—where I bought my first camera—when I was twenty, and the sight of so many Chinese in one place was both bizarre and fascinating. In Duluth, where I grew up, there were very few. It seemed that the only people around who looked like me were either relatives or restaurant employees.

Most of the Asians on University Avenue and within Frogtown are recently arrived Laotian Hmong refugees.

In fact, the Hmong are the area's largest ethnic minority, comprising about a quarter of the population.

I have the conceit that I can guess the ethnic background of Asians I see. I think I can tell if a Chinese is ABC (American-born Chinese) or FOB (fresh off the boat). But most people can recognize the Hmong. The older women—wearing a distinctive, festive clash of multi-patterned blouses and pants, their hair in tidy buns—especially stand out. The men, even when they wear Western-style clothes, have a certain wandering-peasant demeanor that seems out of place on the city streets; it is as though their souls have not yet emigrated from the mountains of Laos. They look, I imagine, not unlike my own parents and siblings must have appeared, years ago, on the streets of Duluth.

My father, Joe Huie, was seventeen when he arrived in Duluth in 1909 from China's Guangdong province. He was nearly penniless at the start. But after years of sixteen-hour days washing dishes, plus an hour studying English (as he often reminded us), he worked his way up as waiter, cook, and restaurant manager. During those years he made several journeys back to China. On one such trip, in 1933, he met and married my mother. He stayed for nine years, fathering my four brothers and sister. He returned to Duluth in 1951 with my two oldest brothers to open Joe Huie's Cafe. The rest of the family followed in 1954. A year later I was born.

Being the youngest of six children and the only one born in the United States, I grew up comfortable in my surroundings. We lived in a small, two-story brick house on what is known as "the central hillside," the closest thing Duluth has to an inner-city neighborhood. There were just a handful of blacks in my area, most of whom I knew from playing basketball. We were the only Chinese family in the neighborhood, and I was the only Asian kid in school, until the tenth grade when another boy arrived—from where I don't know. Curiously, I always avoided him.

Although I was the sole Asian in my circle of friends, I was rarely reminded of that fact. It's not as though I grew up with a mirror in front of me. Indeed, I think that for much of my childhood I forgot that I looked different. My role models and interests were the same as those of my friends. And somehow I kept the consciousness of my family life and the world outside my home separate, so that at times my own family seemed exotic to me.

My parents were not greatly concerned about my knowing or keeping Chinese traditions, except for holidays such as Chinese New Year. On those occasions, my mother would make me pray with her in front of our makeshift household altar, decorated with fruit and incense. The only times I spoke Chinese were at home with her, and those became fewer as I grew older. By the time I was fifteen, my broken Chinese had become barely comprehensible; this did not seem to bother either of my parents. Like most immigrant parents in America, their main concern was that their children do well in their adopted country.

After returning from my trip to Hong Kong, I took a photography course at the University of Minnesota, Duluth, and considered becoming a photography major. But like many college students in the wake of Watergate, I decided to become a reporter instead. I moved to the Twin Cities, enrolled in the journalism program at the University of Minnesota campus there, and graduated in 1978. During the next two years I took photography workshops led by Frank Gohlke and Garry Winogrand.

Before long I found freelance work writing and taking pictures for local publications. The idea for one of my first articles came to me on a walk through an unfamiliar middle-class neighborhood. Very curious about what went on behind the shuttered windows of those ordinary facades, I hit on a ploy to gain me entrance: I would knock on doors and ask residents to photograph their "most prized possession." To my surprise, many people invited me in and readily complied with my odd request. (That tactic only worked in the city. In the suburbs I never got past the welcome mat.)

Another idea I had was to photograph a neighborhood with a diverse ethnic mix. The Twin Cities were rapidly becoming less the "land of the Vikings" and, increasingly, home to a variety of nationalities and cultures—African American, Native American, Vietnamese, Hmong, and Latino. I was intrigued by the notion of finding out what kinds of interaction, or lack of it, were going on among people of disparate backgrounds who, in the early 1990s in some metropolitan neighborhoods, lived next door to each other.

The thought of photographing Frogtown itself did not occur to me at first; my experience of it was restricted to University Avenue. I was vaguely aware of the neighborhood's boundaries and of the fact that there weren't any "Welcome to Frogtown" signs to clue me in to its official whereabouts. When I had on occasion driven through parts of it, something about the way people glared made me glad I was in a car. One beautiful spring afternoon in 1993, however, bolstered by the weather and an especially satisfying meal at the New French Saigon Restaurant, I decided to take a walk into Frogtown.

What I noticed first were the boarded-up houses that made the area appear desolate. But there also was a familiar feel to it. In many ways it resembled the neighborhood where I grew up. The houses were of the same era, built around the turn of the century. But many of the ones here were badly in need of repair, their yards littered with debris. There were a few well-kept homes, ones whose idyllic flower gardens and quaint lawn ornaments made them look out of place.

For several blocks I didn't see anyone. It seemed as though everyone was hiding. But then I turned a corner and was struck by the sight of a mélange of families, all on the same block—Asian, black, and white—out on their respective porches enjoying the day. And there were children everywhere, spilling out from the curbless sidewalks onto the street. Then I saw a nun in a full white habit, walking through this jumble of life like an angel, or an aberration. It was intoxicating to witness such an exotic mix in such commonplace surroundings. I felt as though I had discovered a strange new territory. It reminded me of a line from a movie whose title I have forgotten: "You don't have to travel around the world to see the gamut of human experience. It's on any city block, if you look closely enough." I decided then to make Frogtown a photographic project.

At first, however, I found it all too intimidating. I spent a few weeks just walking around without a camera. People looked at me suspiciously. The first person to say hello was a prostitute. She got angry when I told her I was a photographer and not a customer. I made a flustered retreat to the café latté confines of Grand Avenue, just a mile away, feeling safe and stupid.

The following week I was back in Frogtown, with my camera. The first guy I walked up to was mowing his lawn. He invited me in for a beer. From his walled-in backyard he proudly showed me his private view of the one-hundred-year-old algae-green steeple and clock of the Church of St. Agnes bell tower, the tallest structure in Frogtown. He had framed his private view by trimming the branches of an obstructing tree to a conforming inverted-V shape. "In all the years I've lived here," he said, "I've never known why it rings two or three minutes after the hour. But it always does."

He told me he had lived in Frogtown for eighteen years but that since the 1992 Los Angeles riots he had experienced a great deal of hostility. "If you're a white guy, you catch it heavily out here," he said. "I'm just extremely lucky that I haven't been shot or killed or beat up. I don't walk around here unless I'm heavily armed. I'm more prejudiced now than when I was a kid. See, I grew up in an all-white neighborhood in northeast Minneapolis, and if you saw a black person, he was on his way to work, driving through. I don't think I'm a racist, but maybe I am. I mean, you can only deal with so much shit."

Several days later I photographed a white sixteen-year-old who was contemplating moving in with his pregnant girlfriend. Though he had grown up in Frogtown, he spoke about it as if it were a war-torn country from which he wanted to escape. He told me about the frequent gunshots and the prostitutes whose catfights on the corner outside his room kept him up nights. He pointed out the crack houses on his block and related his confrontations with gangs. He also talked about a Hmong family who lived across the street. "I've never seen them leave their yard," he said. "There's one guy, he goes to work and comes home. The rest of the family, they lock themselves in the yard and just sit there. You wonder what the hell do they think is going on? I mean, I feel sorry for them. This is America, you know. You should be able to walk around the block without getting harassed or getting your ass kicked."

Many residents I met, however, lived in Frogtown by choice and felt that the press had given the area an undeserved reputation. One woman told me she had purposely moved to Frogtown so that her children could grow up in a diverse atmosphere.

Before long, the routine of asking people if I could photograph them became easier. I met most of my subjects on porches, in the streets and playgrounds, and at church, social gatherings, and backyard barbecues. I frequently gave people pictures I had taken of them. Often they would invite me in, which gave me the opportunity to take more photos.

While the photographic results of several months' walking the streets of Frogtown were encouraging, I nonetheless felt I was just getting to know the area. I started looking for funding, and in October 1993 I received a research grant awarded by the Minnesota Historical Society. My proposal read, in part: "By the end of this project I hope to have a body of photographs and interviews that approaches in variety the myriad realities that coexist in Frogtown."

The following year I received additional grants from the University of Minnesota/McKnight Photography Fellowship Program, the Cultural Collaborations Program of the Minnesota State Arts Board, and FORECAST Public Artworks. The four grants together enabled me to work in Frogtown several times a week for the better part of two years.

Instead of taking a systematic approach, I relied on serendipity to show me where photographs might be made. At first I only went up to those people who seemed approachable. Often they would introduce me to or suggest other people. It was in this circuitous fashion that I came to know Frogtown. The process was hardly a democratic one; and there were certain touchstone people and blocks that I photographed repeatedly.

One of the groups I initially avoided were teenagers who looked like gang members, which to me was anyone wearing a hooded jacket and baggy pants. When I finally managed to meet a few teens through their families, I realized that most were just ordinary kids. As I grew more comfortable with Frogtown, I made it a habit to say hello to everyone I passed on the street. Although many were startled by my greeting, most returned it. I admit that I don't usually greet strangers, but then there are many things that I wouldn't normally do without a camera around my neck.

I don't know what combination of personal traits—curiosity, arrogance, stubbornness, genuine interest, or just an absorption in photography—made me want to intrude on people's lives for the sake of a picture. Not that people necessarily minded that kind of intrusion. In fact, most were flattered by it. And it amazed me what intimate details were offered with that camera lens beckoning.

My approach was straightforward. I appeared matter-of-fact and earnest. I was never pushy and did not press if I was refused an opportunity to photograph. I identified myself as a professional photographer rather than an artist (people were more impressed), and I made it clear that they were doing me a favor by letting me take their pictures. Sometimes I was invited into their homes right away, which to me is as exhilarating as hearing a secret you don't have to keep.

After a while, people on the street were calling me the "picture man," and I felt I could approach anyone with my camera. Although I heard many accounts from residents of shootings and other mayhem, I never felt threatened, heard a gunshot, or witnessed any violent acts.

In addition to taking pictures, I taped more than a hundred interviews with Frogtown inhabitants about their lives and the neighborhood. From these I extracted the remarks that accompany many of the images in this book. Interviewing is in a way much like taking pictures: I don't think you can record what someone says and have it reflect the "truth" of that person any more than you can capture it in one photograph or a hundred photographs. A photograph can be as much a piece of fiction as it is a document of the real world—these realms are separate yet somehow complicitous. Indeed, the most compelling photographs shed light on reality in much the way good fiction does.

In the spring of 1995, having worked in the neighborhood for two years, I displayed my results—173 photographs, some of which were accompanied by quotes from the interviews—in a vacant grass lot at the corner of University Avenue and Dale Street in Frogtown. I had considered various indoor sites in Frogtown but finally decided to have the installation outdoors, where more people could see it.

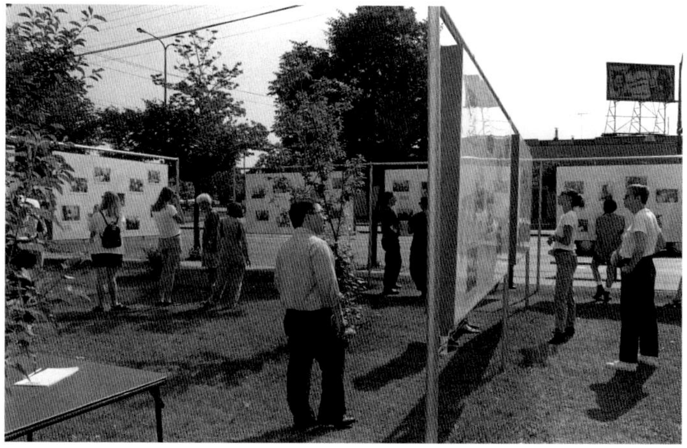

My artist friend Owen Ekman devised an ingenious display solution that would both appeal aesthetically and help the photographs withstand the elements. The eleven-by-fourteen-inch prints were covered with shrink-wrapped clear plastic and pinned to large Styrofoam panels. These were supported by metal rods and wooden frames. Each of the ten panels was attached to galvanized-steel fence posts that were anchored in cement.

The exhibition, *Frogtown: Portrait of a Neighborhood*, was up for a month, twenty-four hours a day. I visited the site daily; there always seemed to be at least a handful of viewers, at no matter what hour. I remember driving by once at 2:30 A.M. and seeing a group of teenagers looking at it. Often there was an interesting mix of neighborhood folk, the art crowd, and suburbanites. People who would never think of coming into the 'hood mingled with people who would never dream of setting foot in a museum.

In a notebook I laid out for viewer comments one person wrote, "I kept seeing people walking by or driving by that could have come right out of the pictures. They are people very unlike me. They are the kind of people, I admit, who I'm normally a little afraid of. Your humanistic art has helped me a little bit to not be afraid."

Another wrote, "Life is different. This is not the same neighborhood where my wife grew up. I'm not sure what I feel. I know this is not where I could live or survive."

When we took the exhibition down, it was 90 percent intact. Six photos had been removed, and some of the Styrofoam panels had sustained punch marks. (You could see the knuckle imprints.) But apart from that, the installation was untouched. It had survived the human elements as well as a couple of severe rainstorms.

Up to the time of the Frogtown exhibition, I had shared the photographs I took for myself only with a few friends. I collected them as one collects seashells; and the act of finding one was as vital as the pleasure of viewing it. Their importance, however, did not go much beyond that. Displaying my photographic obsessions in a public setting as I did in Frogtown, though, awakened me to possibilities for the medium that I had never considered.

People often ask what I think of Frogtown after having spent two years photographing it. I don't quite know how to respond. I'm not sure if what I did helped me understand the place better, or made it more mysterious.

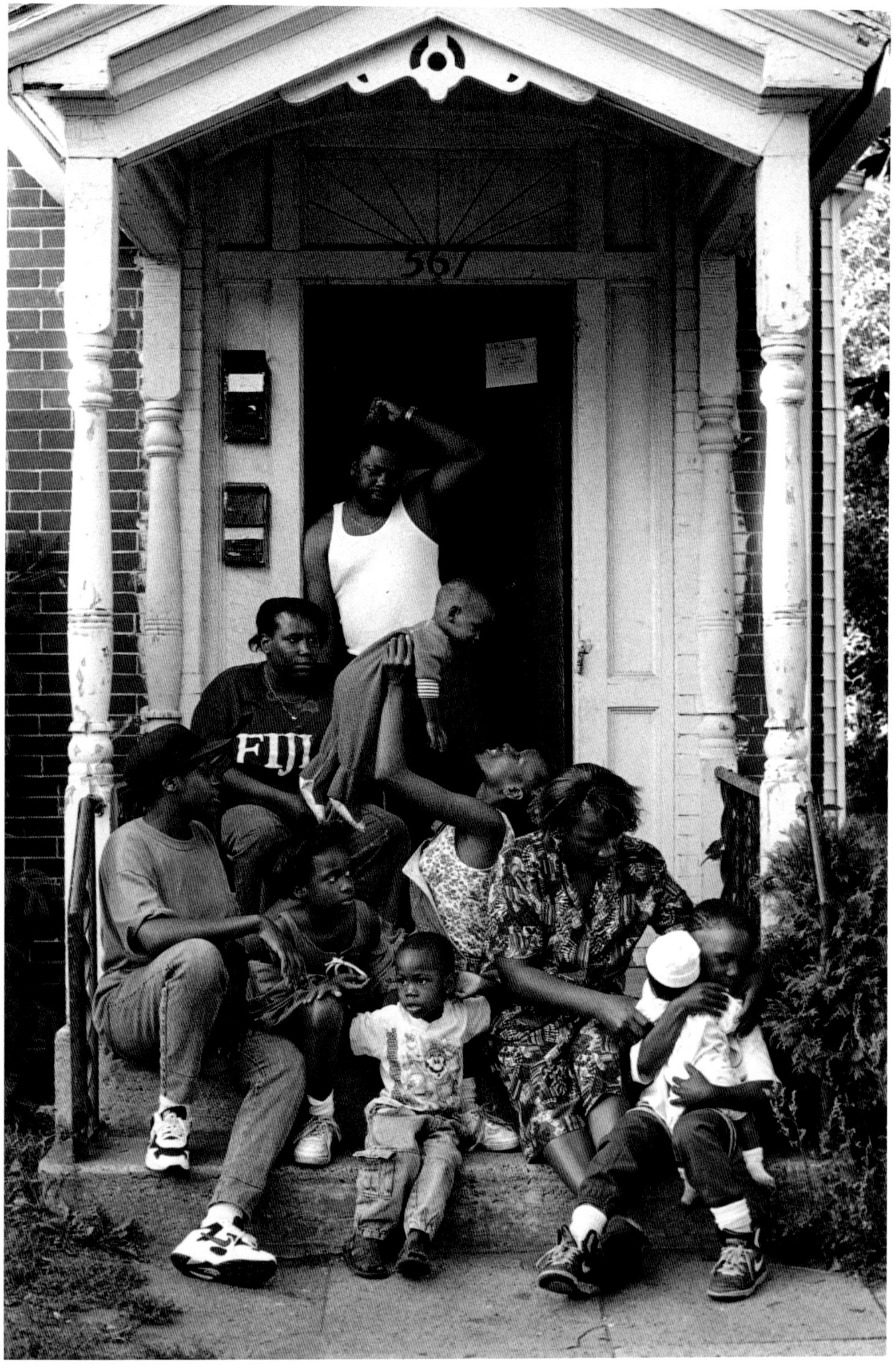
567
FIJI

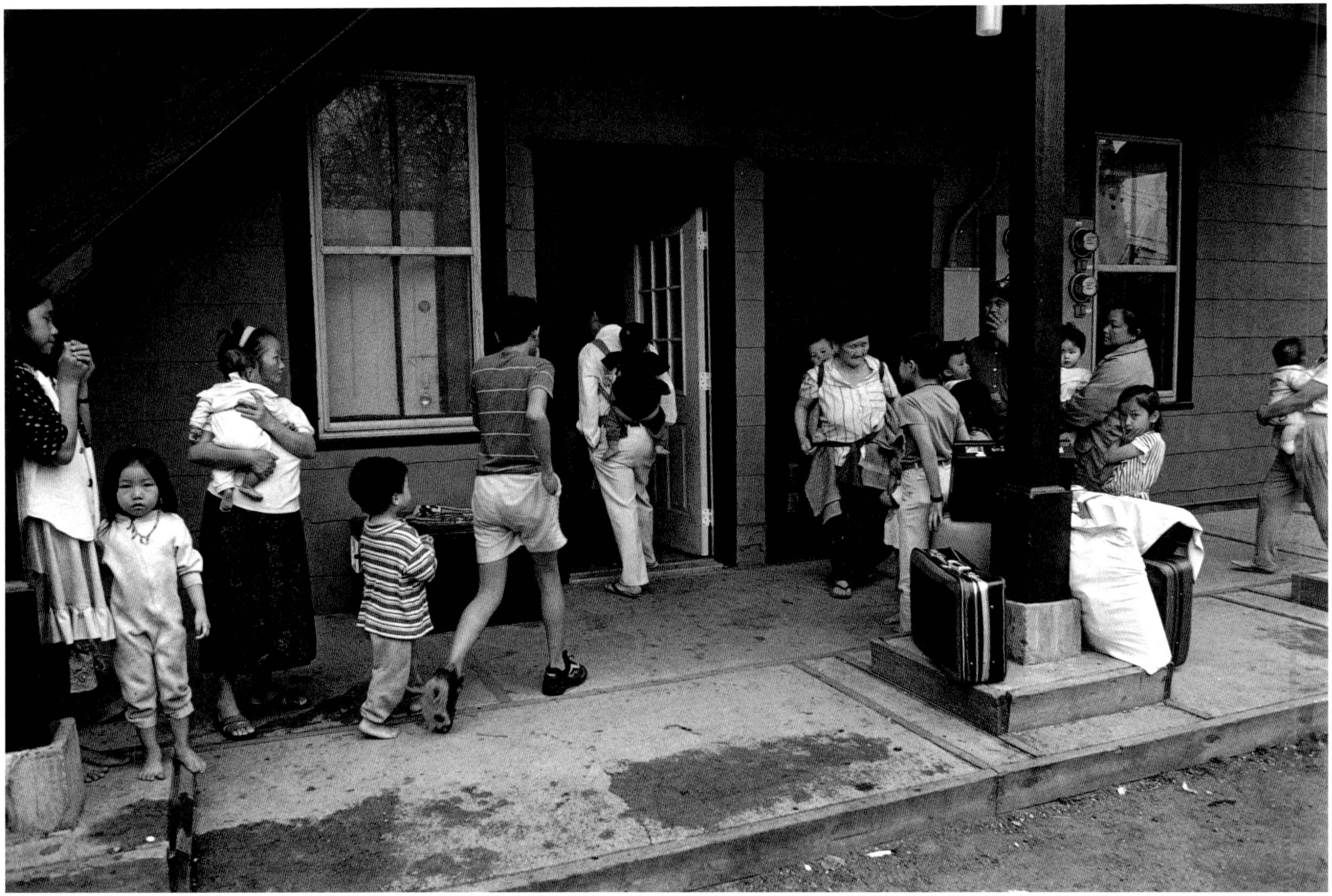

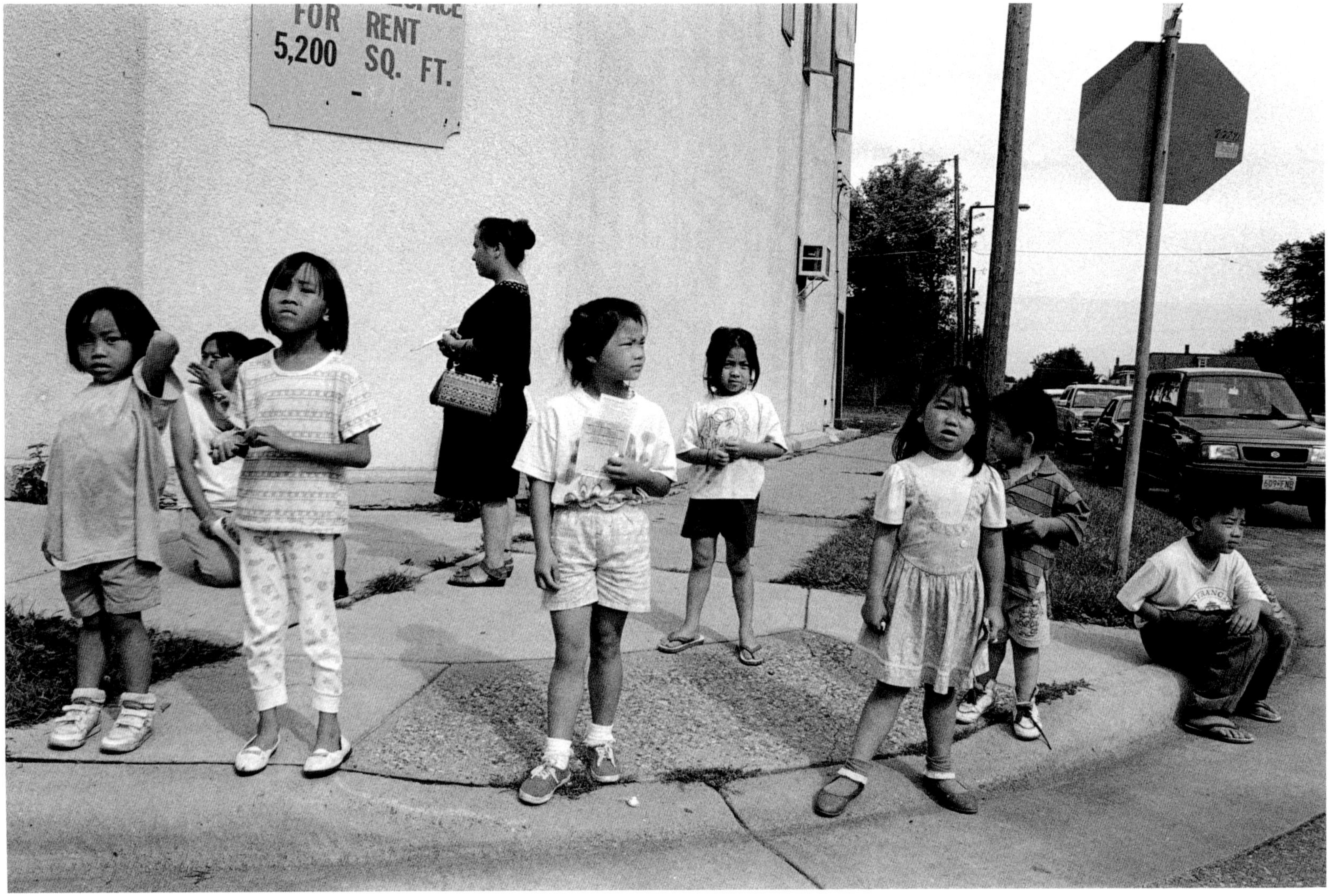
FOR RENT
5,200 SQ. FT.

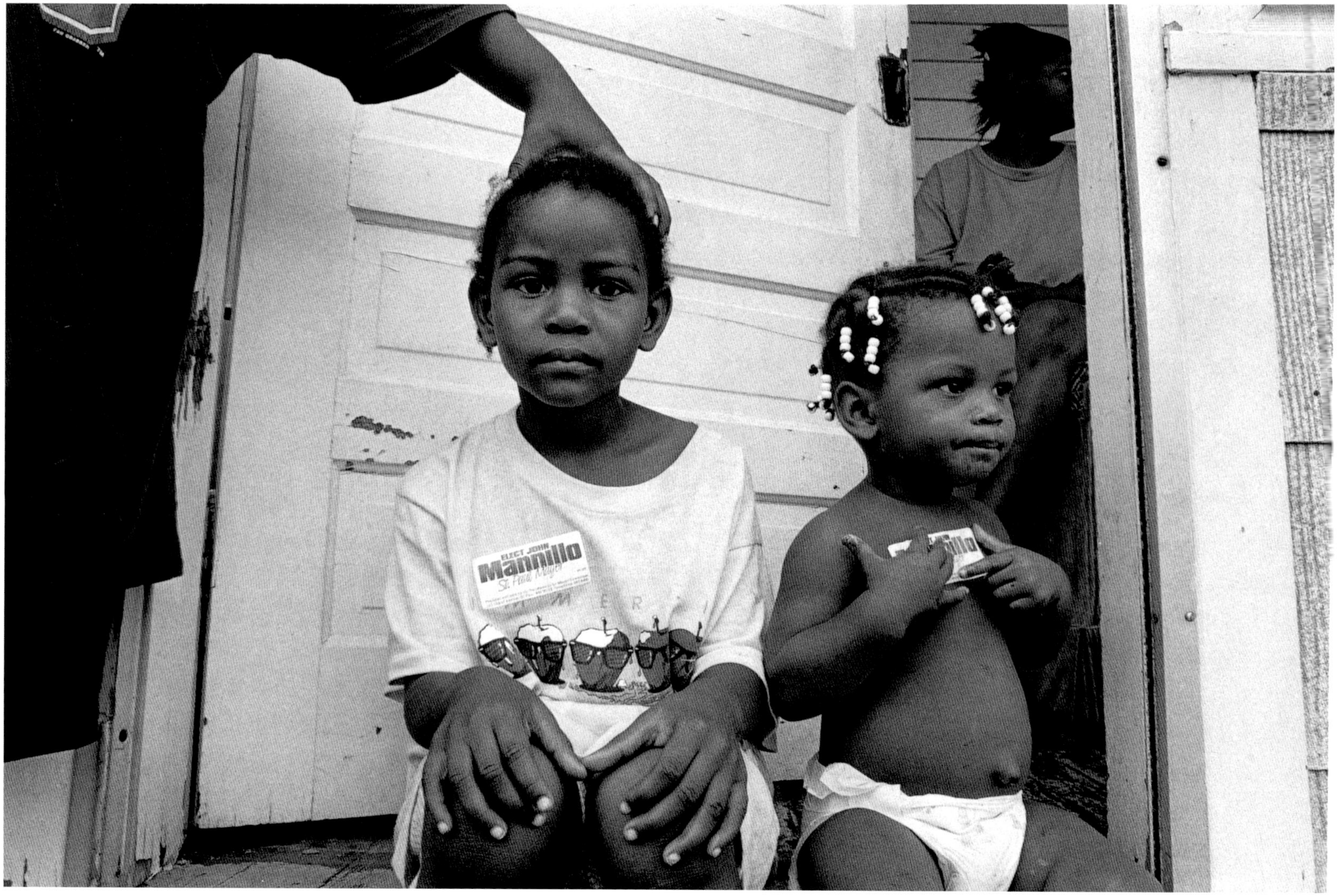
ELECT JOHN
Mannillo

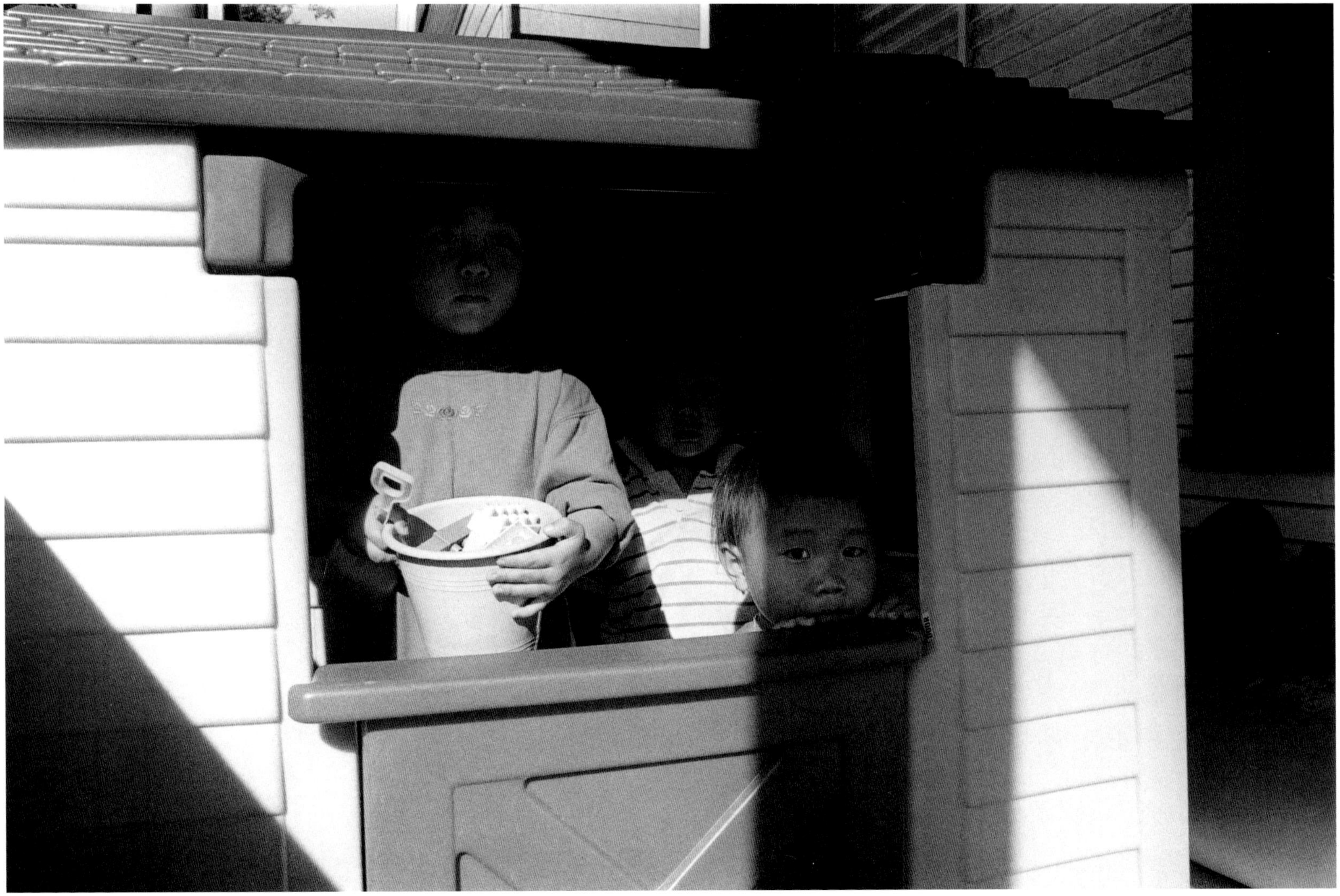

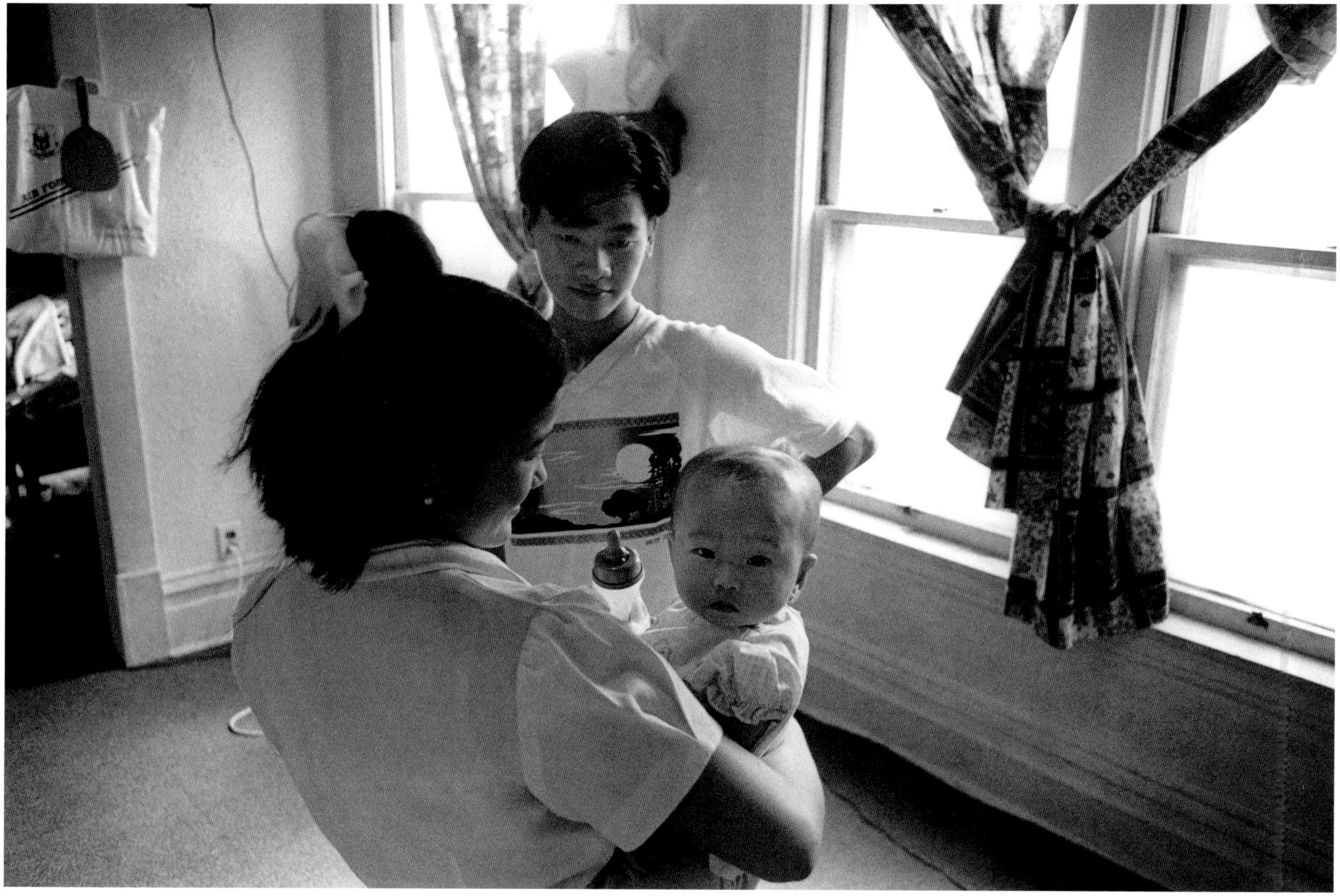

We've been here eight months. We came straight to St. Paul from a camp in Thailand. I met my wife at the camp. We've been married for one year. I was sixteen when I got married. My wife was fourteen. It's common for Hmong to get married at that age and have children.

I'm in the ninth grade at Como Park High School. I'm taking an English writing class and algebra. I do a lot of studying. That's all I do: Go to school and study.

Everything is different here. The snow is not difficult, but the ice is very smooth. Very slippery. Even though it is cold, there is less sickness. We are better off here than in Thailand.

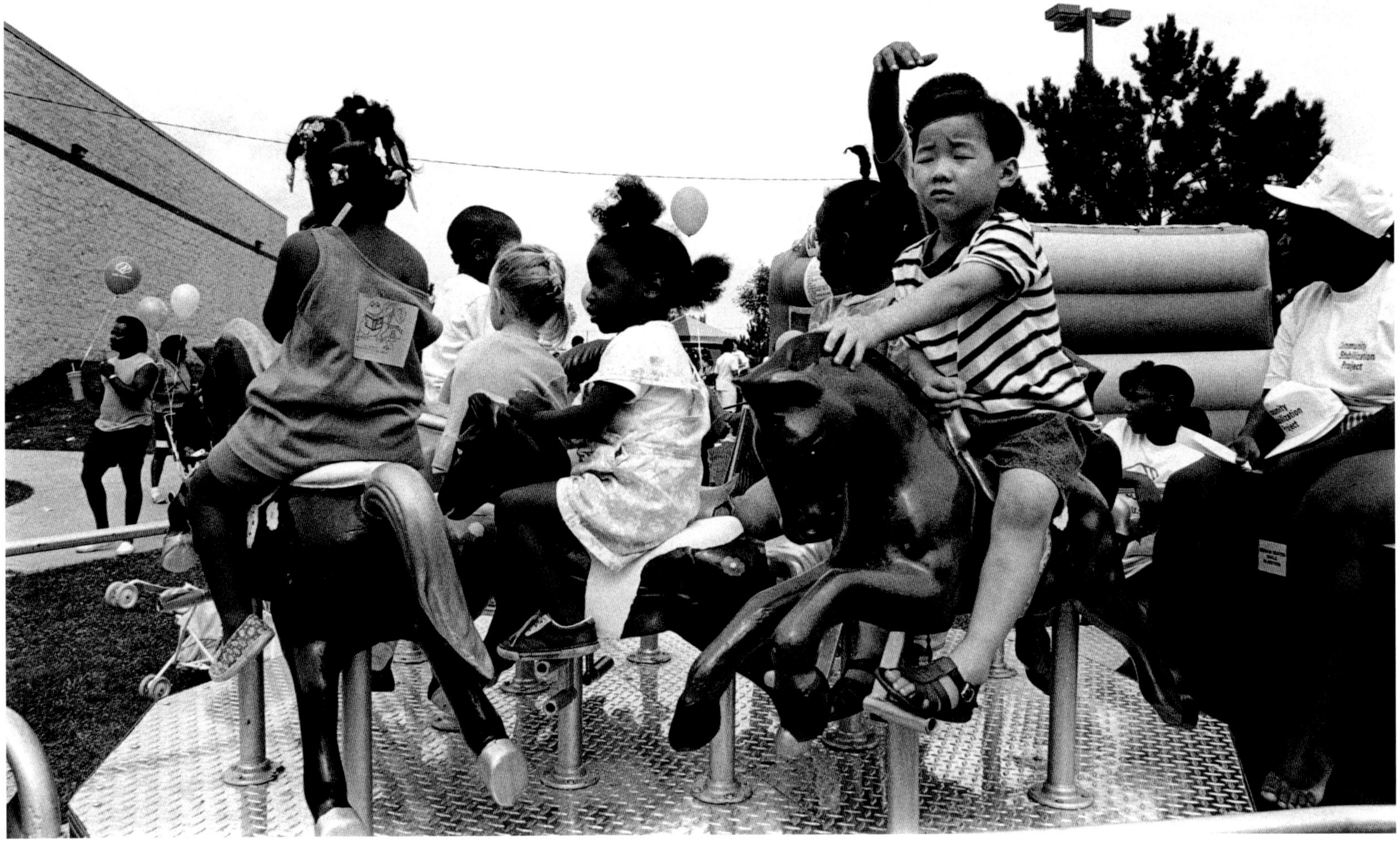

Several years ago we had a man down the block shot right in the street—over his dog. A little girl got shot sitting in her high chair in a drive-by shooting. Same block. So we as a block started taking action. It was quite a process. It took a year for us to get recognized by the police department that we wanted something done. It took a lot of lobbying from certain neighbors on this block. But eventually things got taken care of. Today we have zero crime on this block.

As I drive down the streets I can pretty much tell you what street has got a block club by the way people intermingle with each other. You can see neighbors talking to each other across the fence. Or you'll see a group of them in their yard helping them plant a garden or something. Then some blocks you won't see anybody out. Nobody. Those are blocks that are having a lot of trouble. They're afraid to come out.

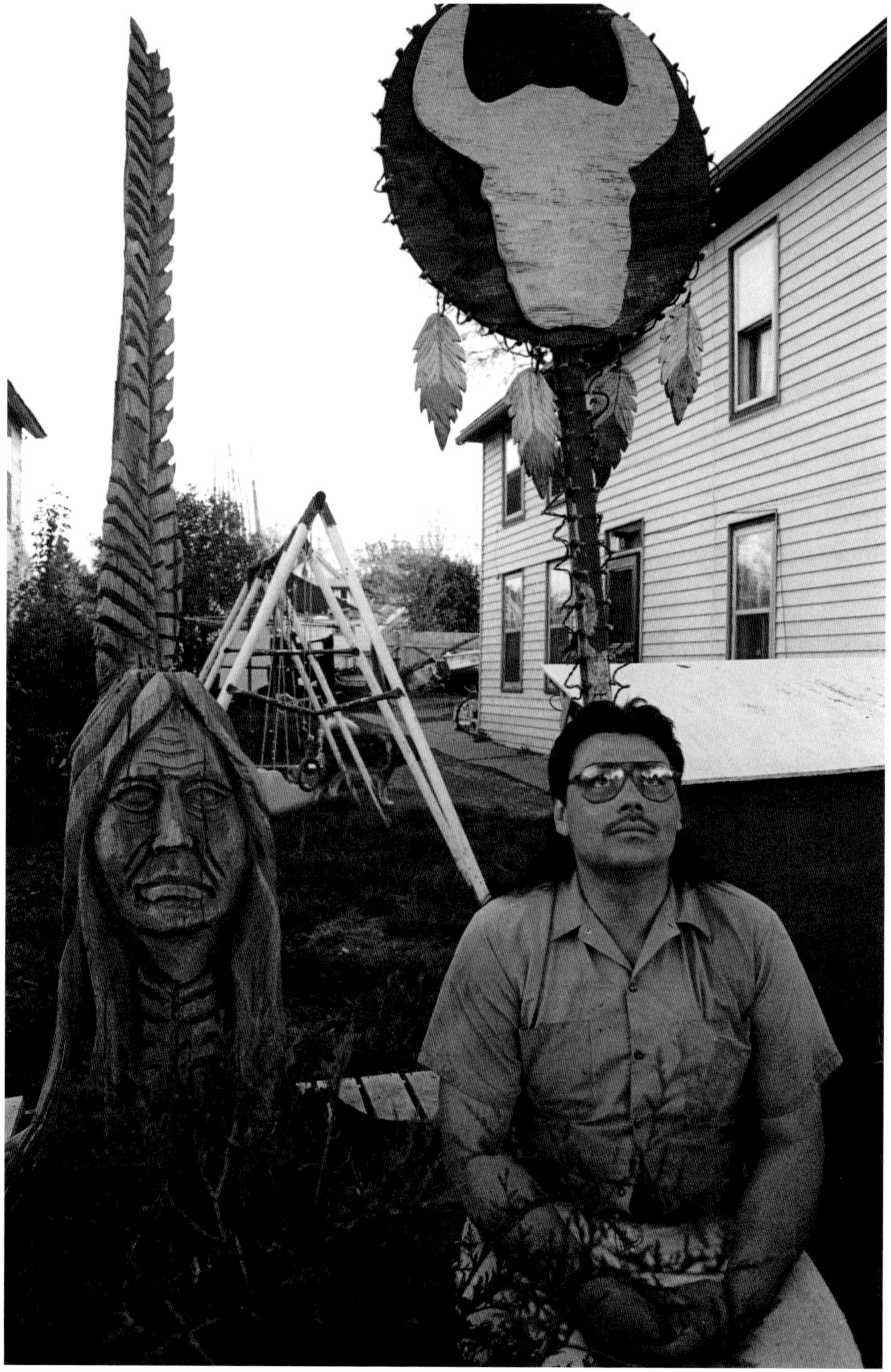

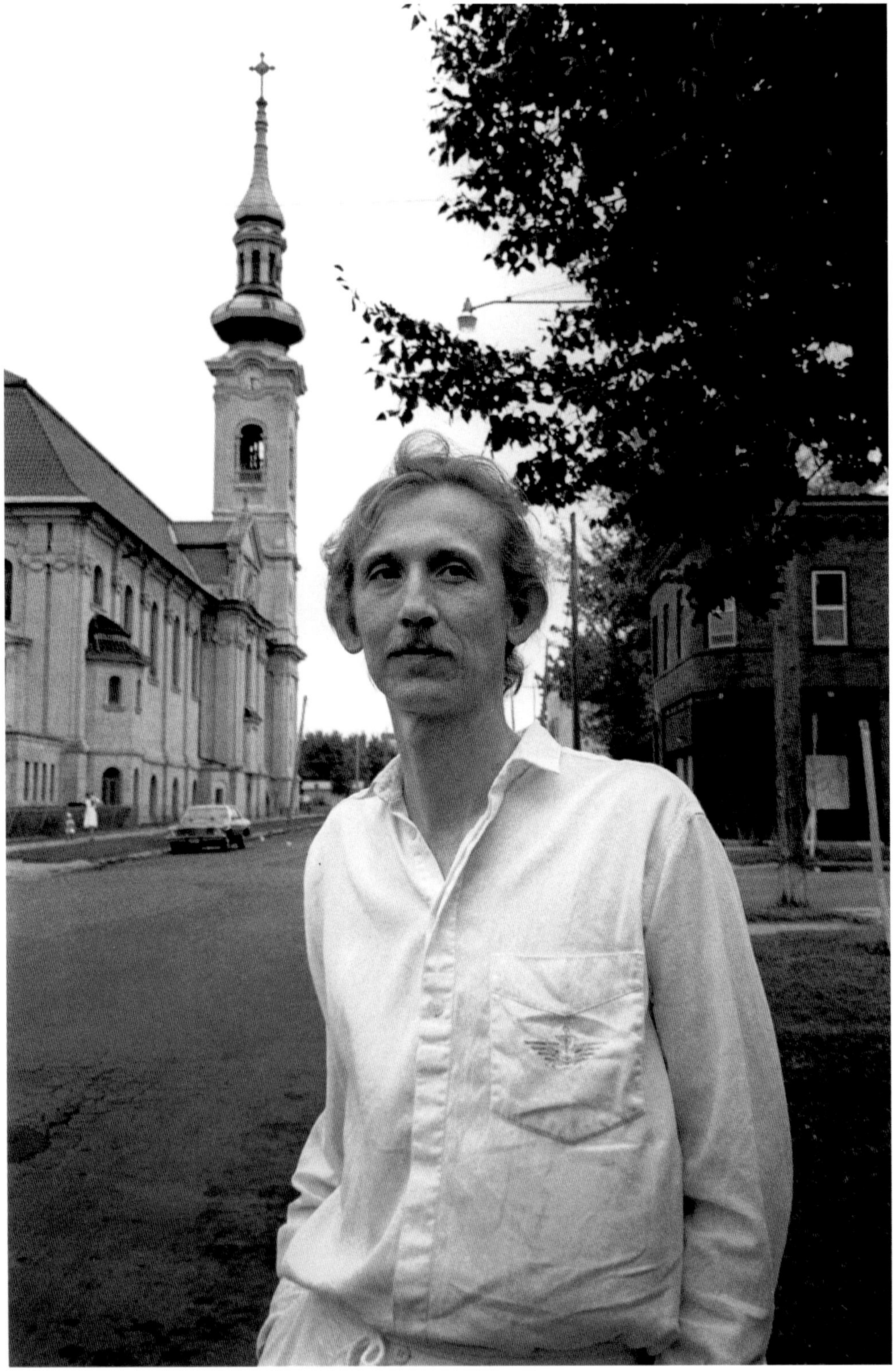

There aren't many neighborhoods like this where you can find such a variety of people living right next door to each other. It's a fairly stirred-up pot. There are some tensions. But it's the kind of place where the experiment of living together has to be carried out. This country has got to grapple with these issues in a way that isn't divisive, that creates an ability for people to really accept each other and work toward something. And this is the kind of neighborhood it has to happen in.

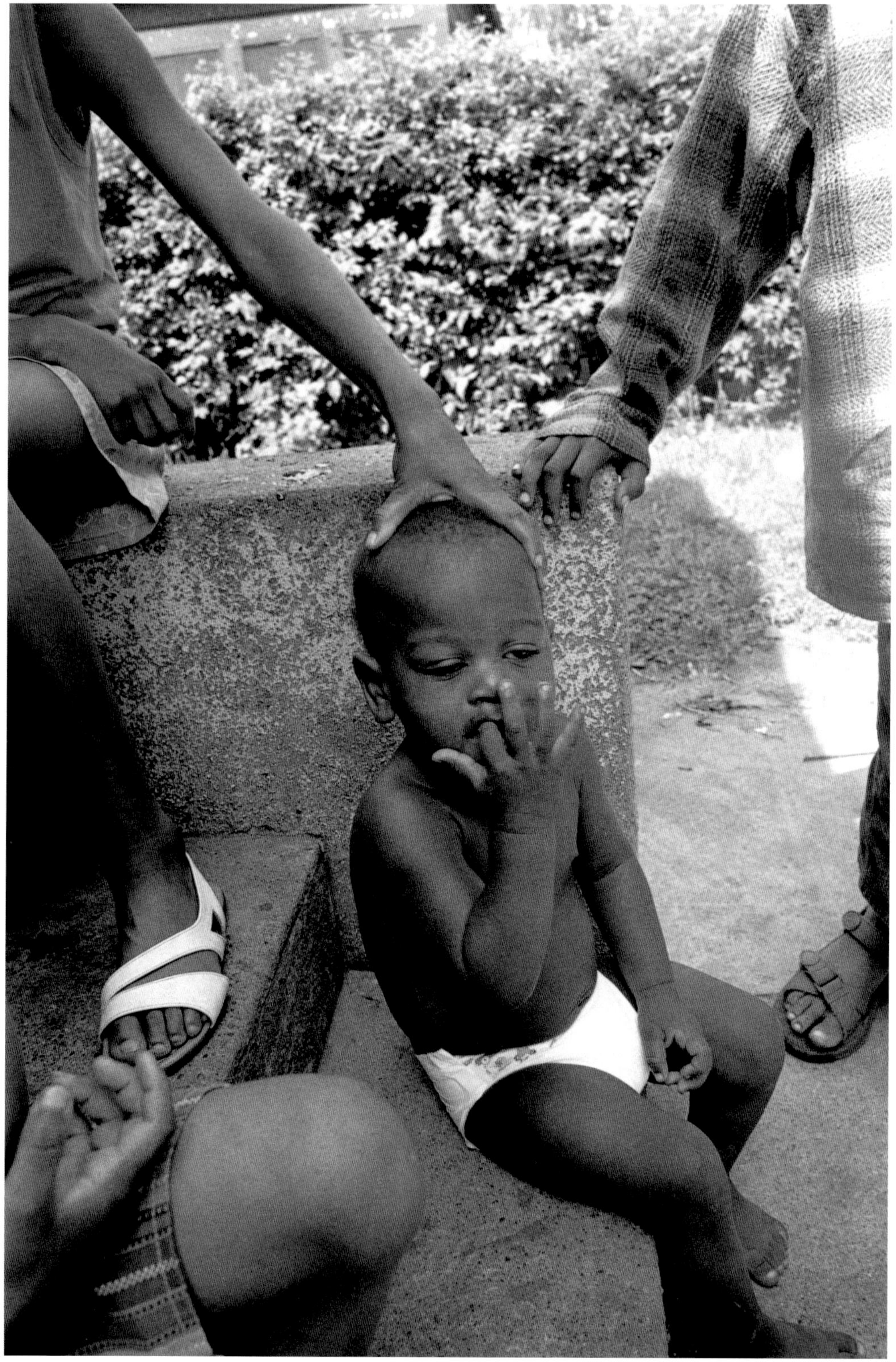

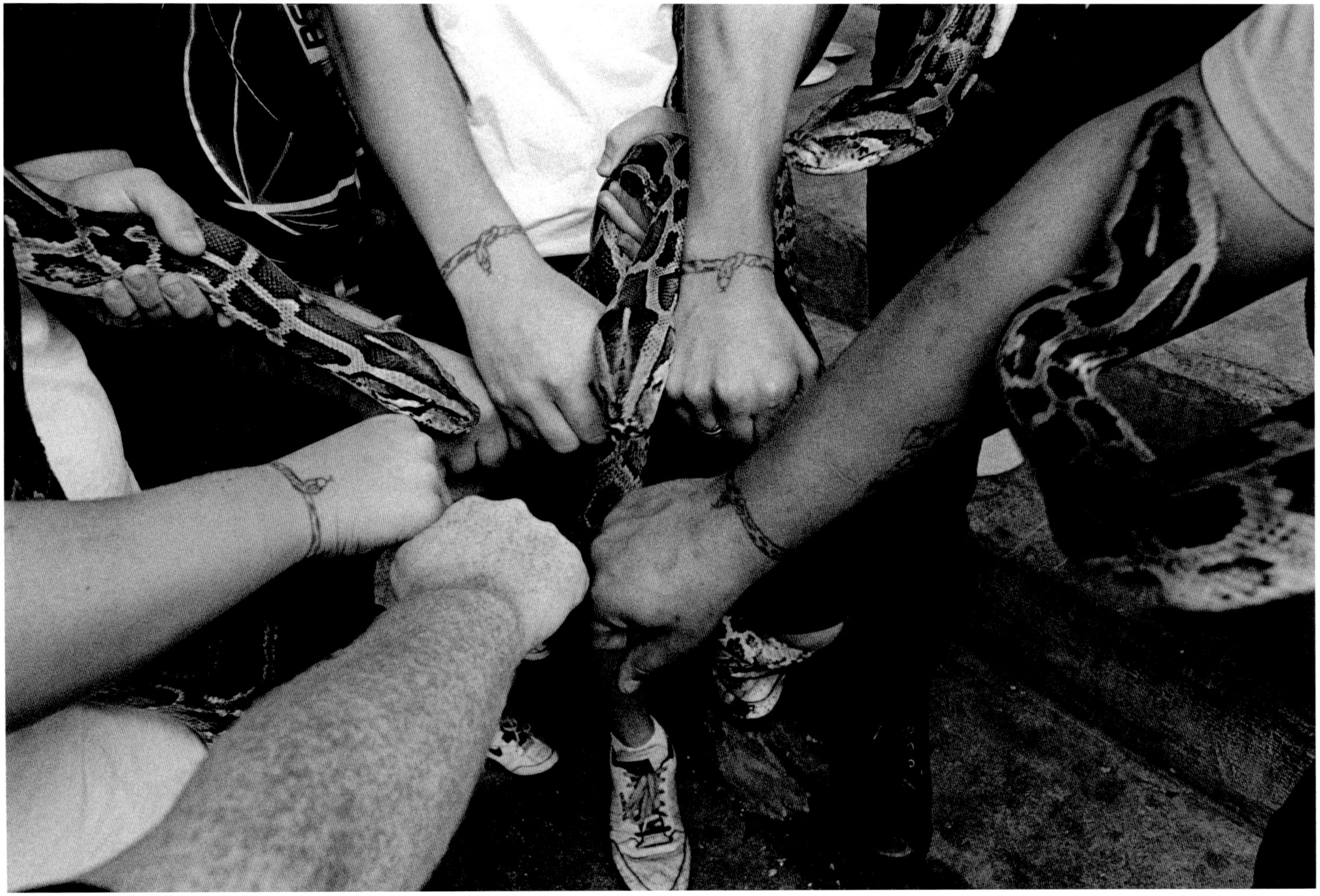

They're like friendship rings. Except you can always get rid of a ring. We're bonded for life.

We call each other "Bubba," you know, like brothers. But we don't want to be confused with the blacks in the neighborhood because they call each other brother and sister. We're not a gang. It's not a race thing. We don't even have a name for our group. We're just really good friends. We don't go out looking for trouble. We just sit here and have fun.

From left to right: Caveman, Hobbit, Face, Chunks, Chief, and Girlie Boy.

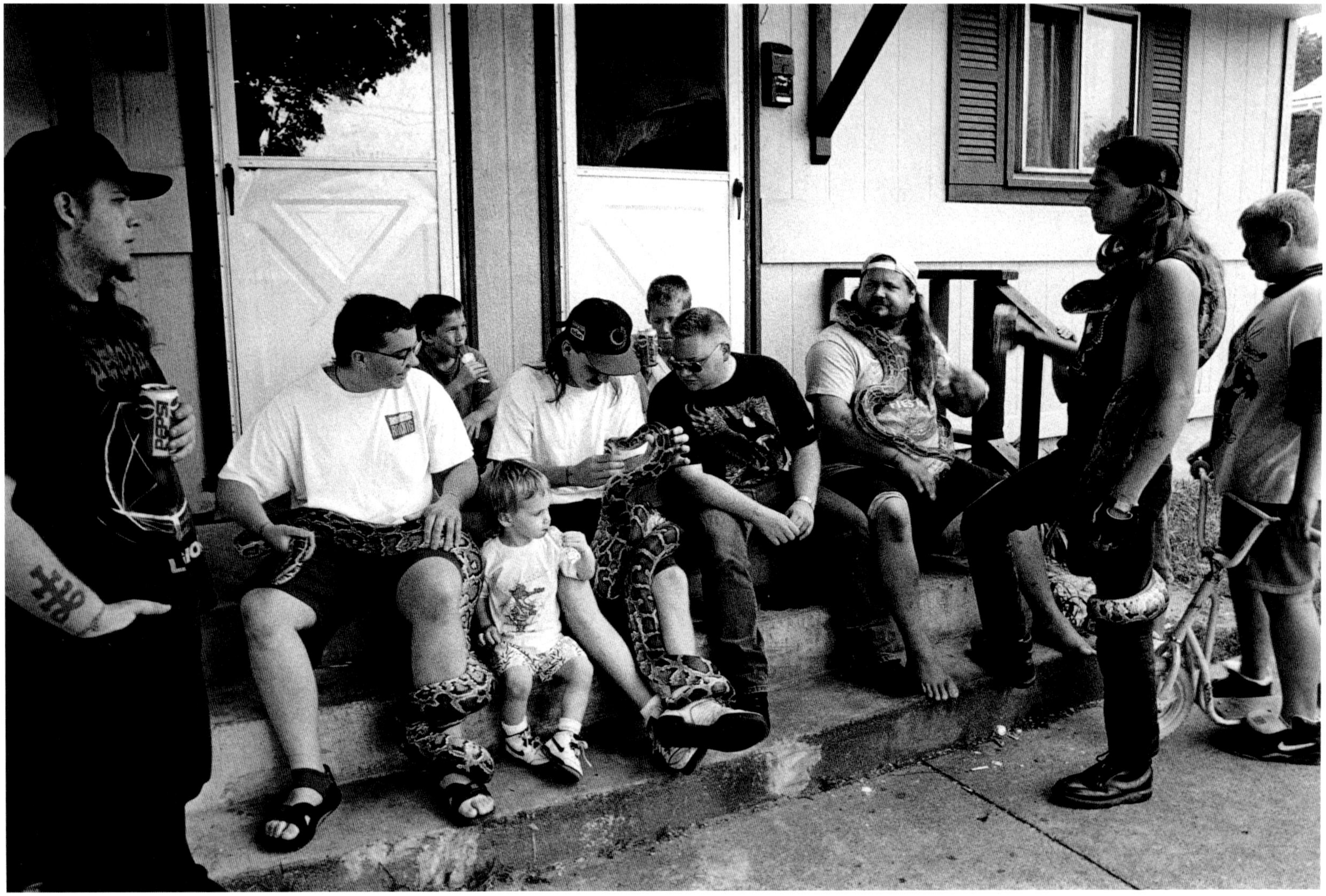

"Church" is one of the first words he was fixated on. He just loves this church. Even though we aren't members there, he insists on coming to the "church porch" almost every day. He'll walk around the whole block with his little hands clasped behind his back, inspecting the premises to make sure everything is to his satisfaction. He looks like he is trying to play the role of monsignor.

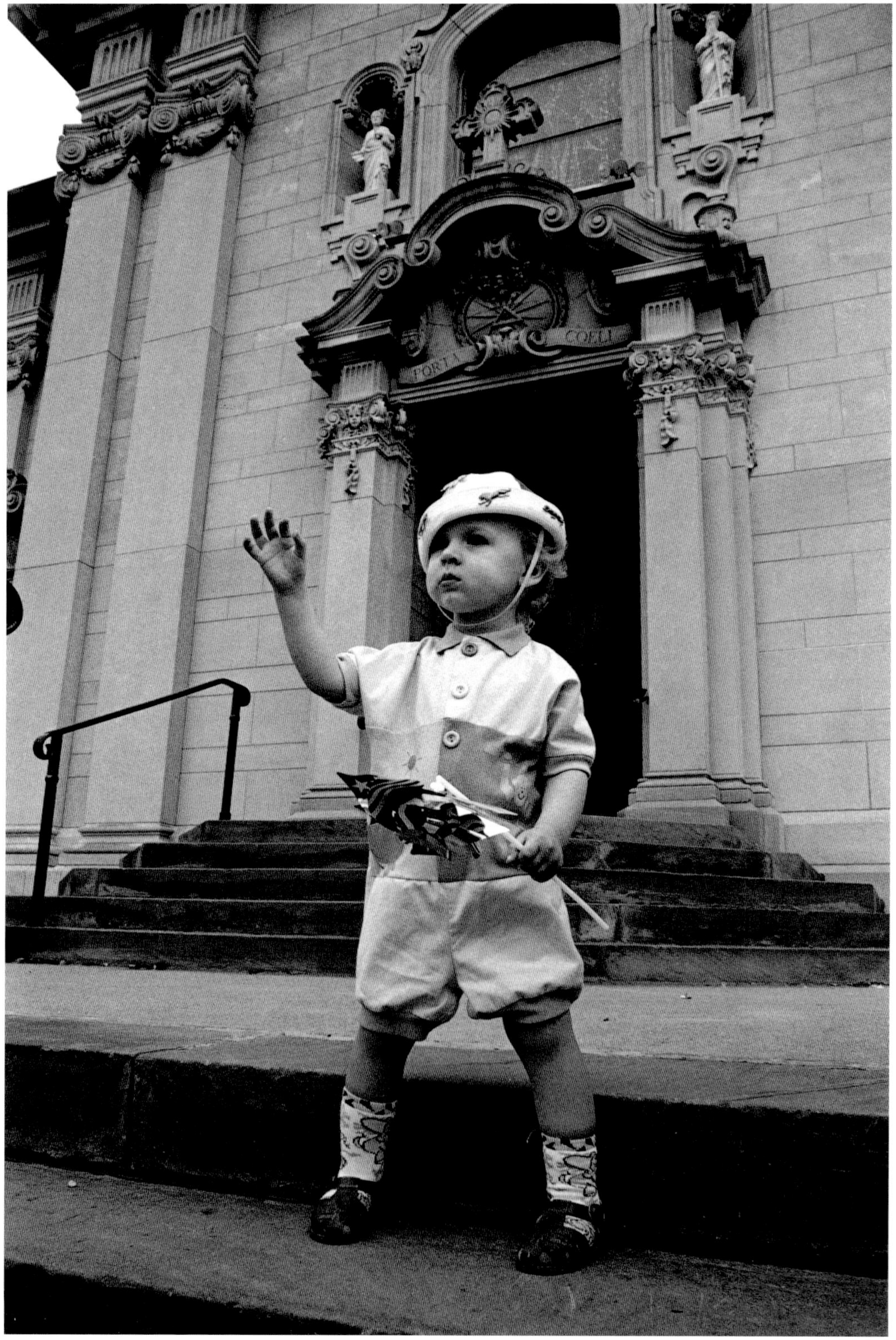

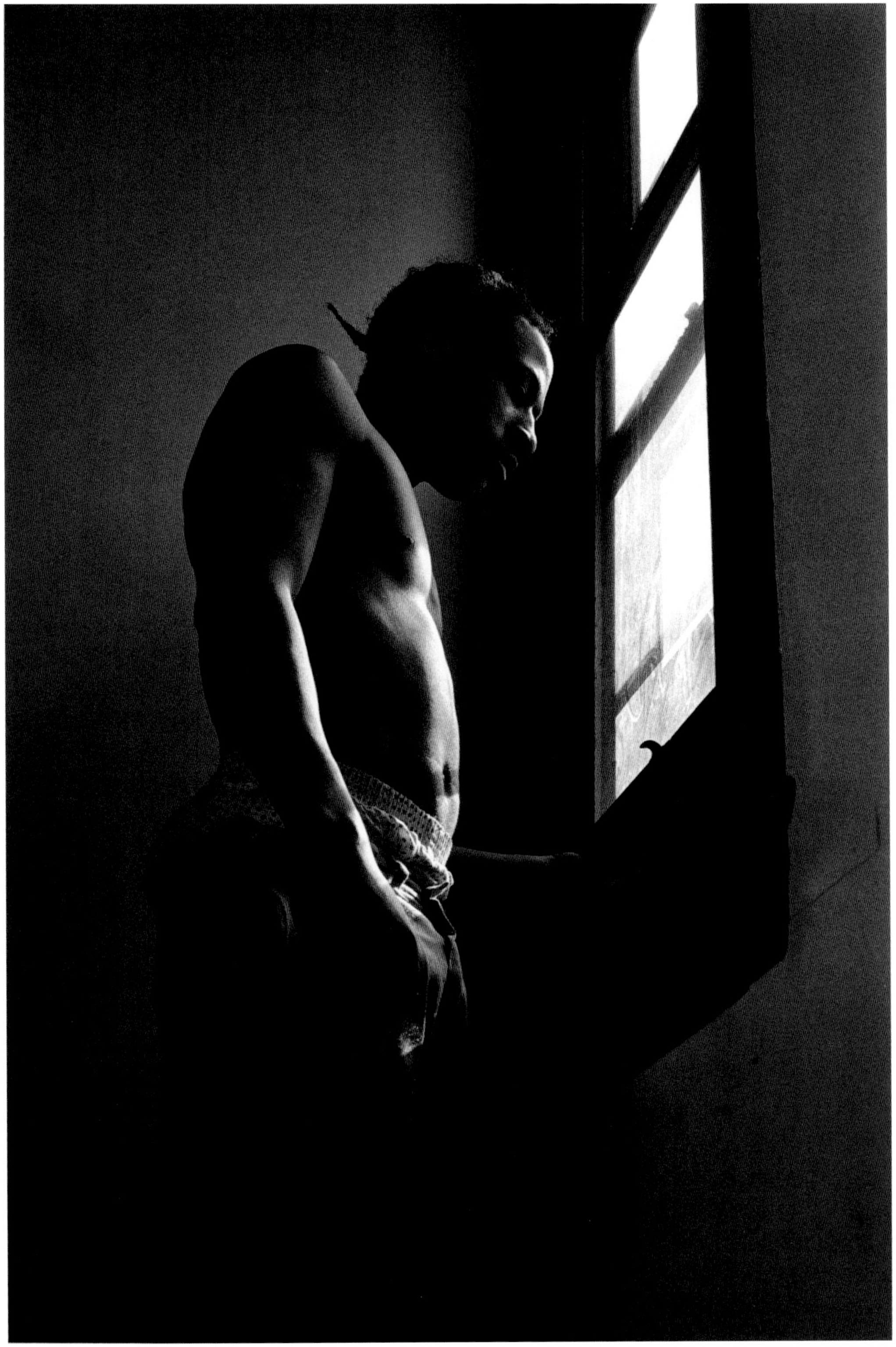

I'm just trying to live, 'cause in this day and age everybody around my age, like seventeen to twenty-five, is getting shot. It's hard to make it out there. That's why I play so much basketball. I used to stay out all night. But if I play basketball all day, then I'll get real tired and just go to sleep. Most of my friends have been in and out of jail, and that's all we do is play basketball. It keeps us out of trouble.

I think the world is going to come to a self-destruct. One person get killed, somebody going to retaliate. Then that person going to retaliate. Then there's going to be a whole lot of retaliation, and it's going to self-destruct. If the countries don't start it first, then it's going to be cities self-destructing.

The police try to get guns off the street. But the more they taking guns off the street, the more guns is coming on the street. They ain't stopping nothing. They think locking someone up helps them to be better. That's making it worse.

I'd like to get a job and take care of my kids. Maybe get a job moving things, 'cause I like lifting. I lift weights. I like being large. I don't like to be a little person.

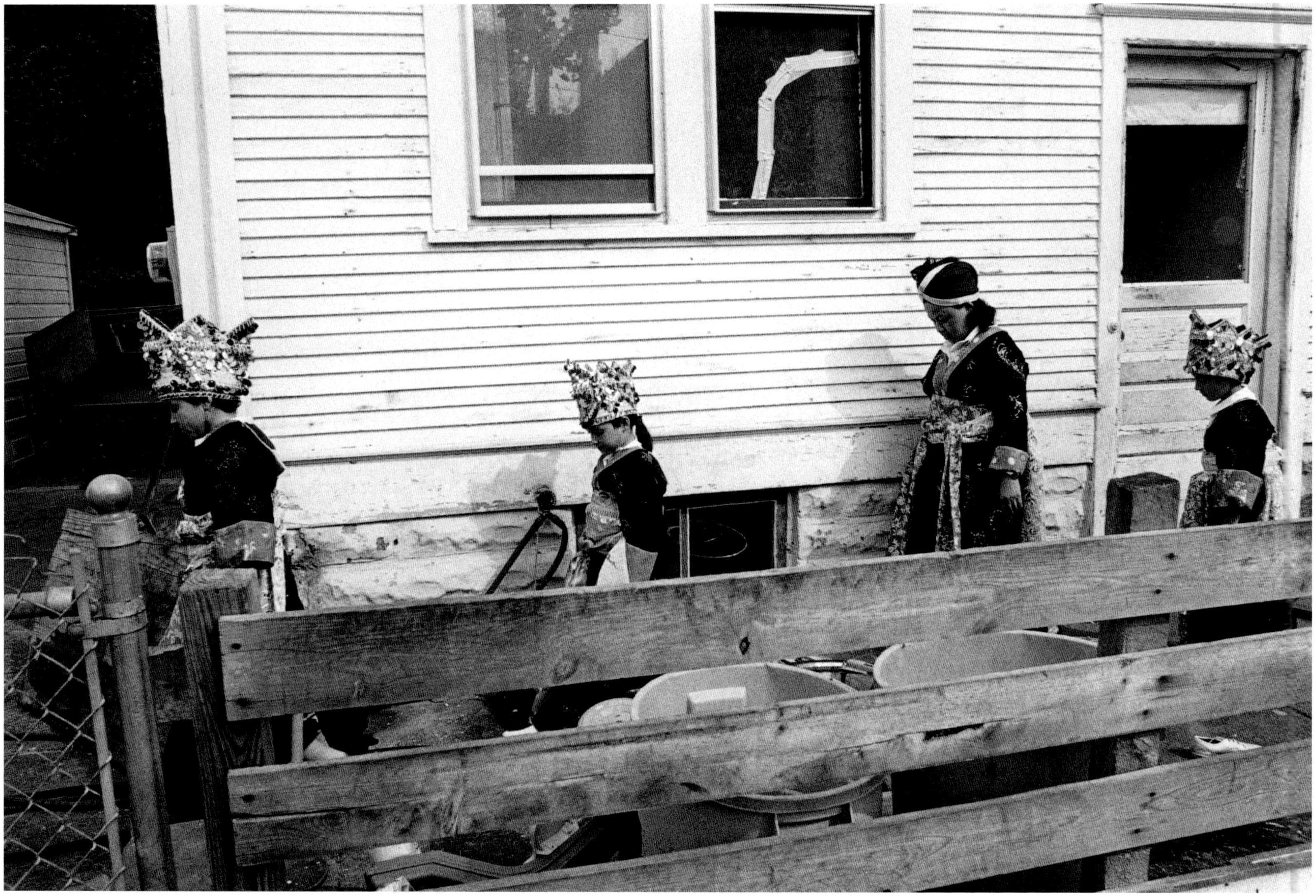

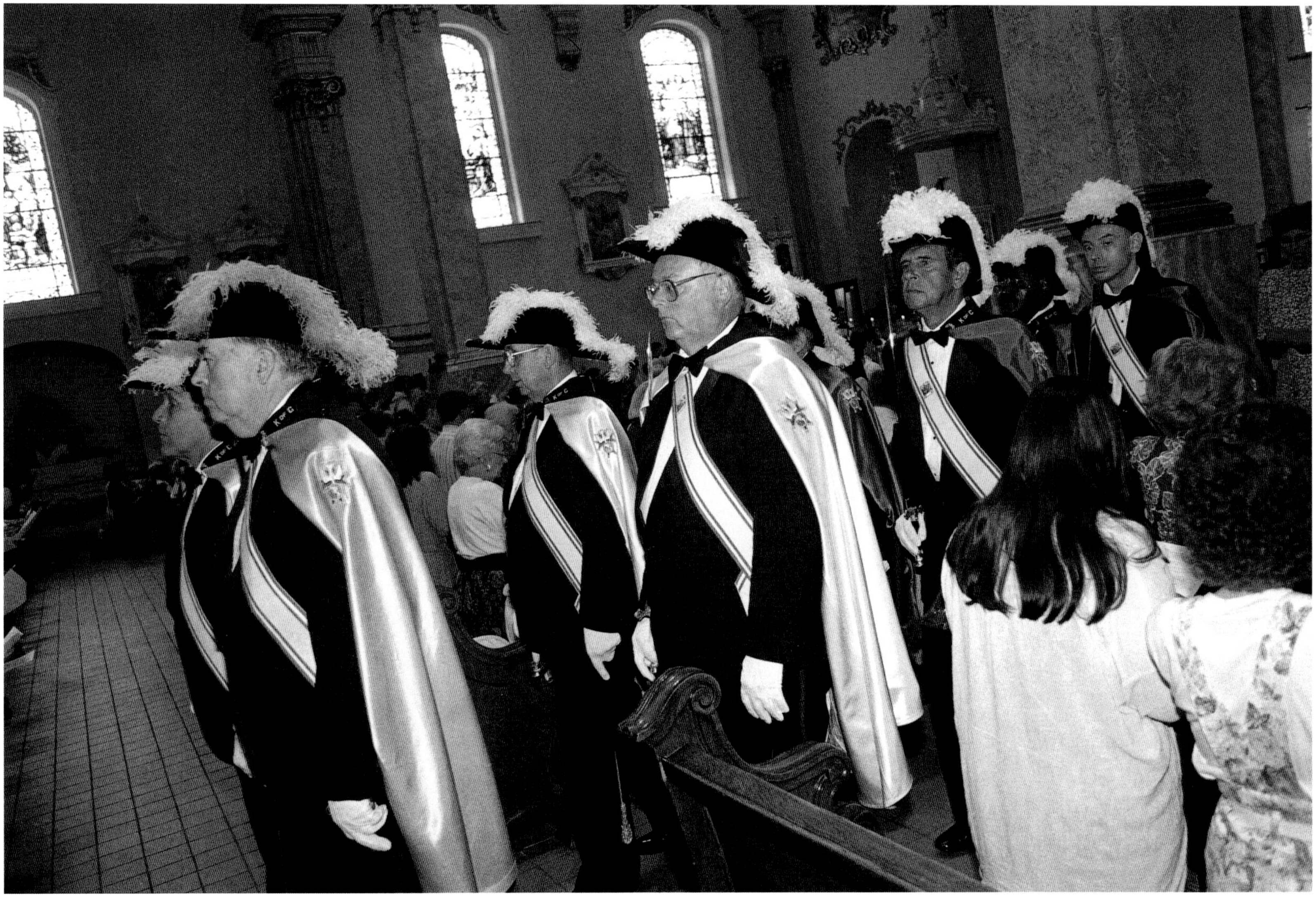

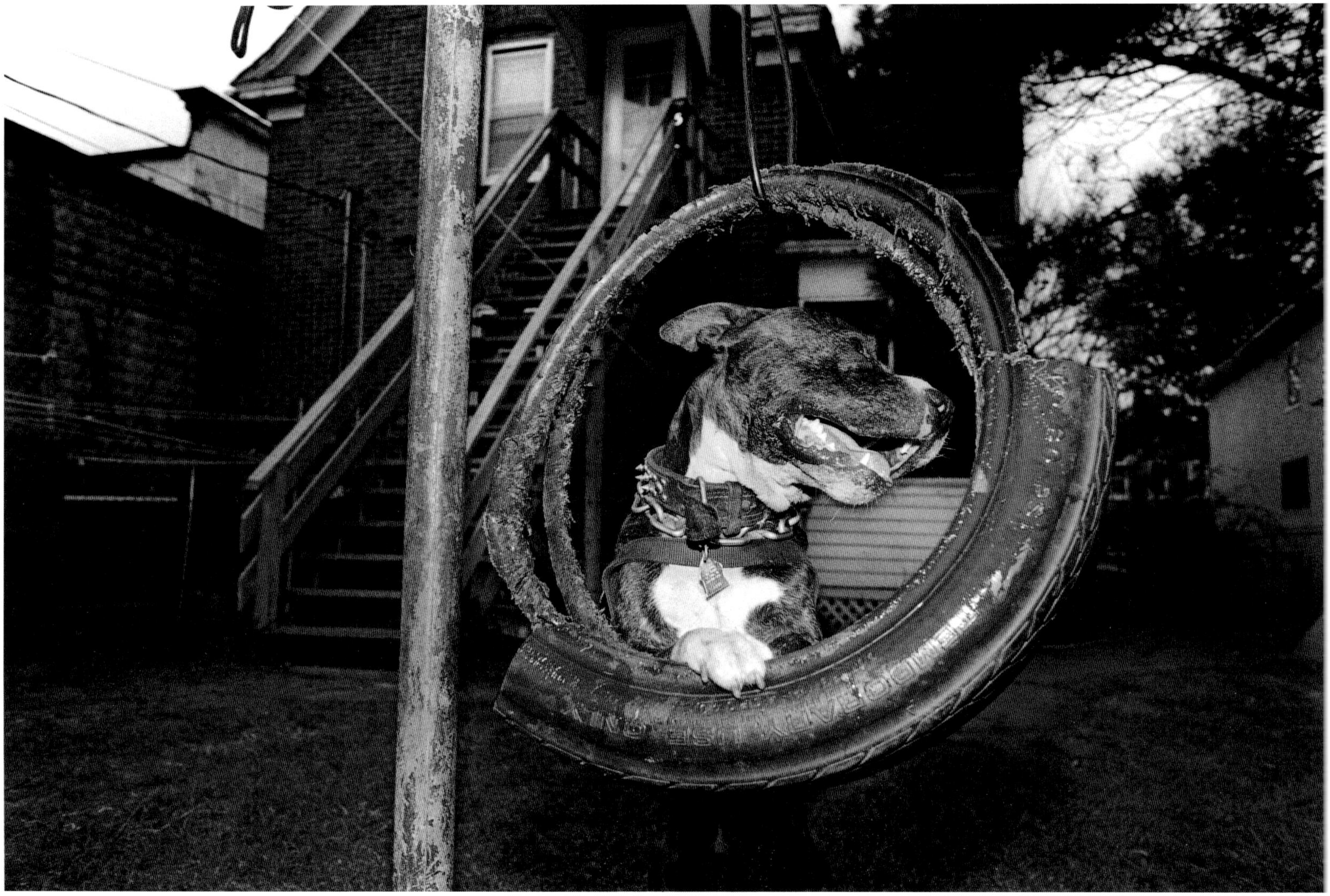

Dogs are my buddies. Outside of my wife, my dogs are first. It's my hobby. Some men like fishing, playing sports, football, basketball. Me, I like training dogs. My wife says it's better to be like this about a dog than to be like this with other women.

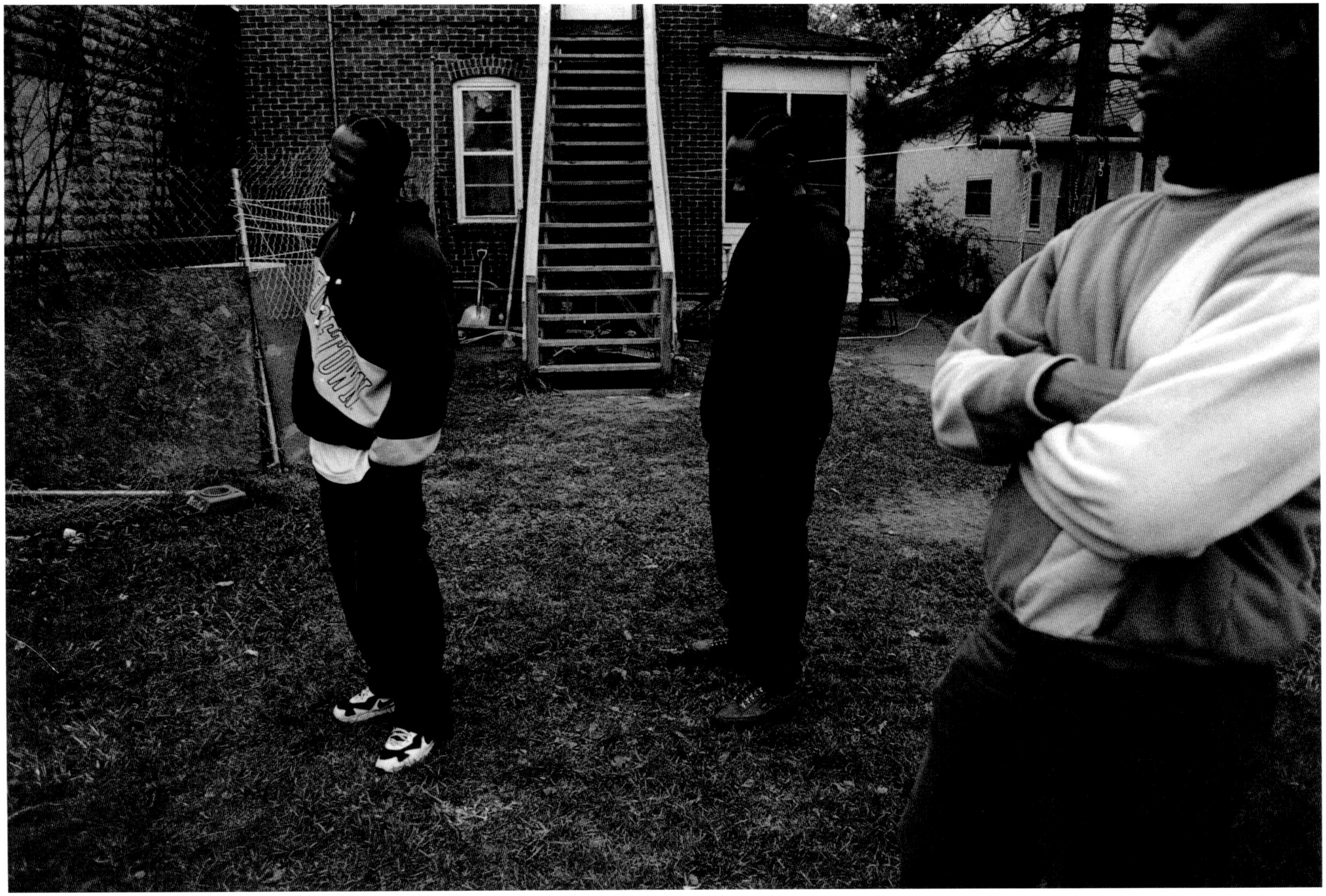

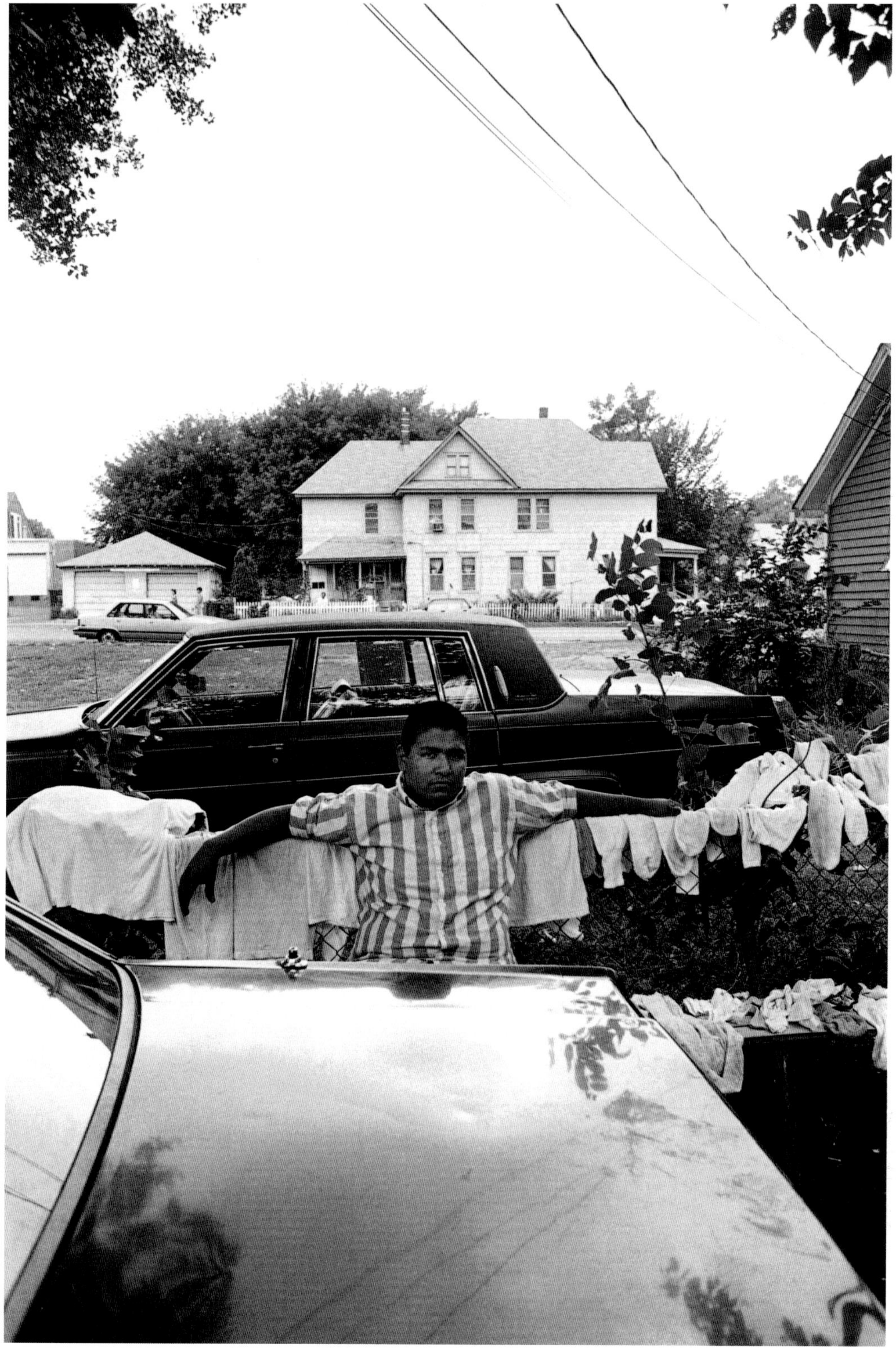

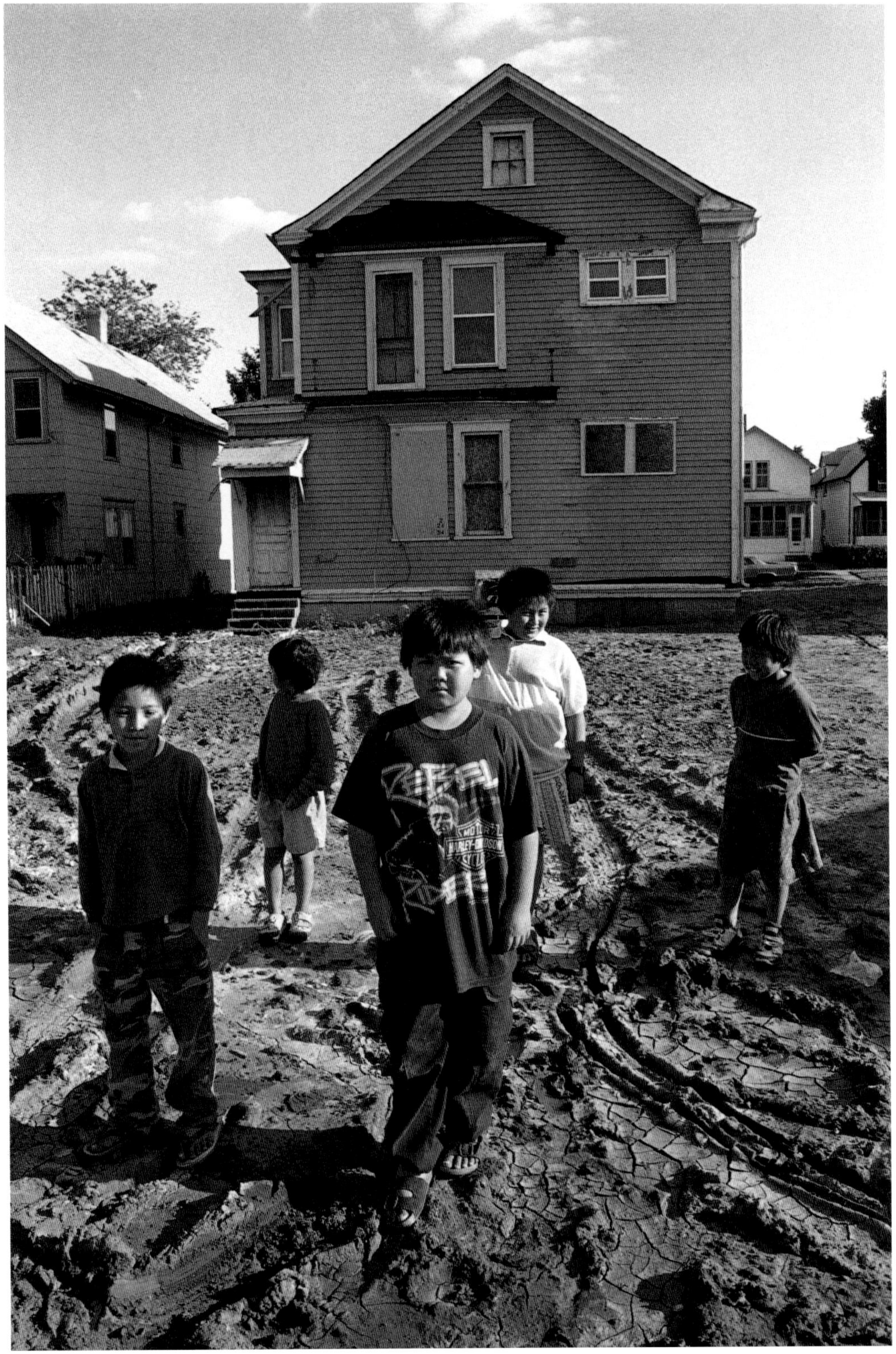

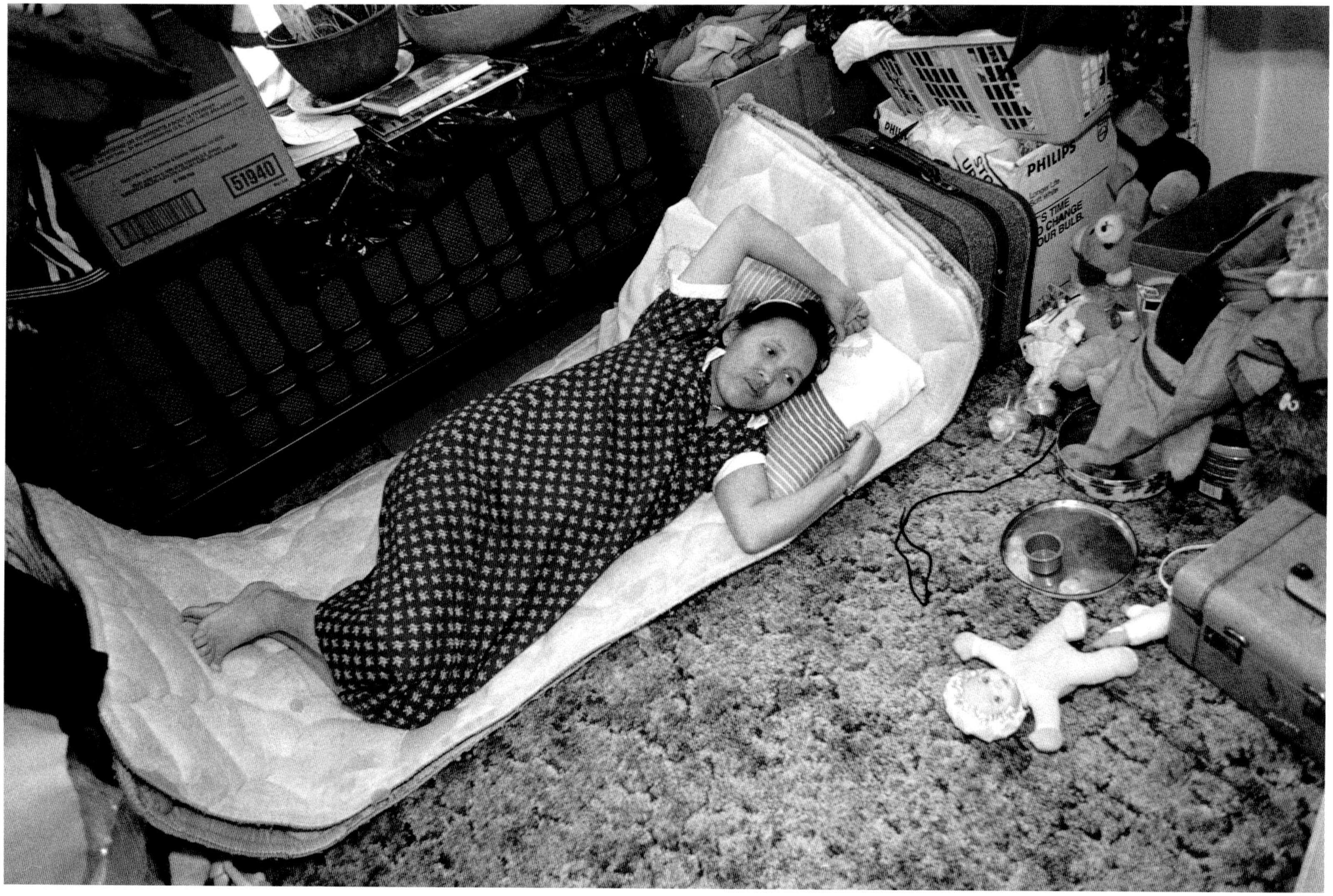
51940
PHILIPS

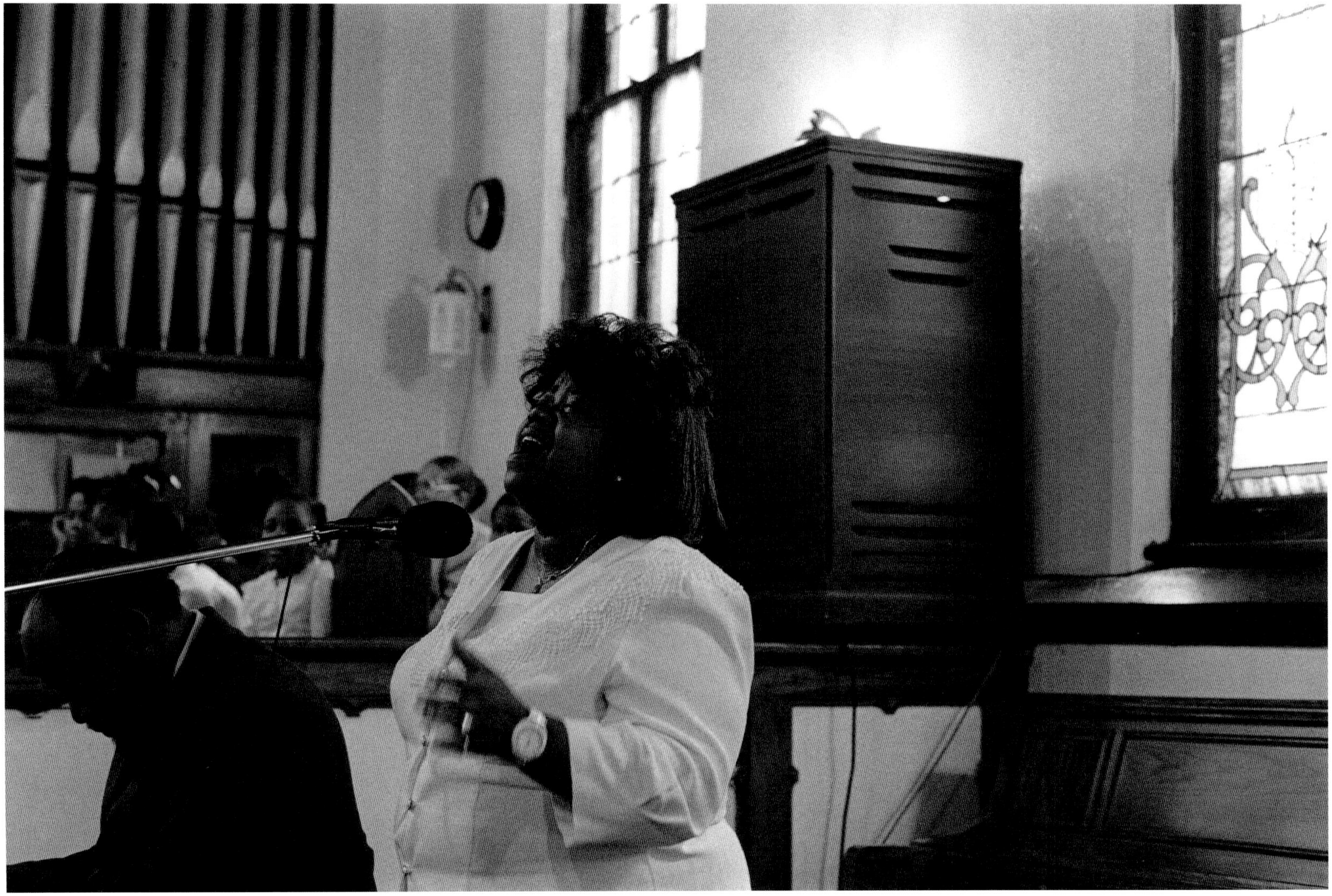

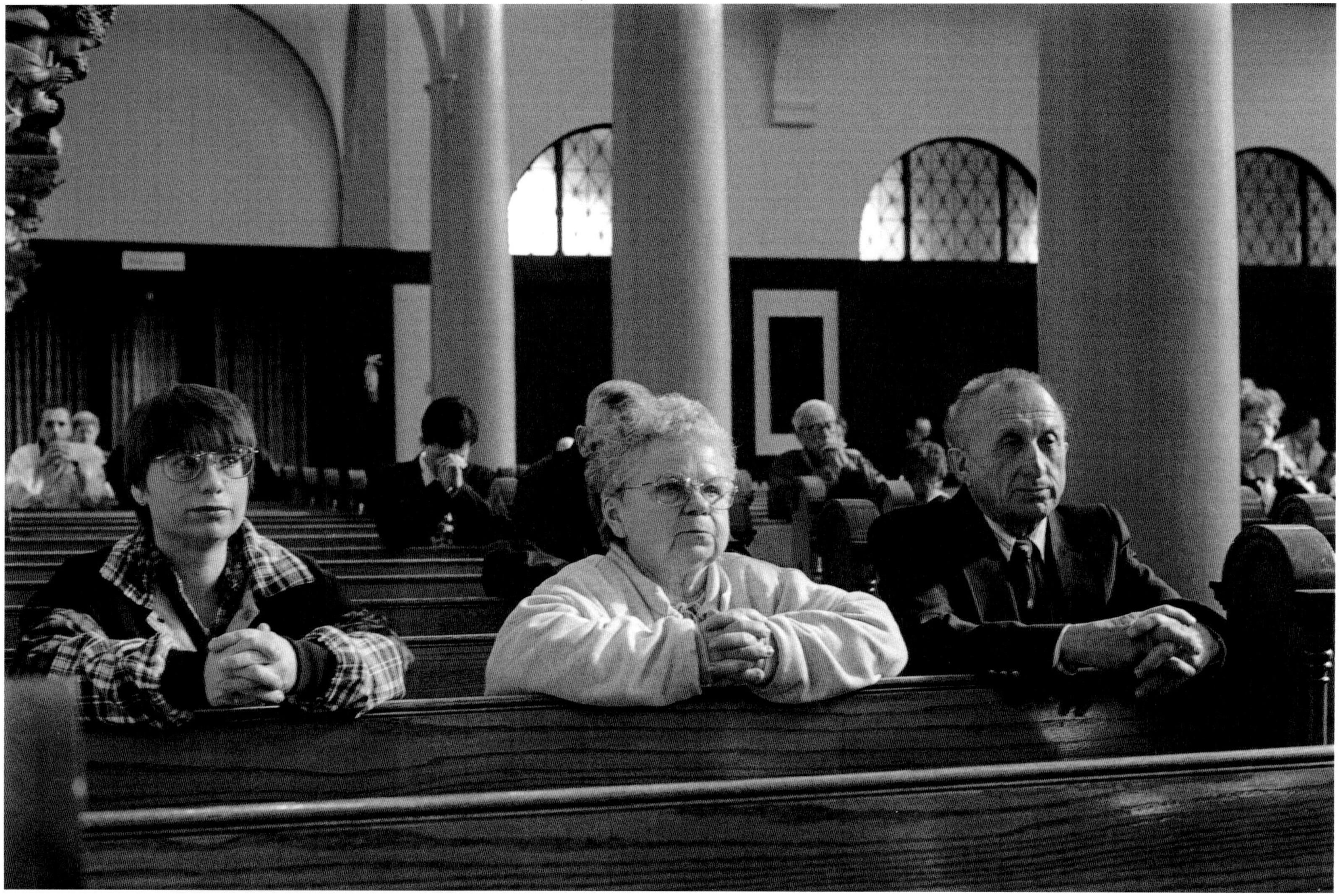

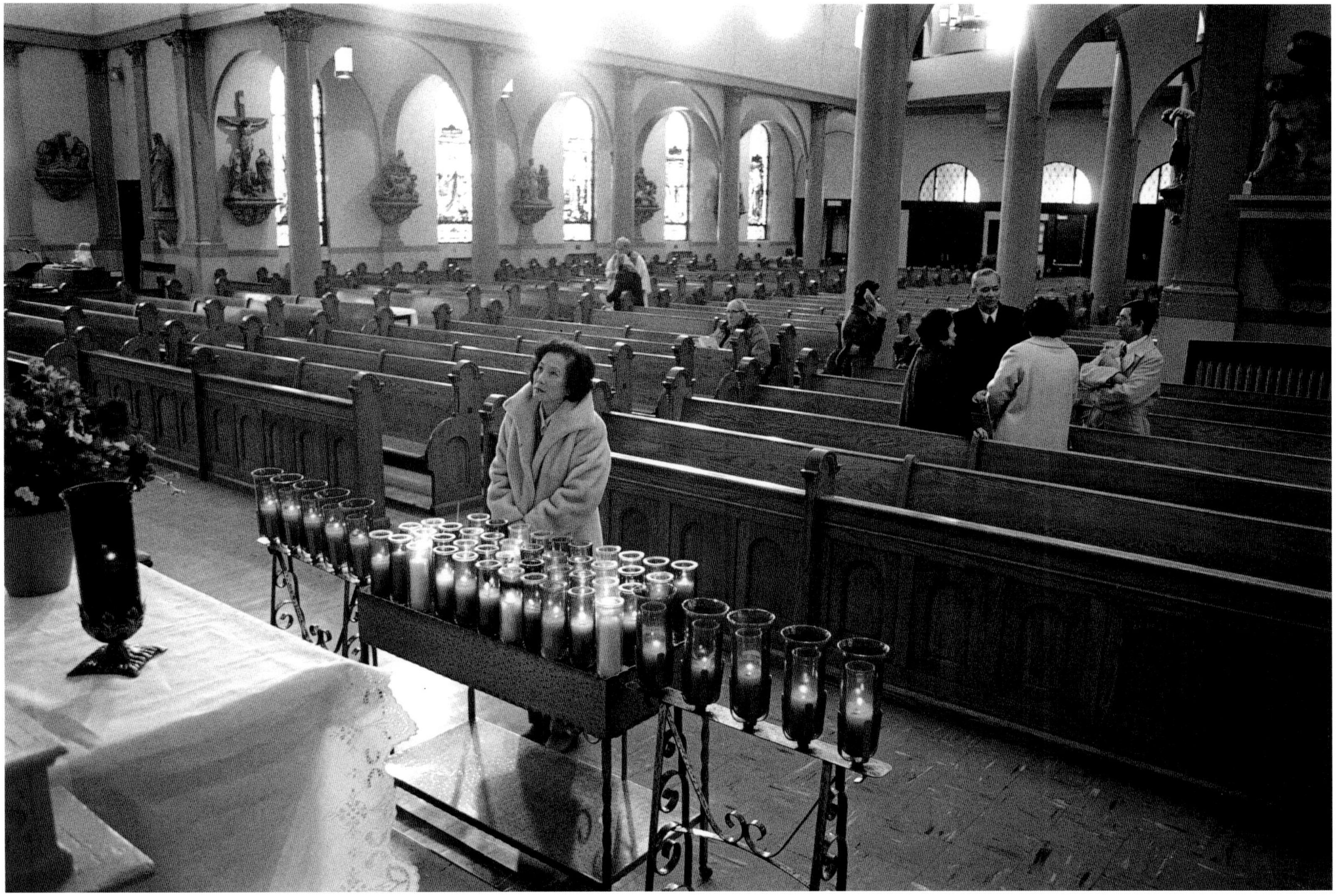

God is the most important thing in my family life. I've been a Catholic since I was born. Both my mother and my father's parents were Catholics. And their mother and father. It goes back many generations. Same with my husband.

The traditional religion in Vietnam is to worship the ancestors. As Catholics we worship God, but we also keep our traditions. This church allows us to do that.

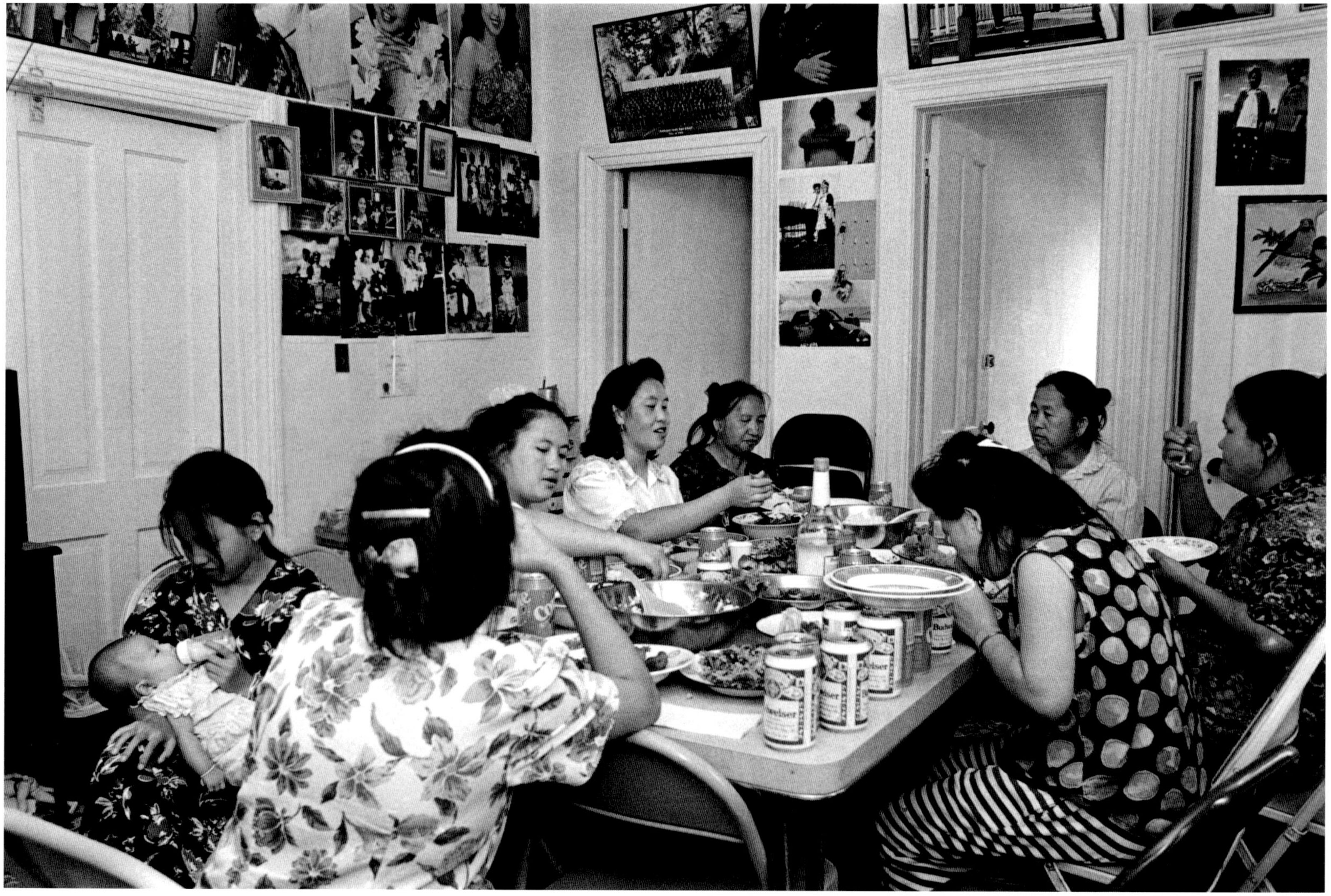

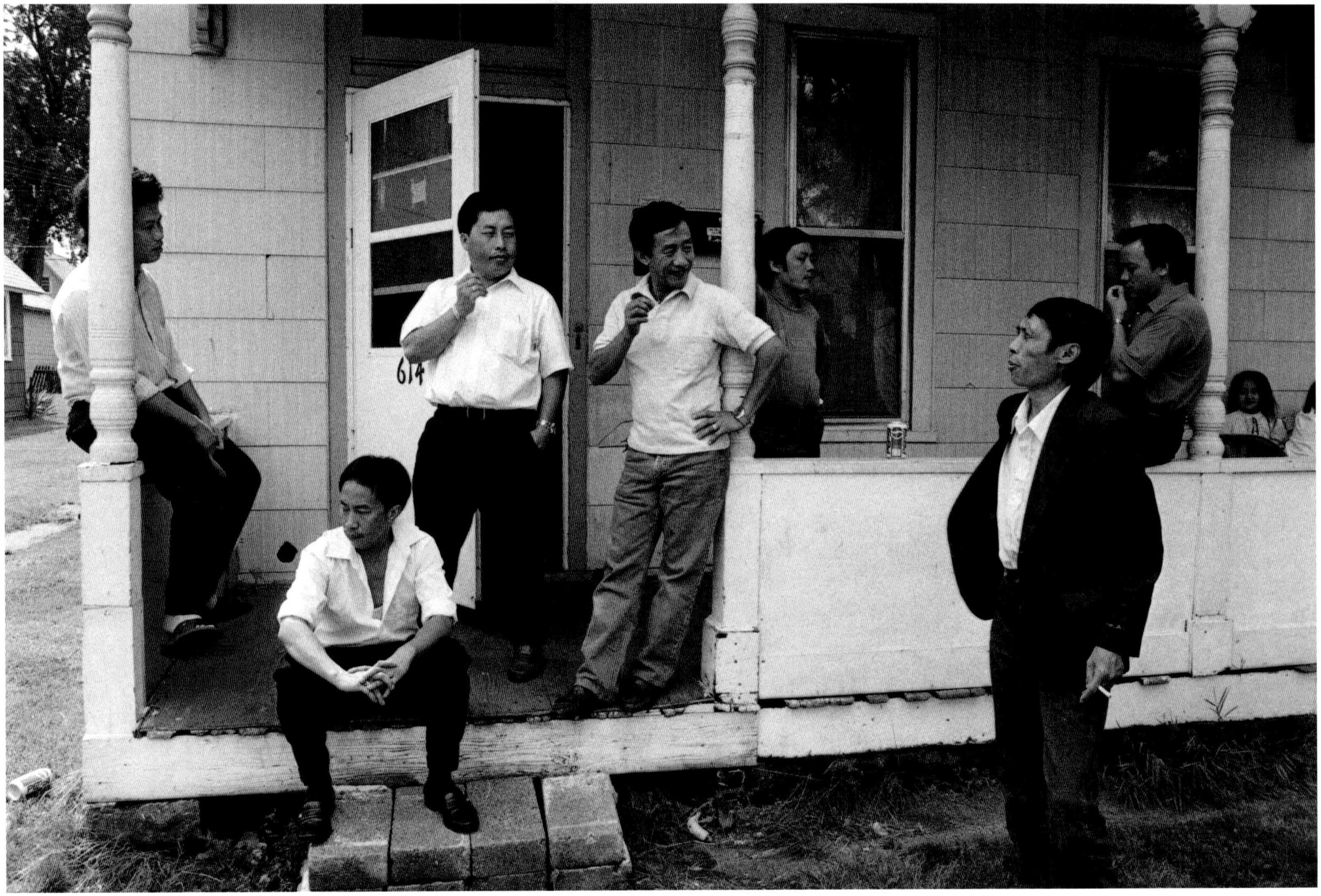

The men eat first, and the women eat after the men. It's our custom. All the old people, that's what they do, so that's what we do. We do what they did.

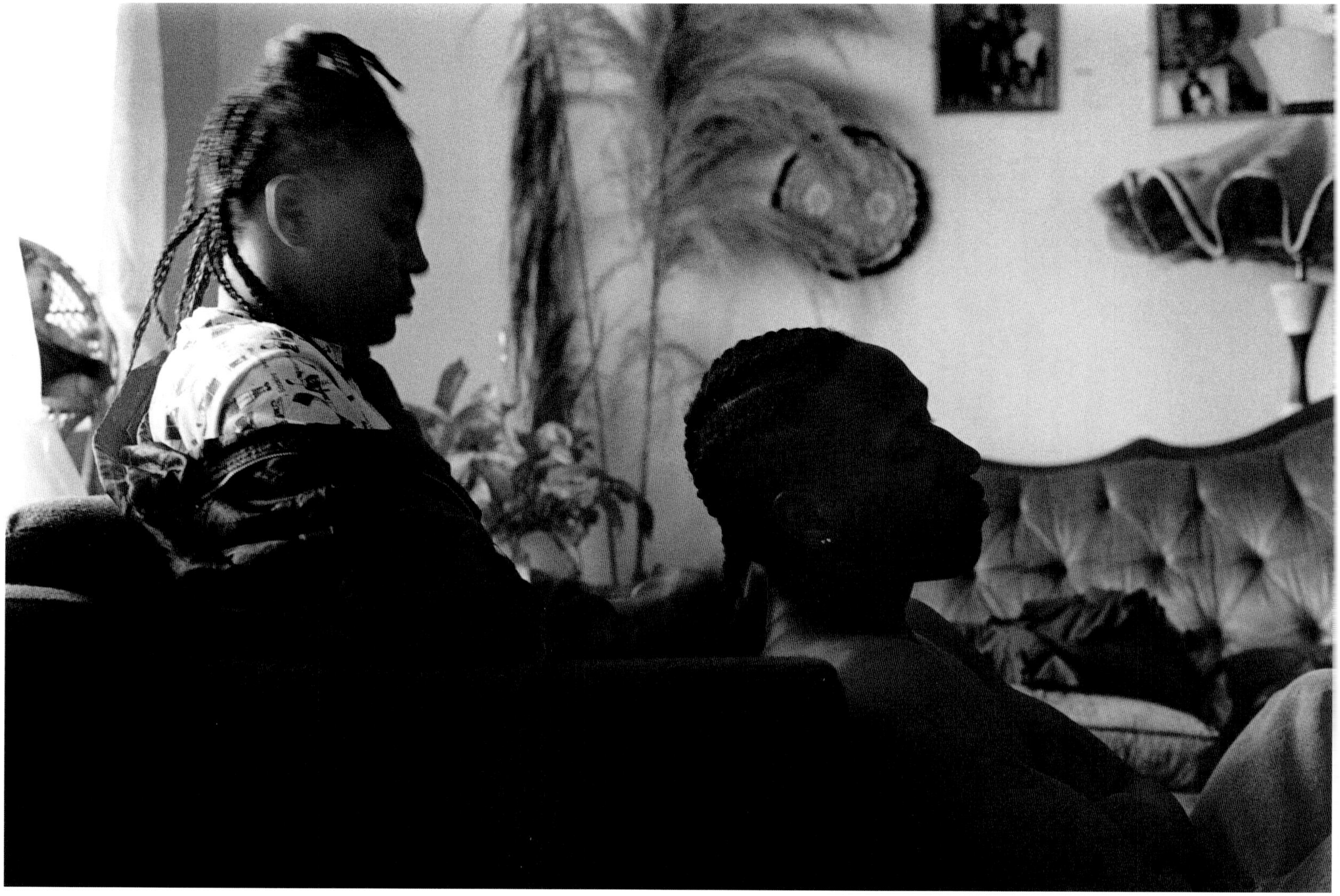

It's tougher being black. There's more black gangs out here. Black people got an attitude. They got a quick temper. But it's not just black people. I know some Asians, and they got the mentality to kill somebody.

It's like everybody got their own little 'hood. Like if all the blacks are standing up there, the Asians know not to go up there.

I'm not your typical gang member, you know what I'm saying? I don't go out vicious, throwing up my hands, running my mouth off. I'm in a gang out there. I could have my hat back or to the side. But when I come in here my hat is always straight or off my head. I never bring that stuff in my mom's house.

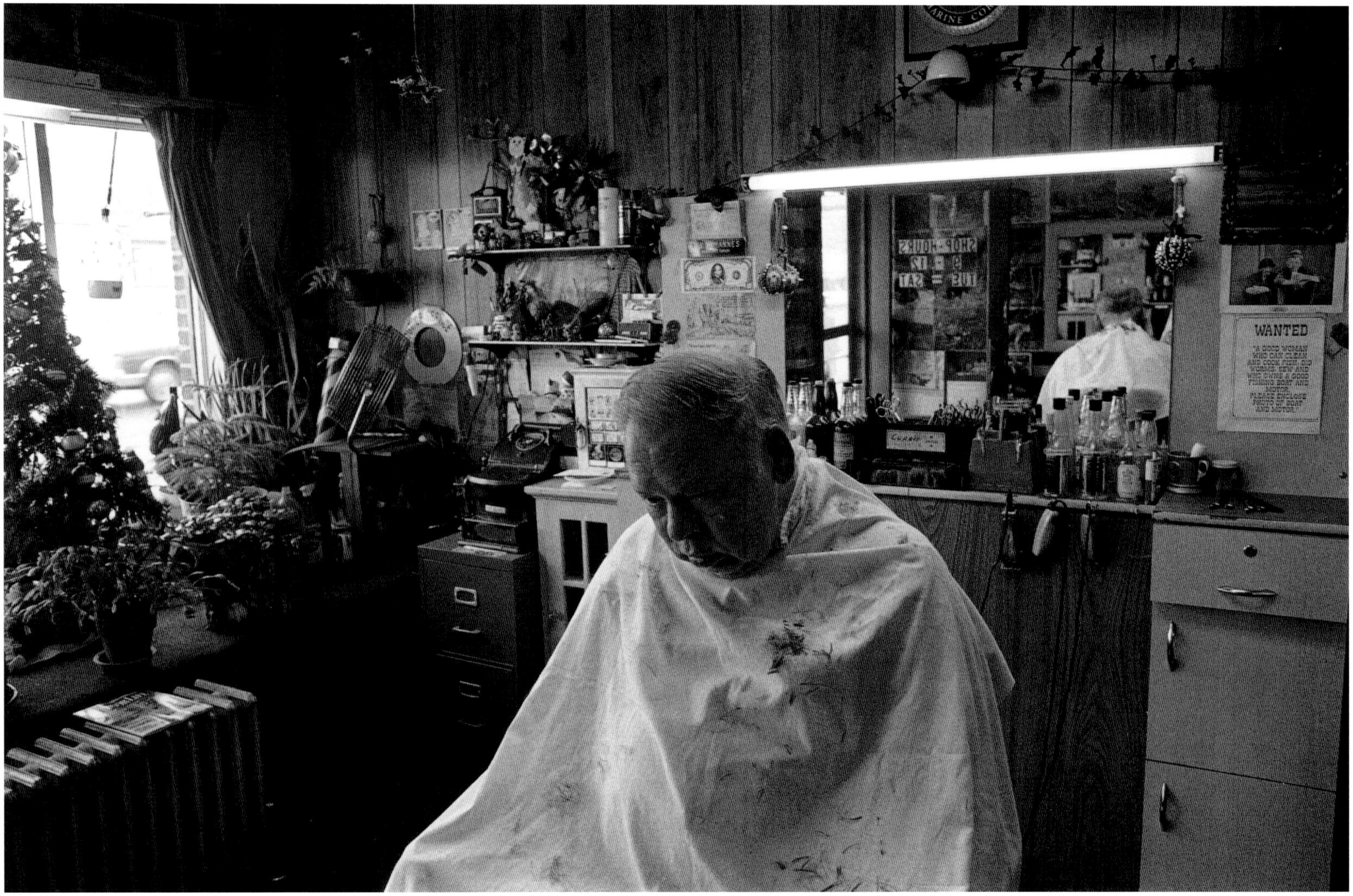
WANTED

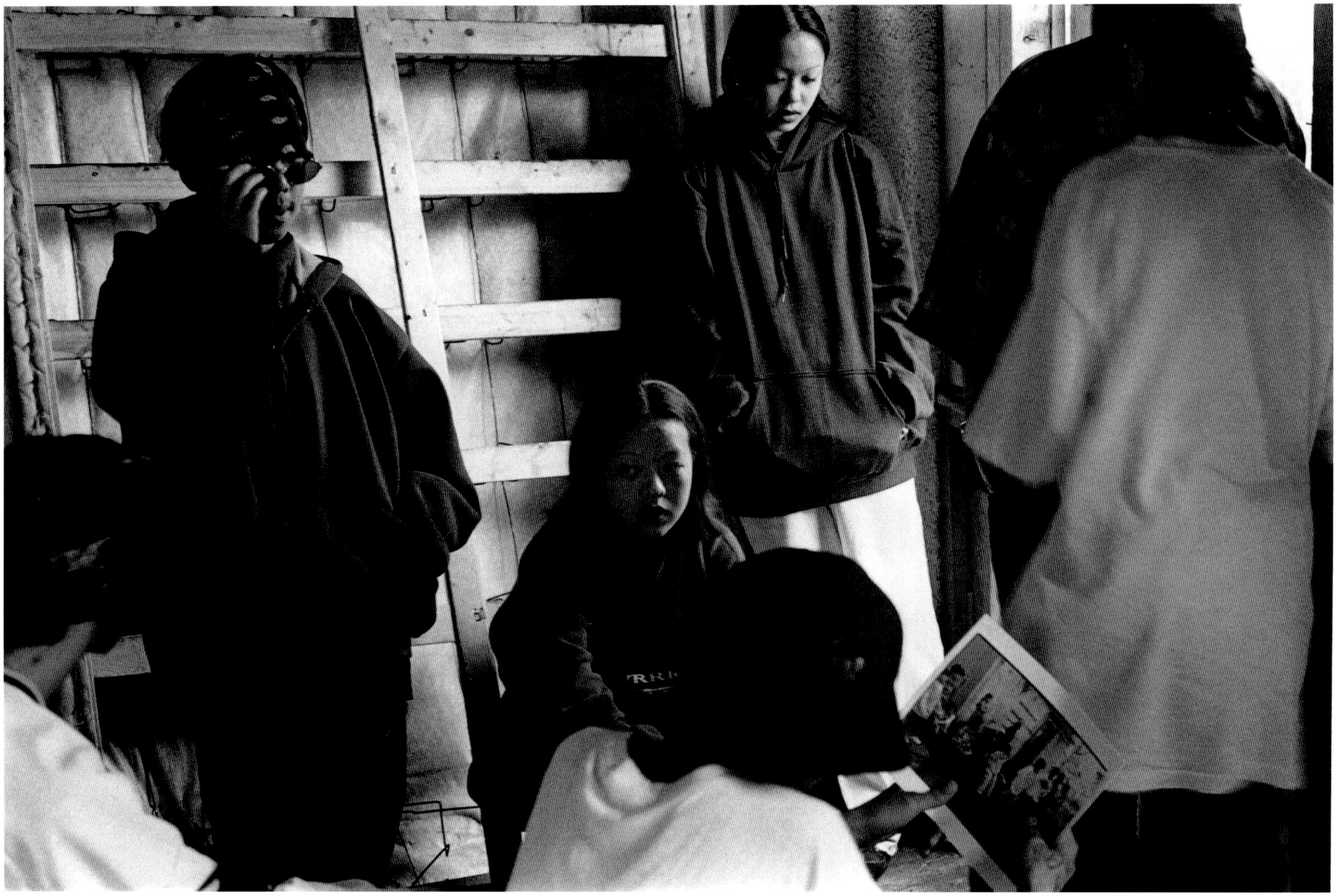

We only hang out with Hmong. We know some black people, but we don't hang out with them. People got their own way. Their way ain't the same as our way. We don't hang with white dudes, either. Some white people are racist. They don't like people like us. Like how we dress. They talk about us. They make us feel disgraced. They be telling us to go back to our country.

[When I asked them about the future, they gave varied answers:]

I want to go to college, but I don't think I'm smart enough. I don't have the money anyway. / I want to become a hustler. / Get a good job, get a good wife. Start my own family. / I think becoming a gangster is the only way. Going to school is a hard time. Nobody is going to make it. Easiest way out is just becoming a gangster and have fun.

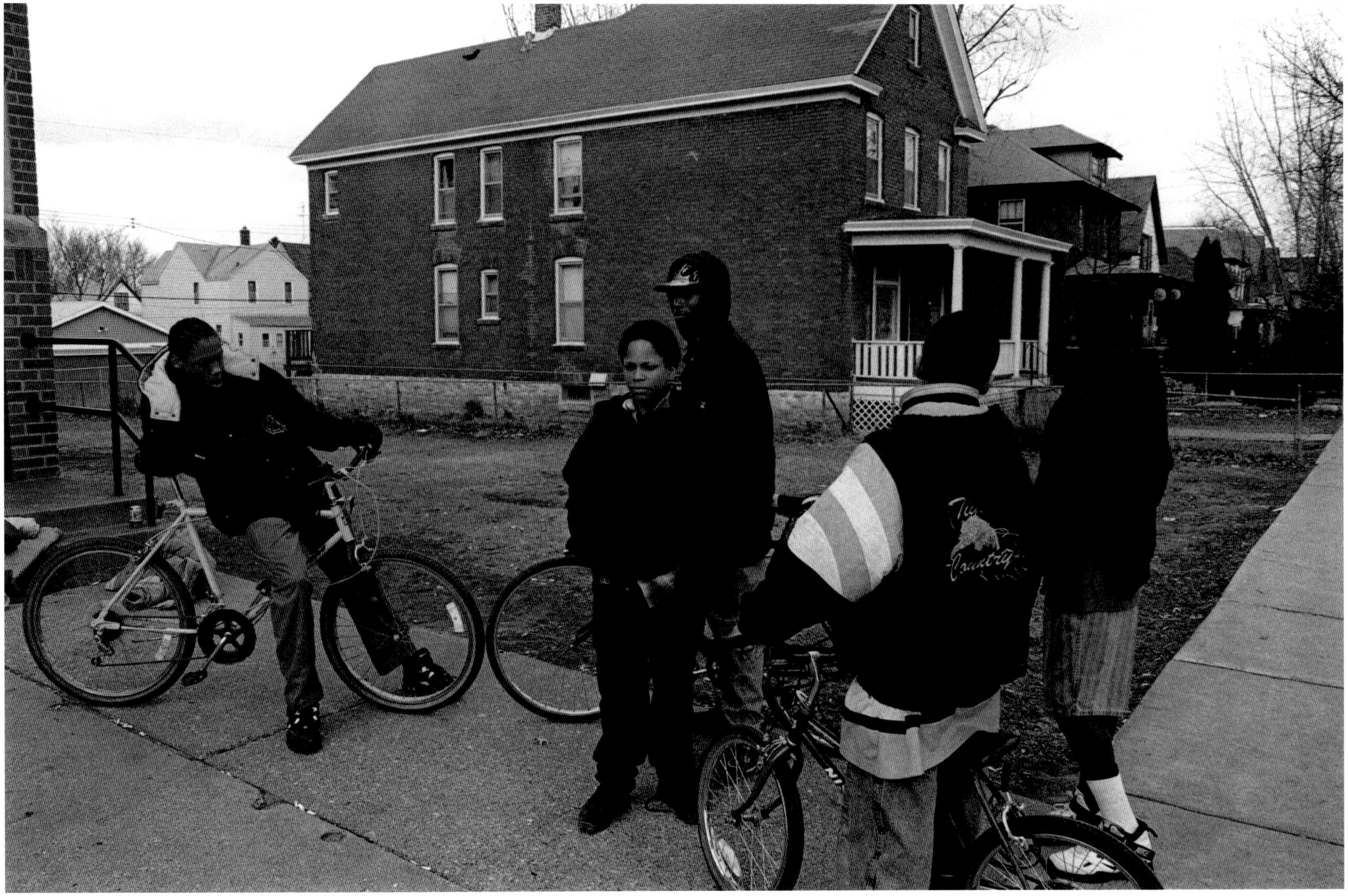
Country

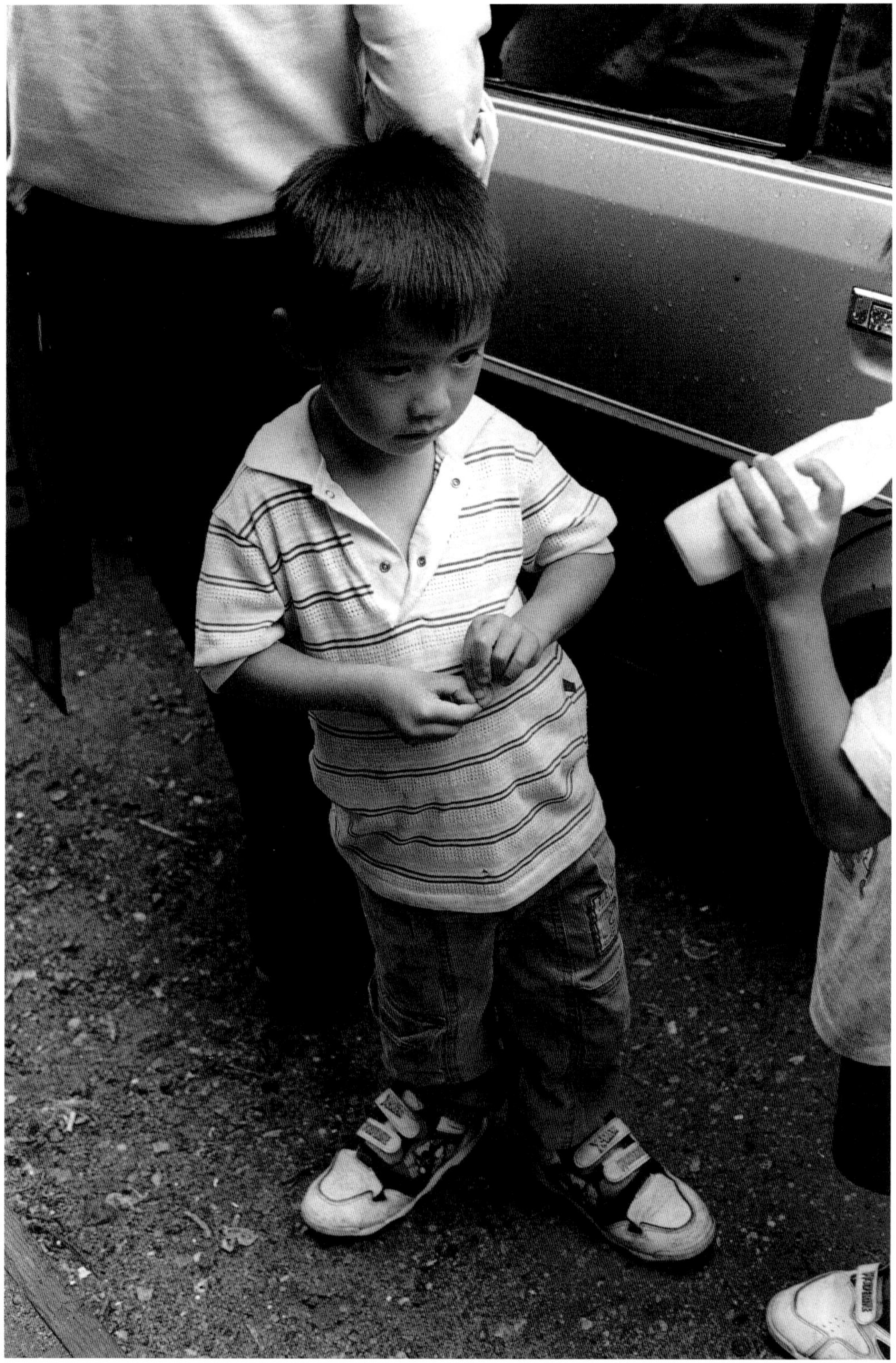

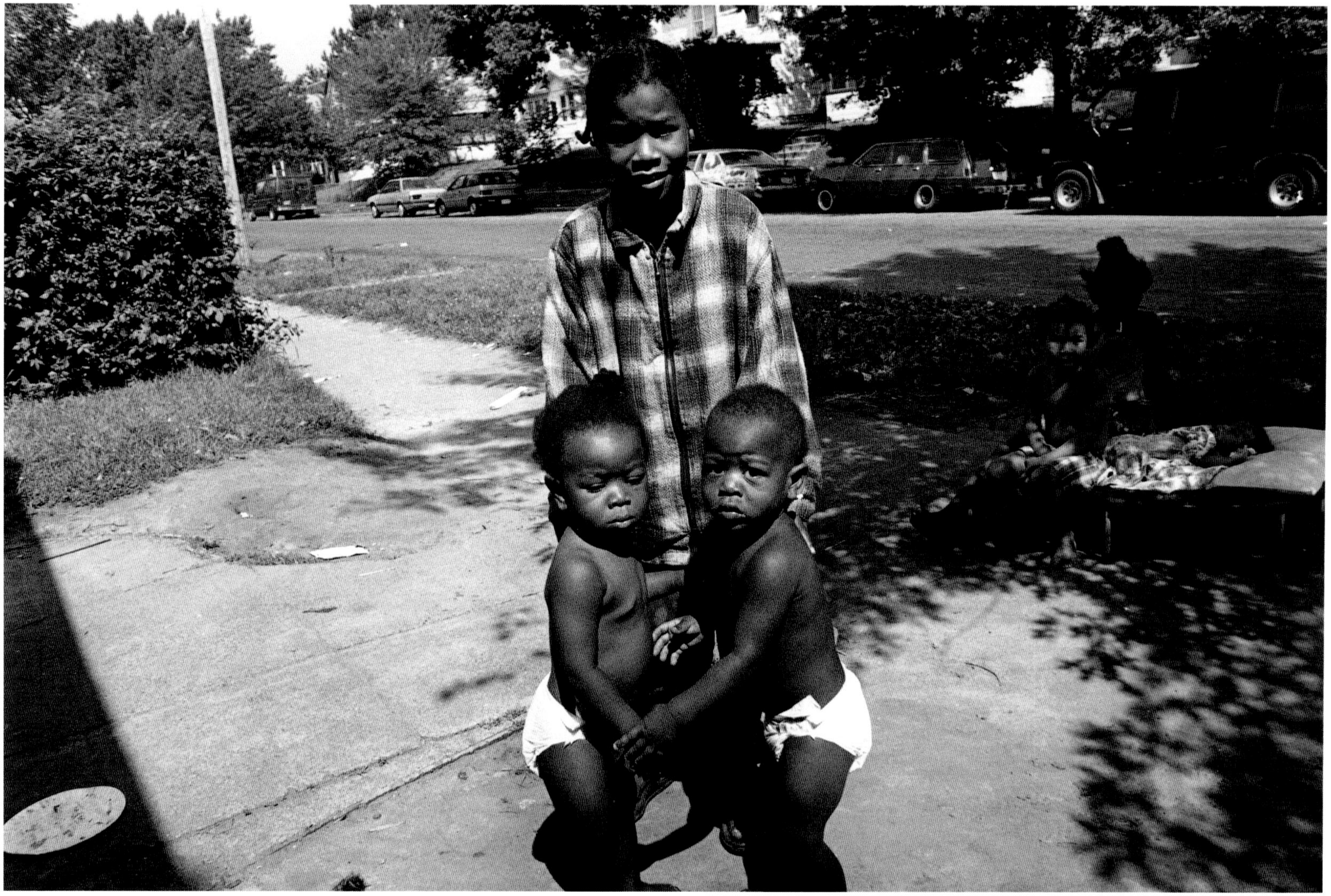

I was just sitting on my back stoop across the street when she walked by, and I said "hi" and she nodded "hi"—and here we are. That was twelve years ago. I've heard stories from the Hmong people that I was one of the first that married a Hmong girl. There was another one in Wisconsin. That's the only two I knew of.

It's difficult to raise seven kids with a person that can't hear or speak. I manage, let's put it that way. My wife doesn't understand a lot of things—money, children, getting them to school on time. But she's a good wife, a good mother. I know that she'll be there when I get home. A lot of the white women, they don't treat the husband right, I don't think.

I'm very happy. I think if 95 percent of the men had a wife like mine, you wouldn't have as much trouble as you do now. Really, it's real nice. They're devoted to the family and the man. I think they're probably like other oriental people: Their main goal in life is to have children and a man and a home. She has that.

All the boys have American names because they probably might have a conflict when they're working or going to school. The girls' names are pretty Hmong names, so I don't think they'll have any trouble.

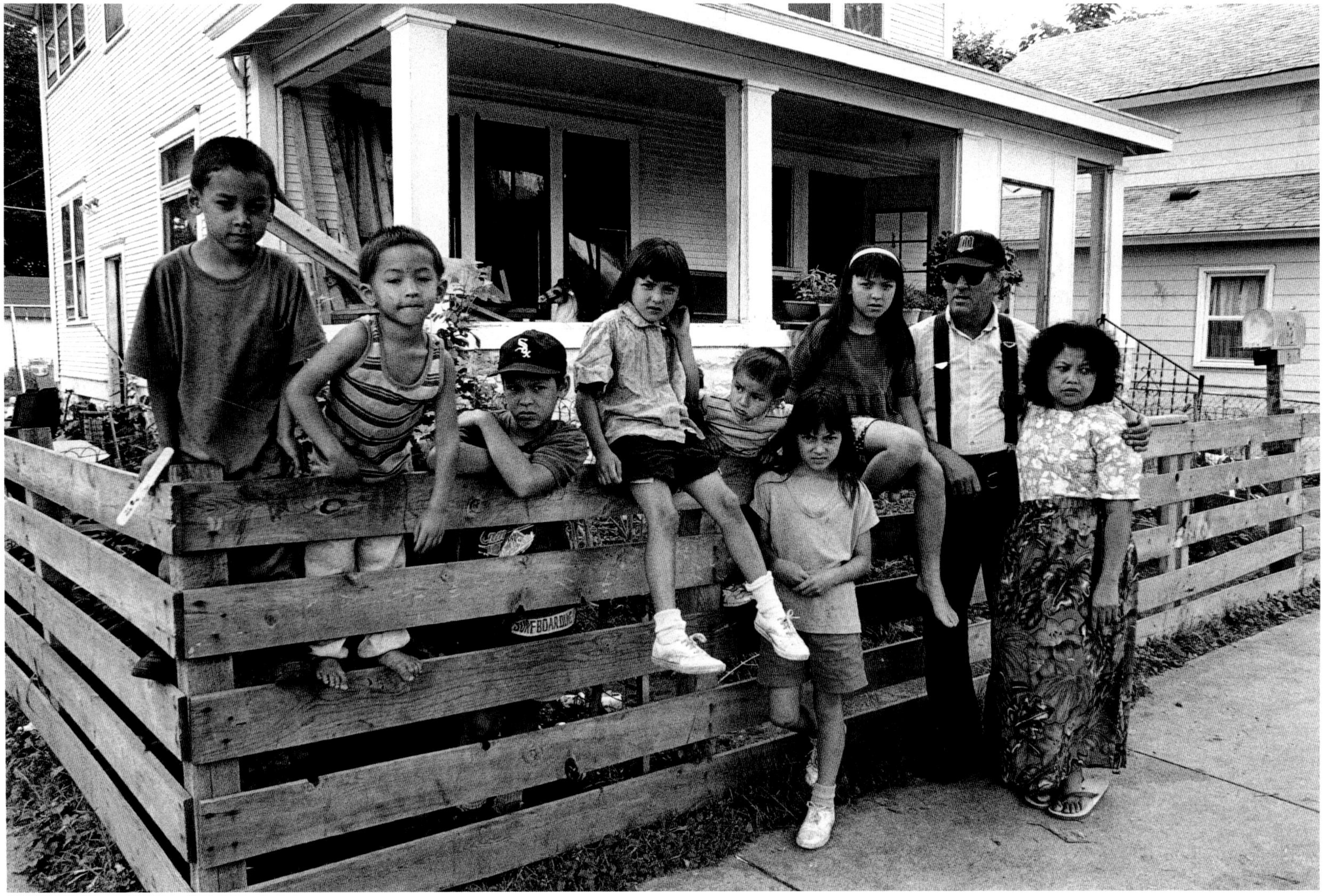

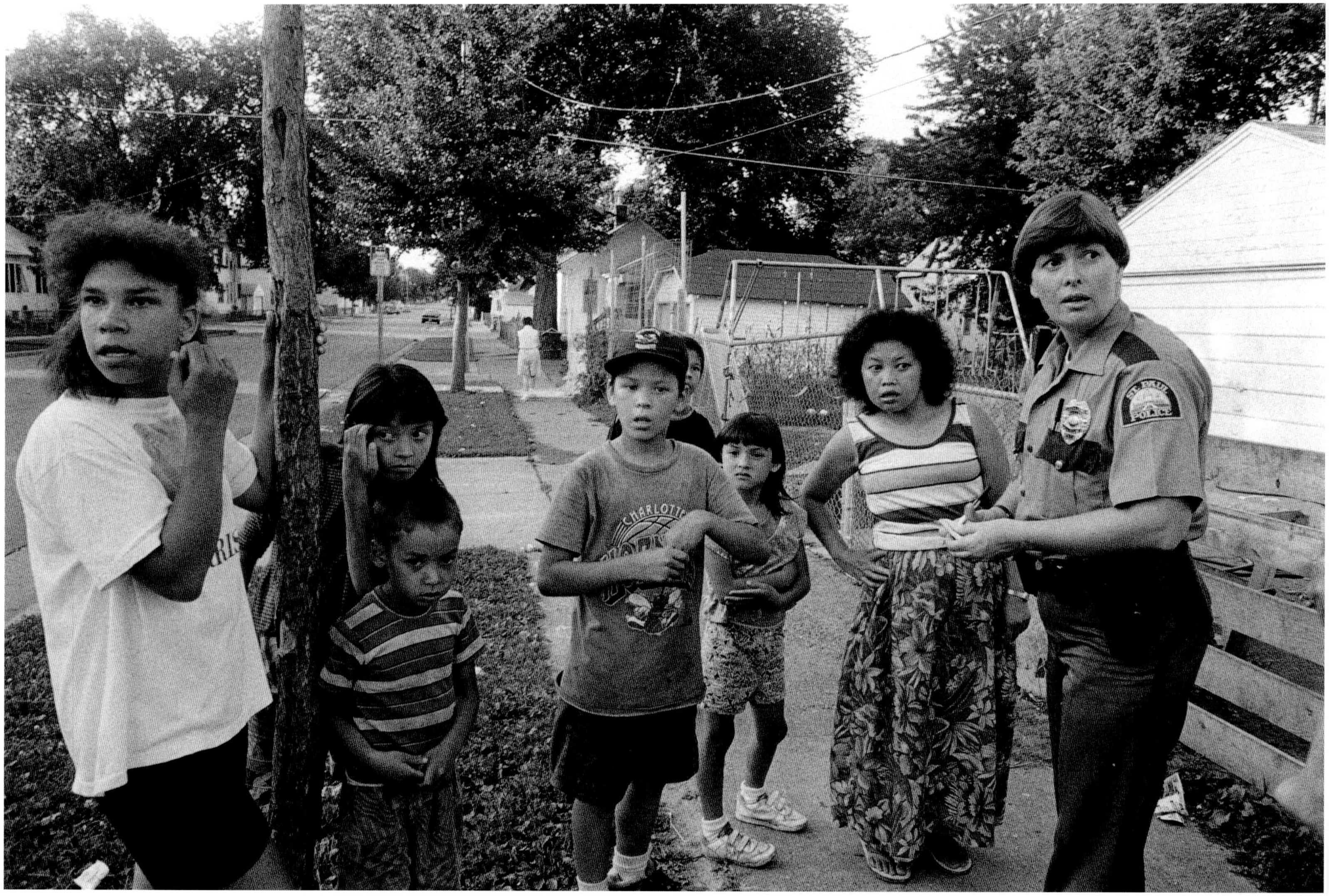

The neighborhood is run down. I think a lot of the people from the Selby area of St. Paul moved over here. We have gangs, prostitutes, shootings. But they aren't going to intimidate me. I'm not going to move. We were here first. The children see the prostitutes and gang people, and it doesn't seem to bother them. We just try to keep them in after dark.

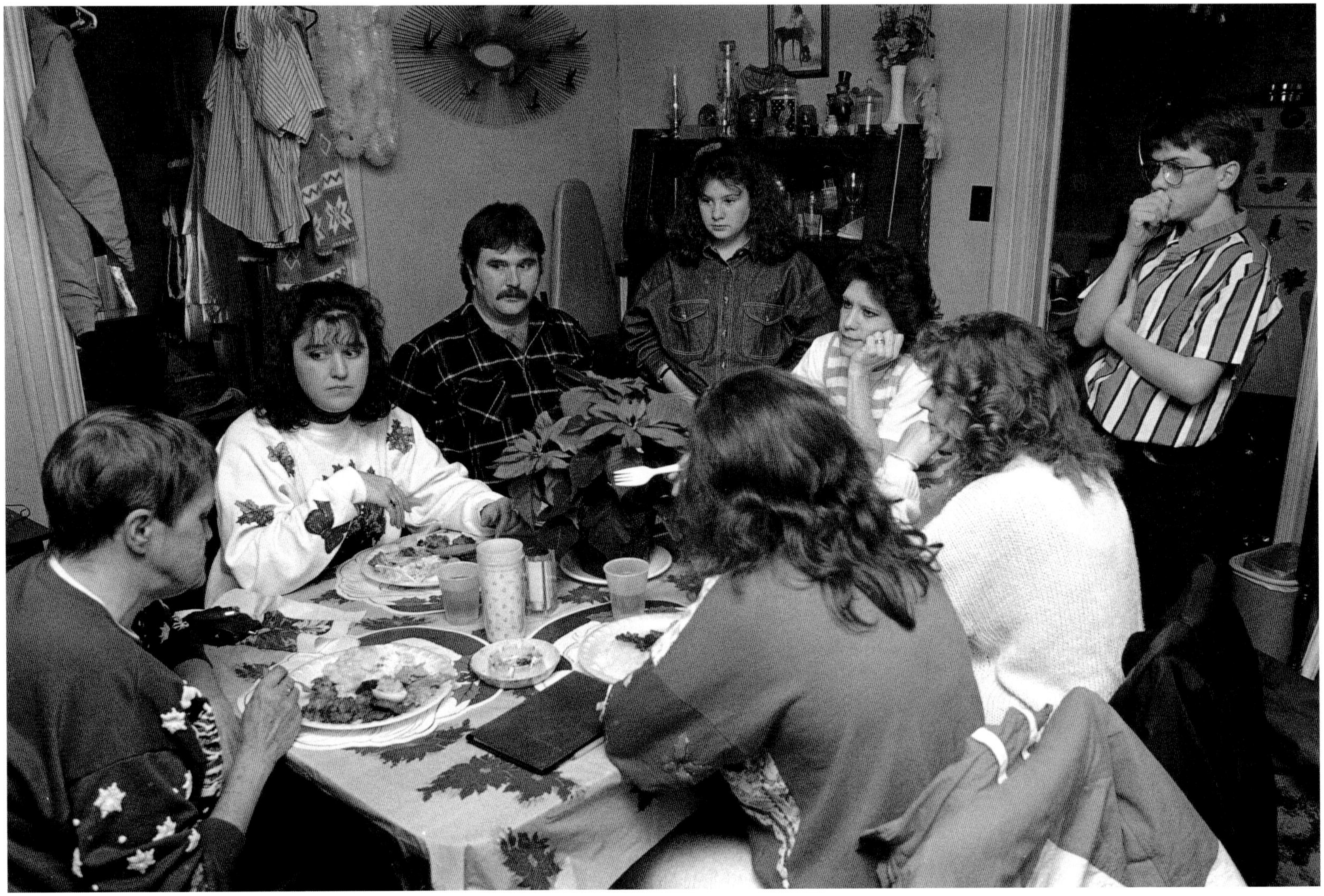

I have no problems living here. I chose to live here. Our world is made up of a mesh of all different types of people, cultures, ideas, activities, dreams, wants, needs. I wanted my child to experience those things. It's educational. I know young black men who cannot deal with being in a predominantly white situation. They can't handle it. I want him to be able to meld wherever he goes but without losing his own identity as a young black man in this society. And I think he's doing a very good job with it.

I was having a conversation with someone who lives in this neighborhood, and it got around to "Well how come all the storefronts on University look like they're Asian-owned? And how come they always got a new car, and how come their cars don't get ticketed on the street? And how come they're allowed to do illegal gambling? And how come and how come."

Personally, I think black people should be the last ones to open their mouths about Asians, because of what we suffered through the last two hundred years. It didn't make sense to me to listen to a black person throwing the same disgusting habits on another group of people. It's like, didn't you learn anything from the way you had to live the last two hundred years and are still living today? I said the reason these Asians have those new cars is because they know how to pool their money. They're not standing around stabbing their brothers and sisters in the back, calling them names, and being jealous of what they have. You know, you all laugh at them because there are thirteen of them in one car, but the truth is, all thirteen helped pay for that car. And two months from now, those same thirteen people will pay for another car, and then there will be six-and-one-half in each car. And then those same thirteen people will buy another car and then there will be—what's three into thirteen? Anyway, that's how they got those new cars.

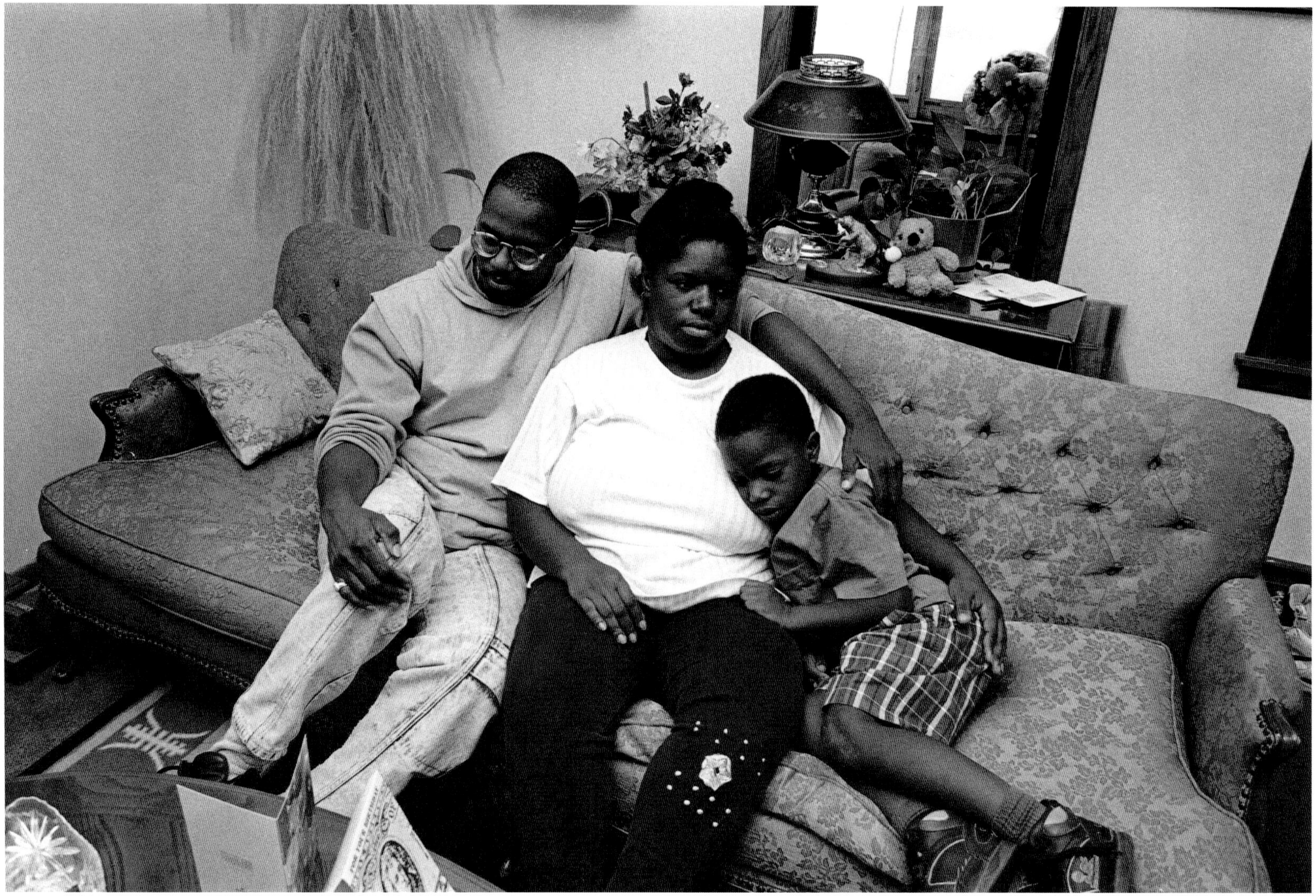

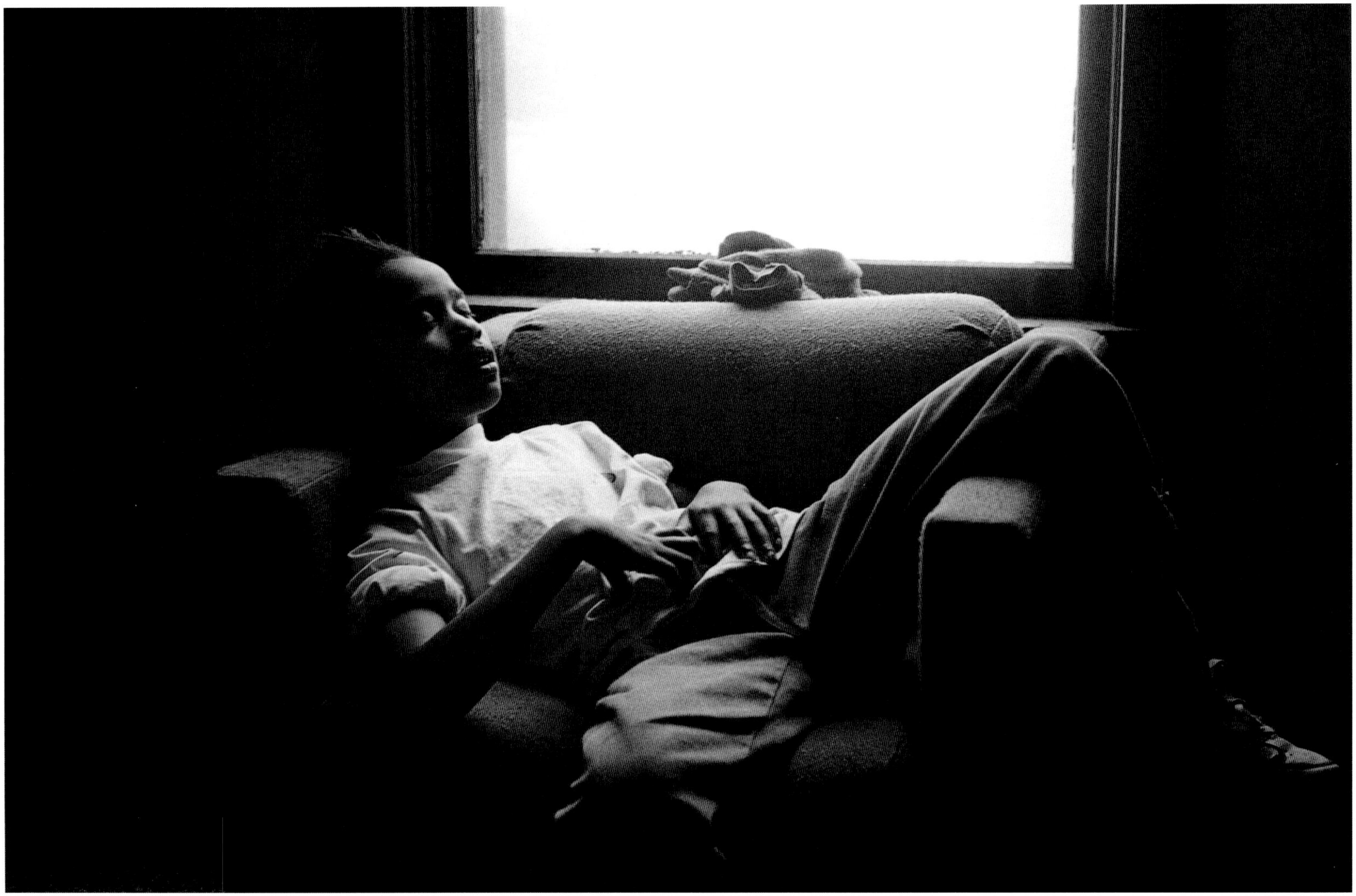

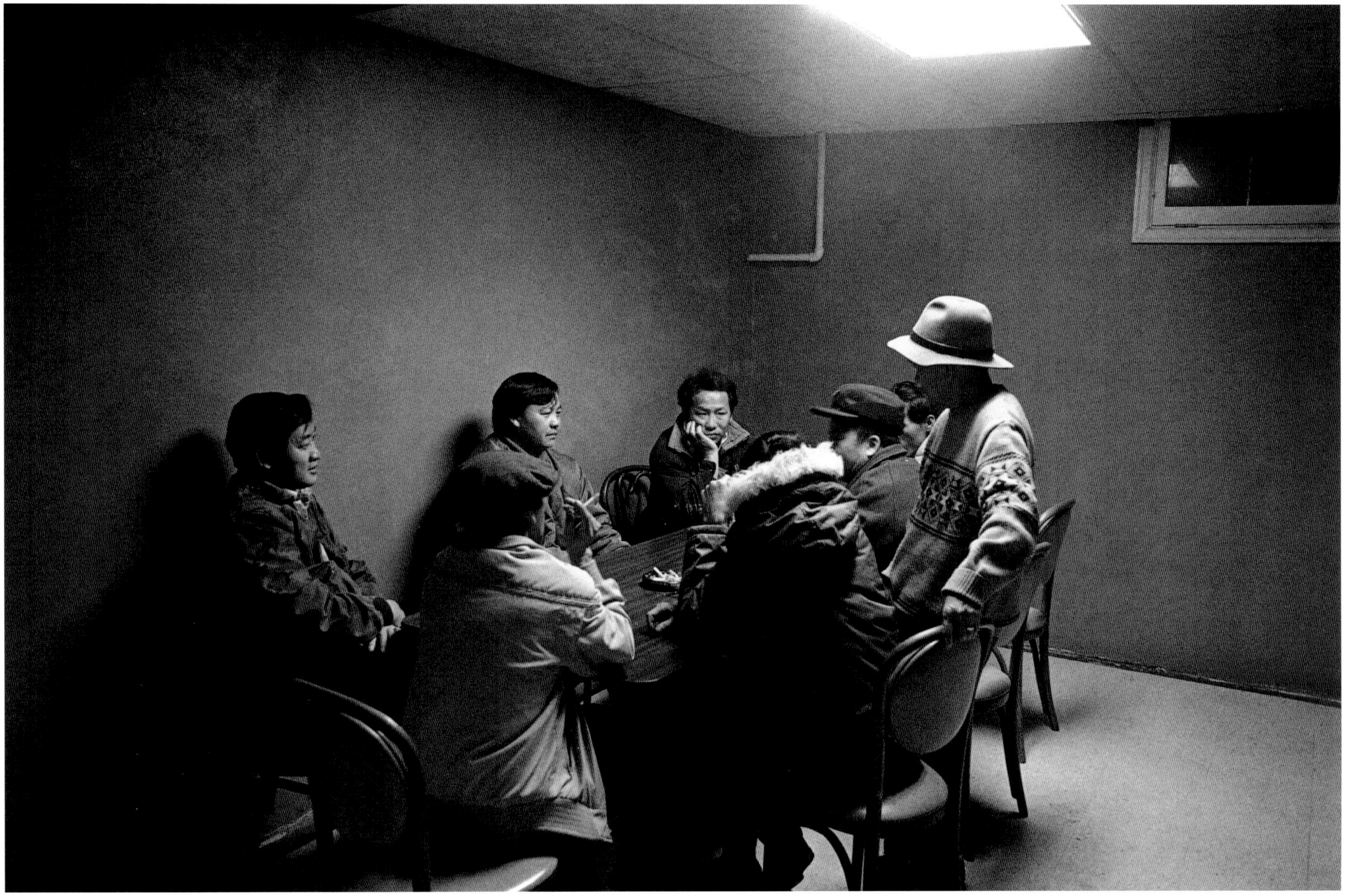

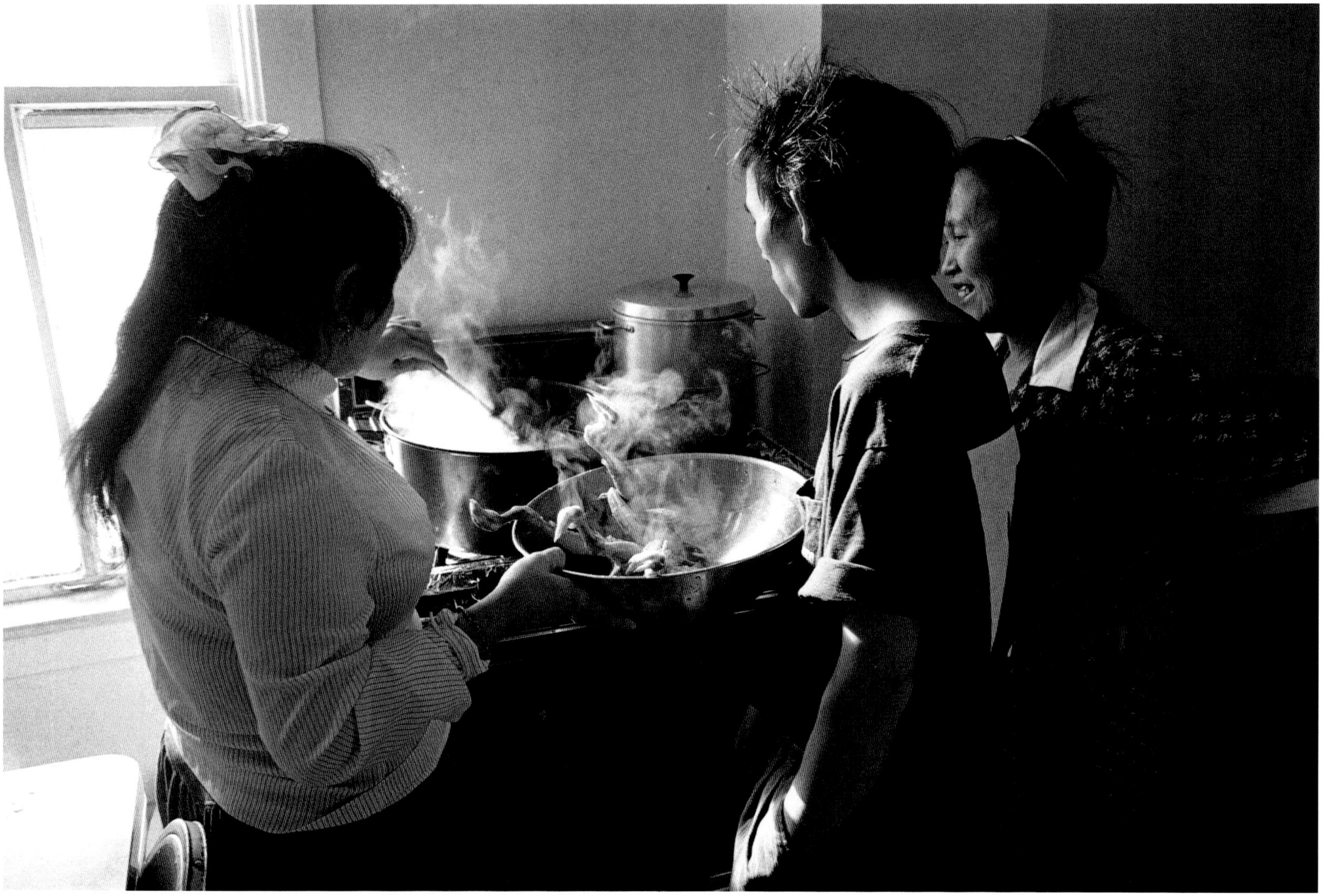

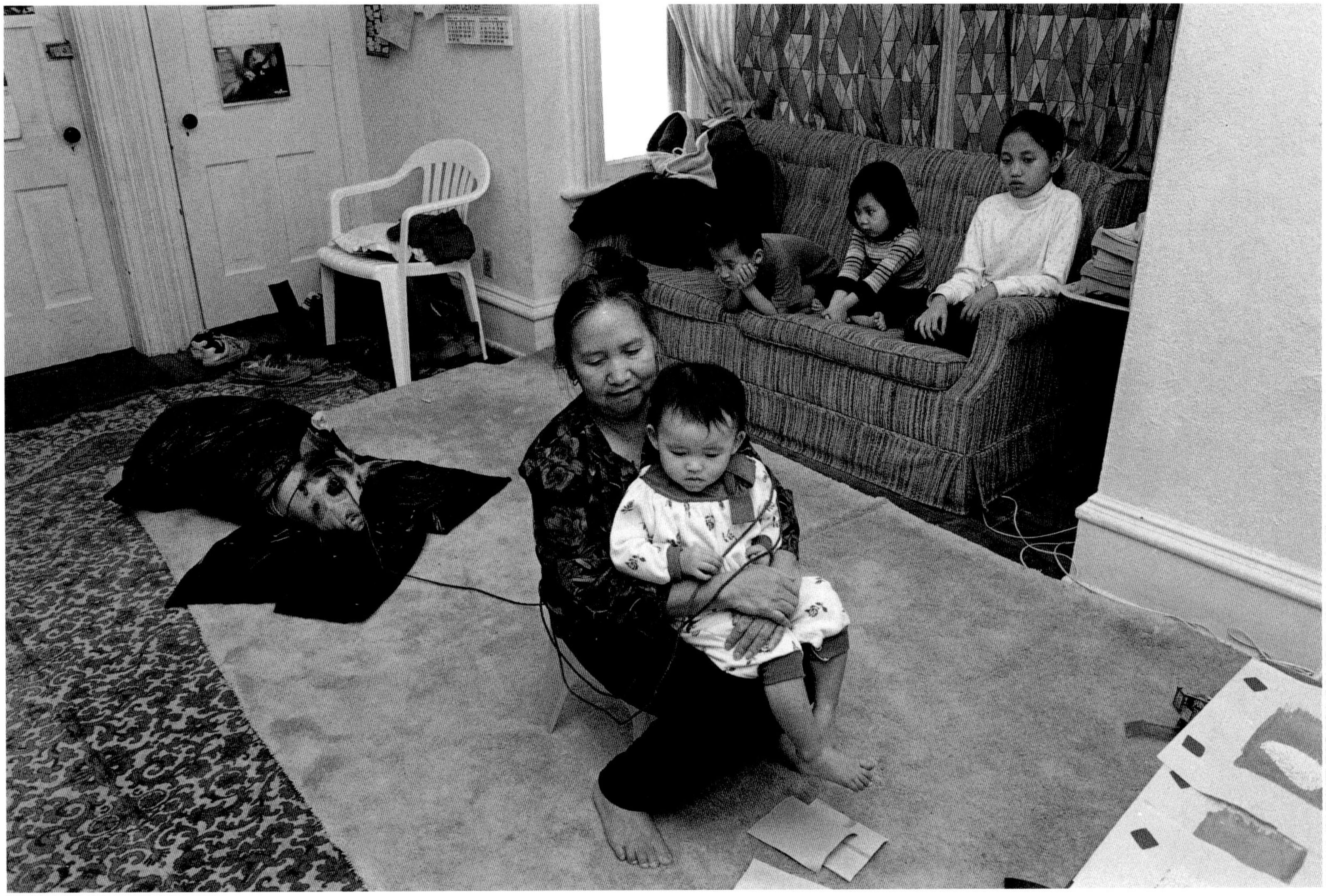

When a child is sick we have a celebration to welcome them back so she won't get sick anymore. In this ceremony we invite a lot of friends and relatives over and have a big meal together.

We hire a shaman to perform a ceremony. When a person is very sick we believe their spirit has gone away from the body. It takes an animal to replace the spirit. We buy a live pig, and after the ceremony takes place we kill the pig. Then we cook it.

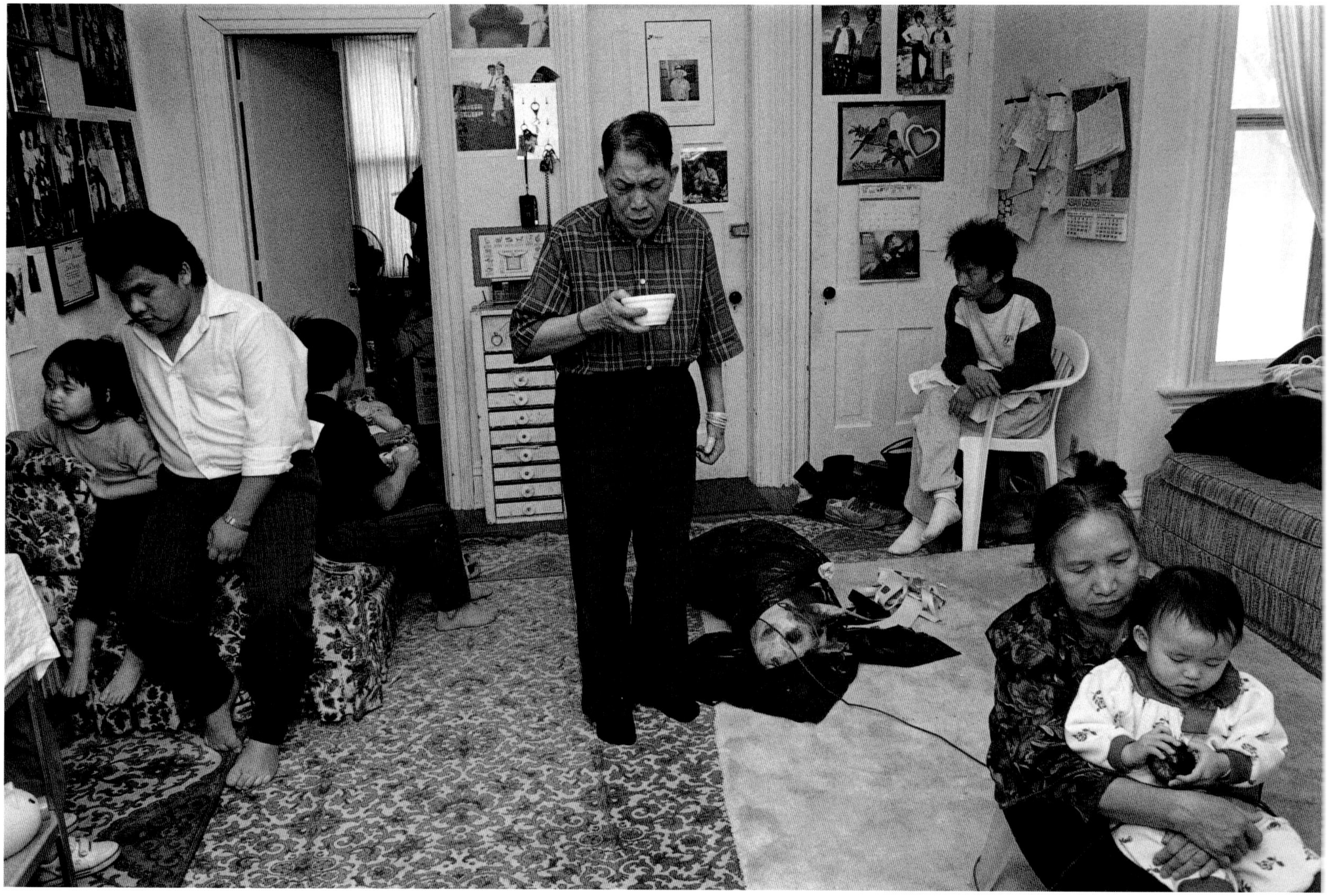

To become a shaman is God-given. It's not for regular people. It takes a special person. This shaman can help cripples become normal persons. He has helped two American people already. But this is just a small part of being a shaman. In Hmong culture we believe that sometimes our good spirits have become lost. That's why people get sick. It is the shaman that calls the spirit back.

There are many powers that help the shaman. During a ceremony the shaman calls the Magic power. When it comes, the shaman and the power will start shaking and chanting. The shaman gives the Magic power instructions on what to do. It's just like giving a computer instructions.

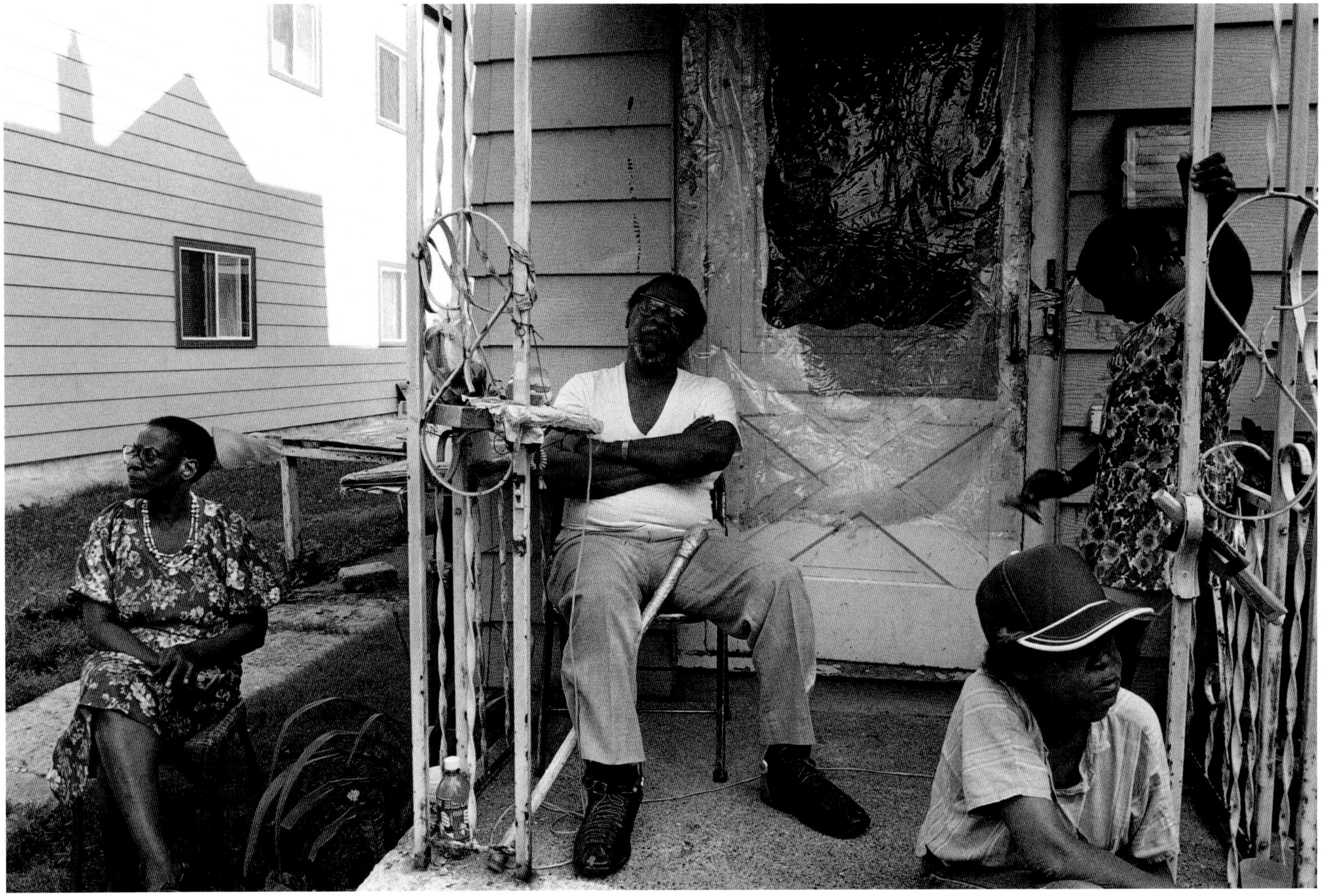

I've lived all over, and this is the best neighborhood I've been in. Because it's more quieter and peoples is more respectful and friendly. They watches over you.

We sit out here and talk, play a little music sometime. And we quiet, so it don't disturb the neighborhood or nothing like that. We give the police respect, and they give us respect. We have us a drink, we don't do it in the open. We don't drink out of cans or bottles. We give them respect.

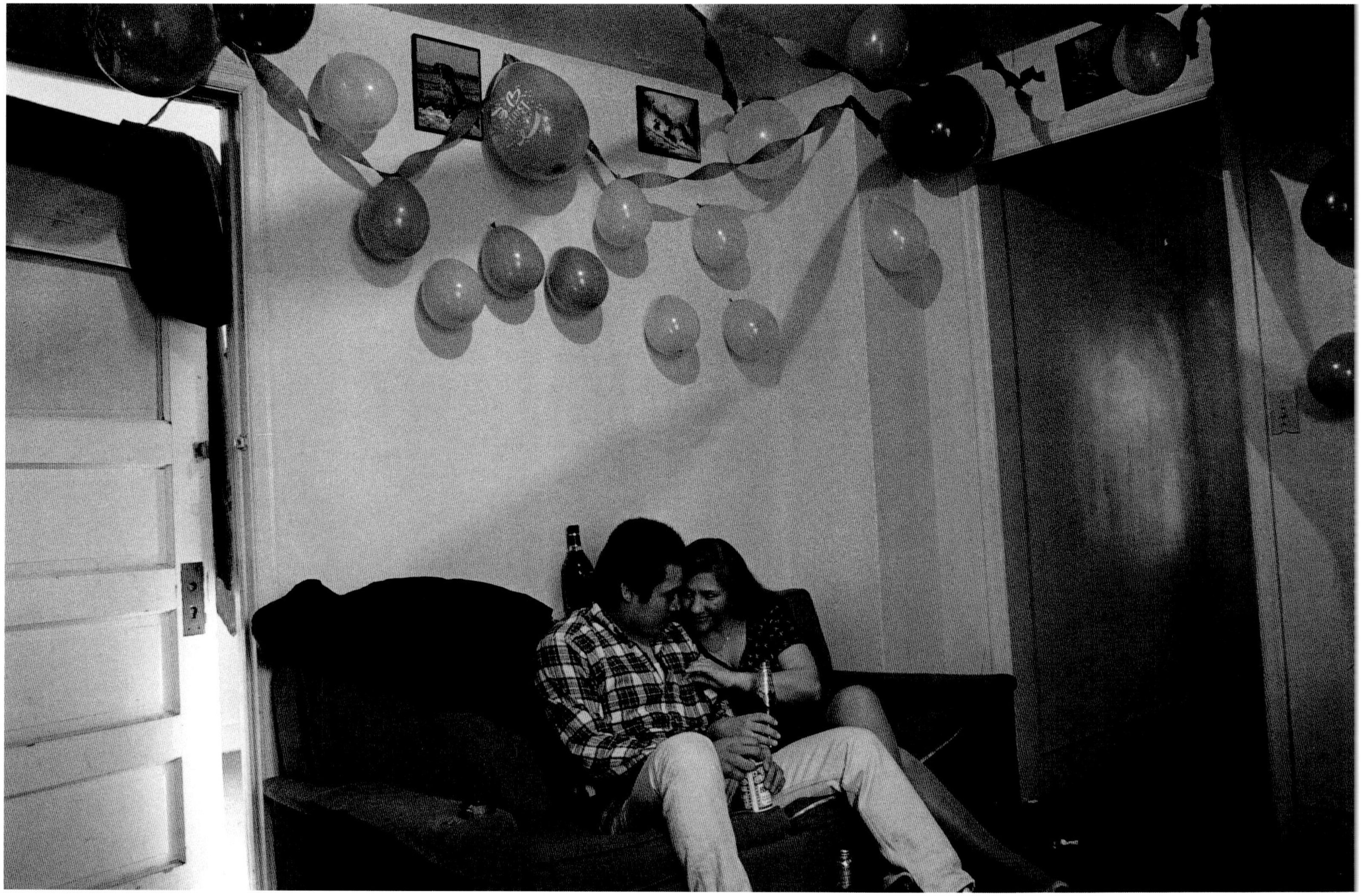

My father is Swedish, and my mother is Spanish. My mother says the Swedish are sweet and the Spanish are hot. So I'm a sweet hot Spaniard.

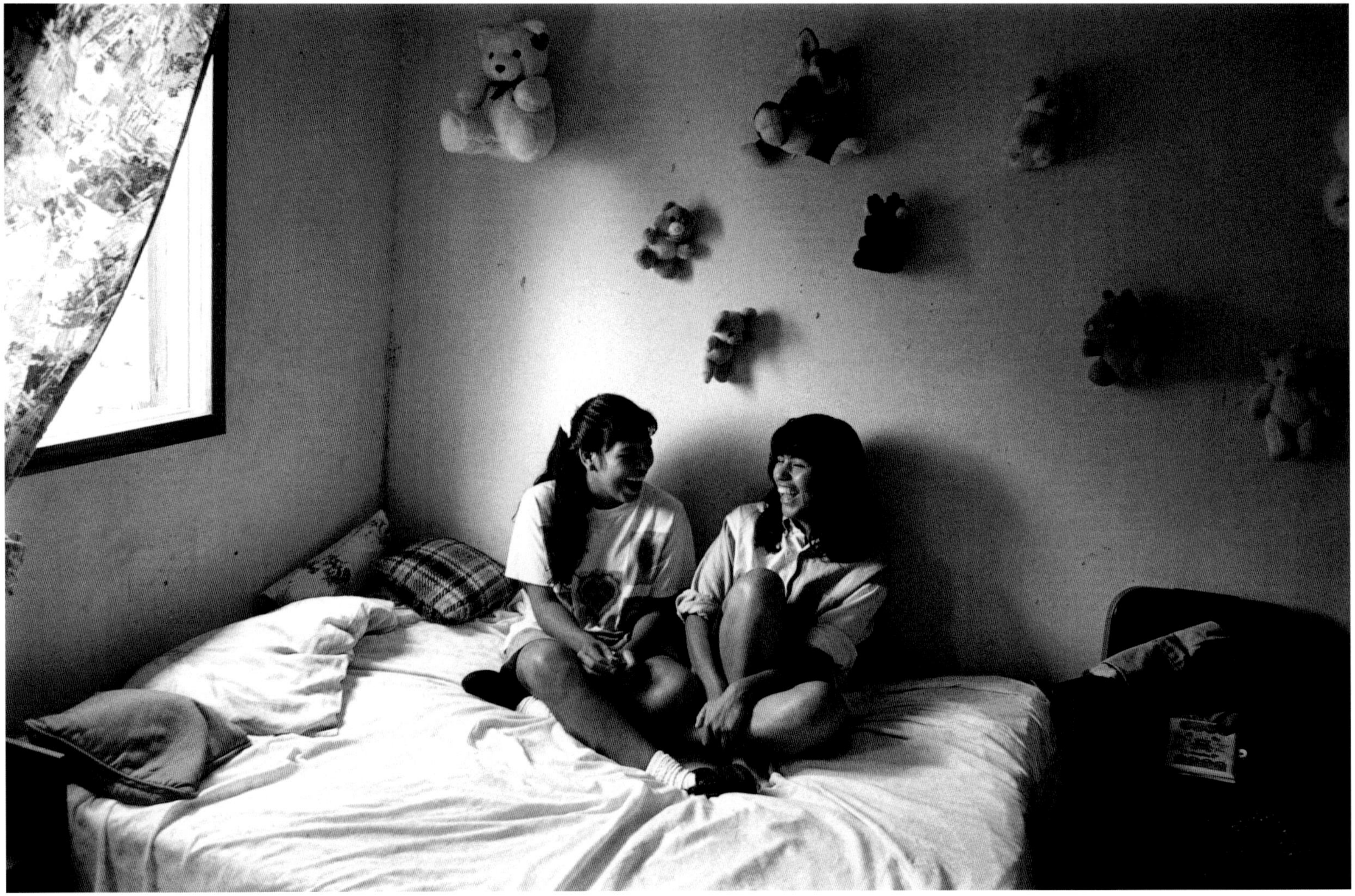

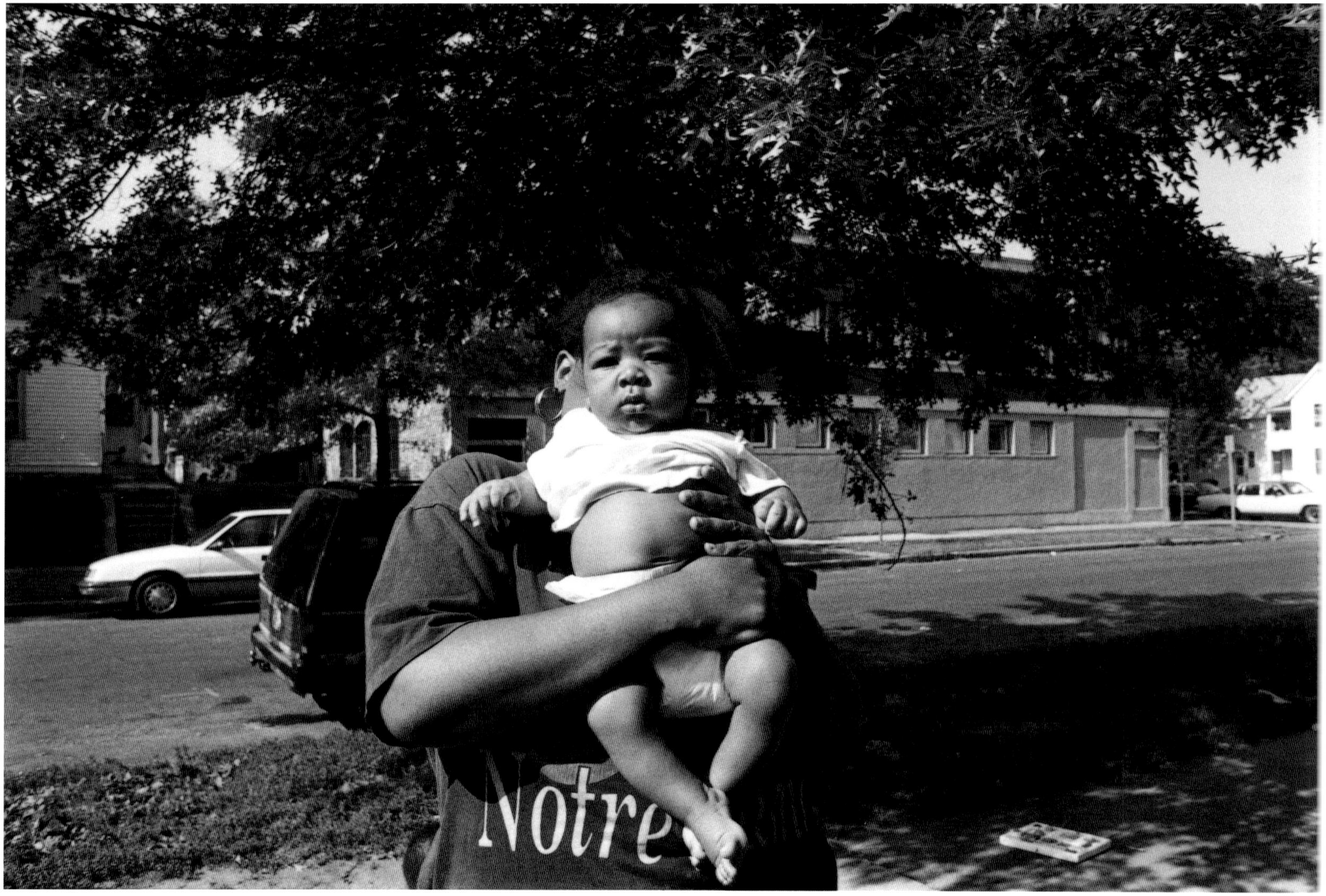
Notre

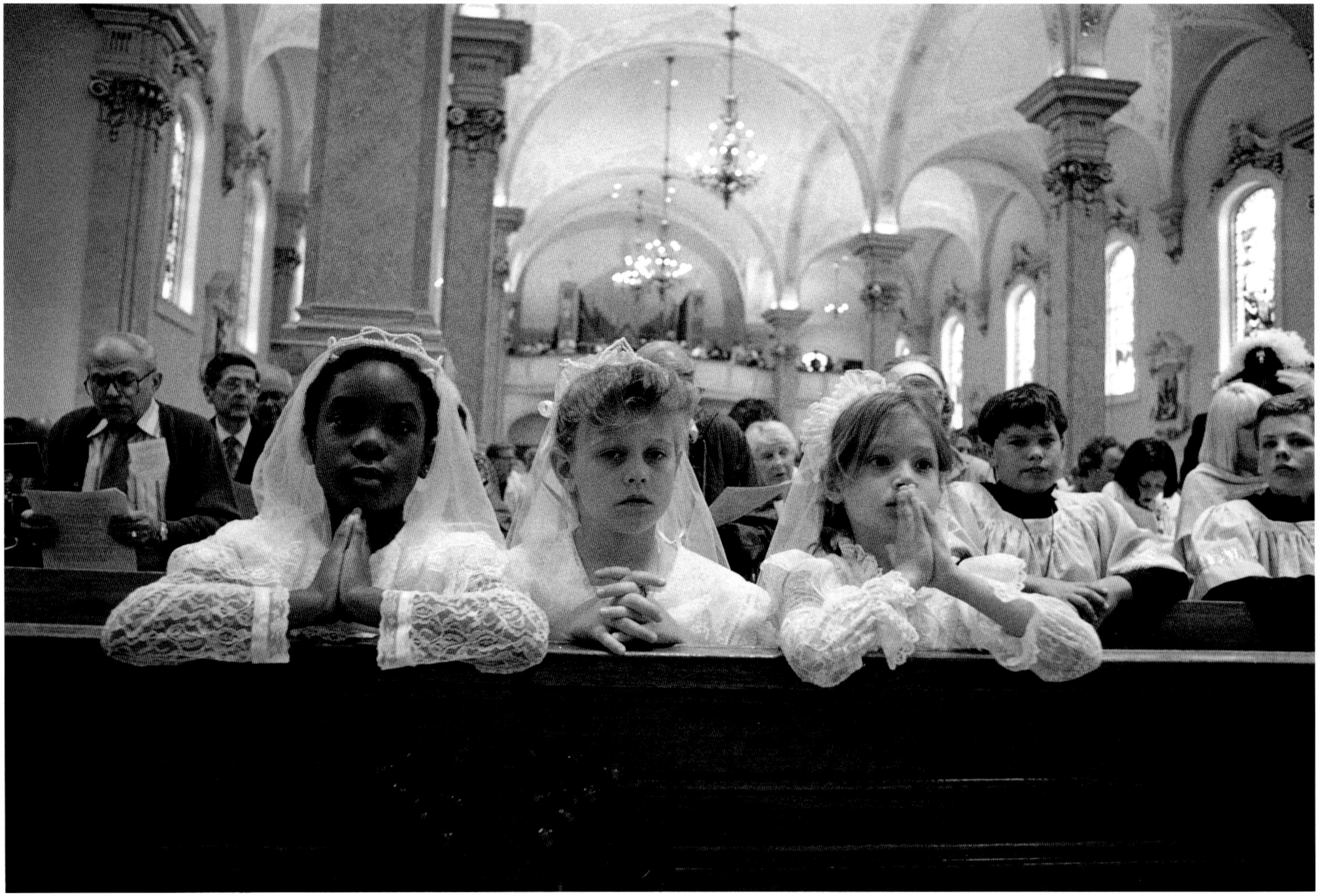

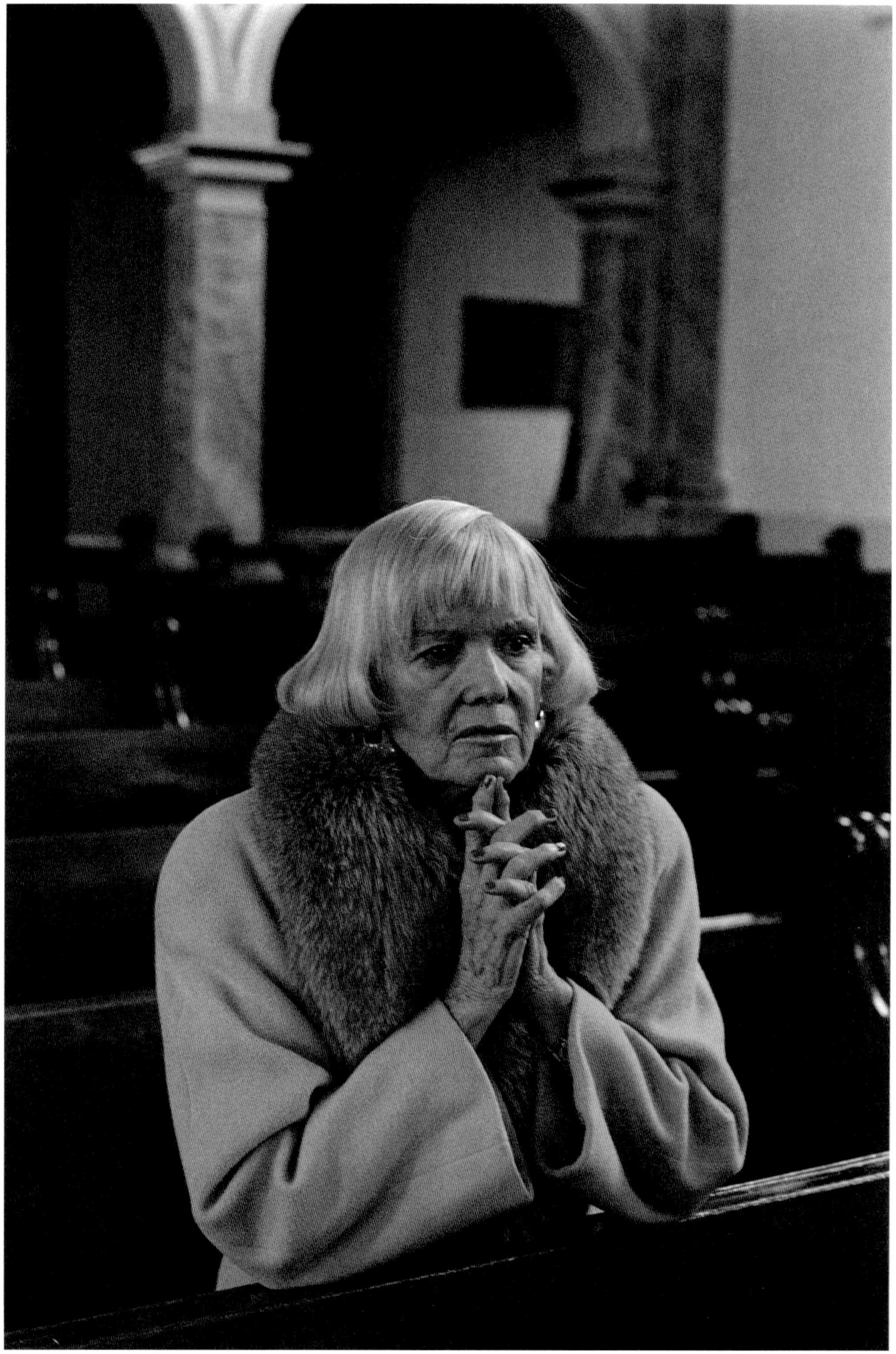

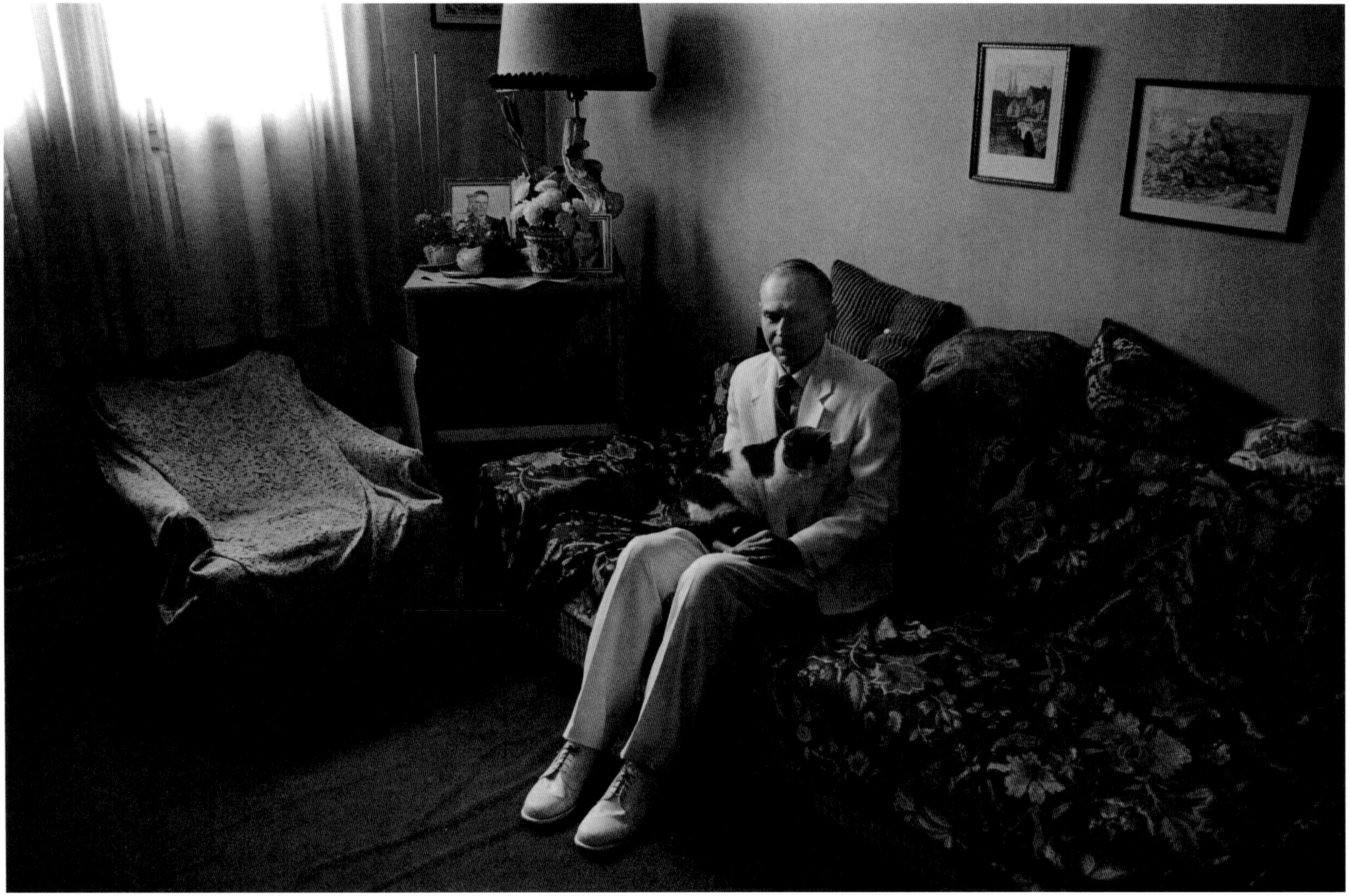

My dad and I are active at Faith Lutheran. In the church brotherhood organization I'm the recording secretary. I'm in the bell choir and the singing choir. I'm in the ushers' club and the friendship club. I go to Bible study Monday mornings. We're members of the Minnesota Historical Society and the Audubon Society. We're active in the Republican Party. I'm the precinct chairman. I'm on the board of the Thomas/Dale block club. My dad is a Boy Scout. Every year we go to a Boy Scouts jamboree.

I got the idea of wearing a white suit from my caddymaster. But I didn't know where to buy one, so I had Agnes from Agnes' Tailor Shop make me one. It's sort of reminiscent of Harry Truman, who wore an ice-cream suit. I remember seeing a photograph that was taken during World War II during the occupation of the Philippine Islands by the Japanese. And everyone in the photograph was wearing a white suit. I remember seeing Saddam Hussein wearing one on television.

I wash it by hand with Purex. It's 100-percent polyester, so it washes well, and I press it with a steam iron. It's my only white suit. I wear it quite often.

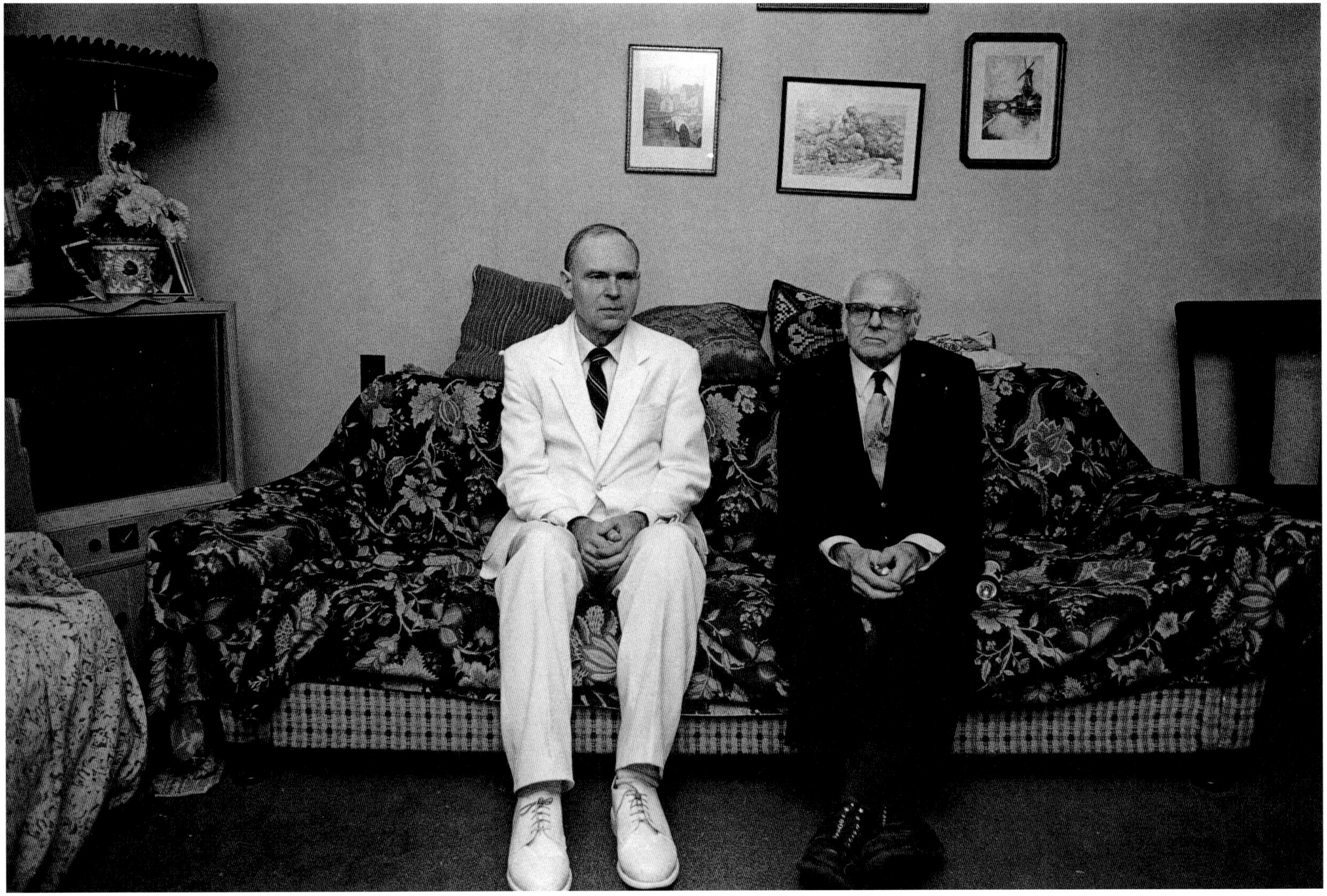

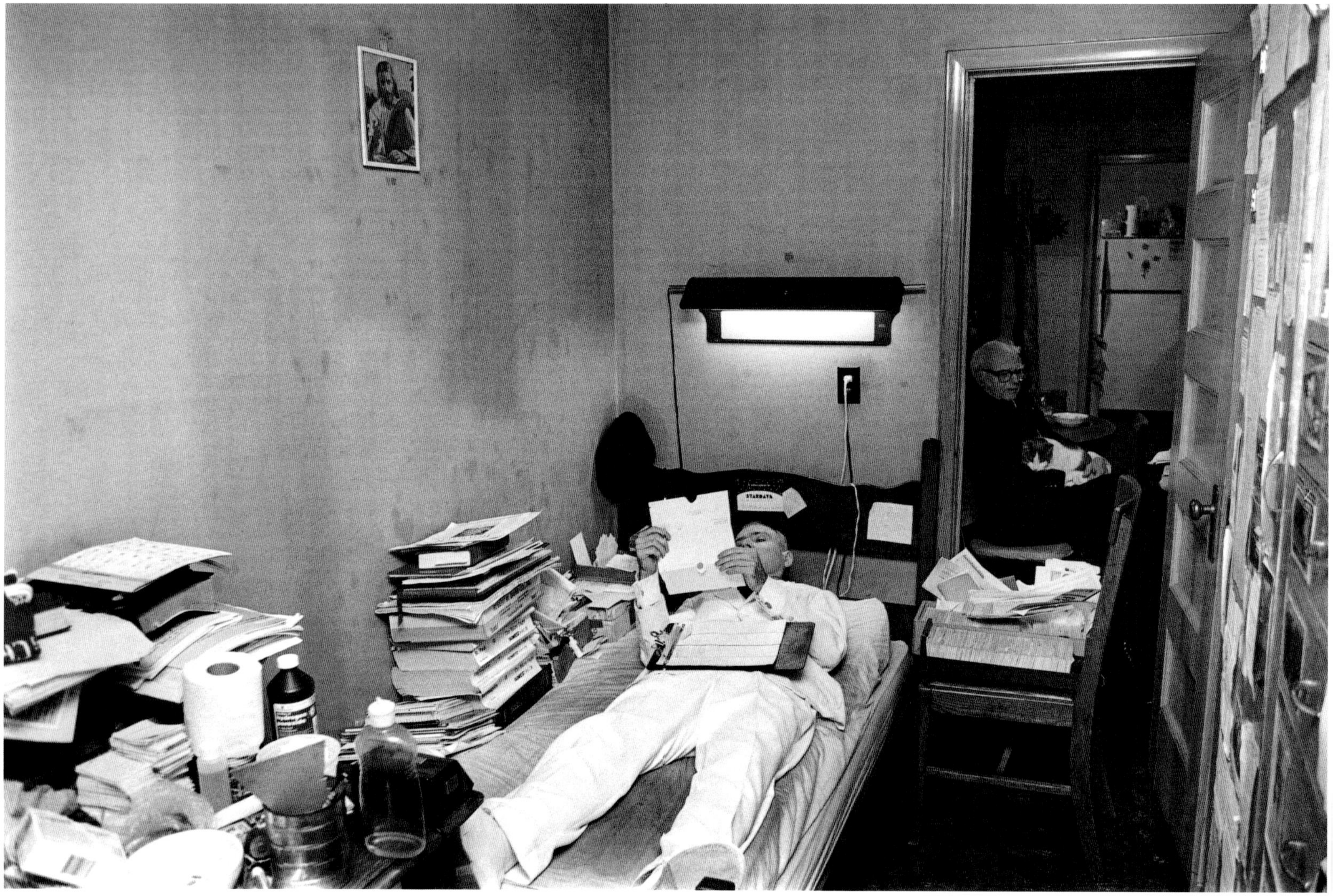

For seventeen years I've been keeping a daily diary on three-by-five-inch cards. I've got a plethora of cards, probably four thousand. I remember seeing photographs of Saddam Hussein, and he would have someone constantly writing down every word he said. I don't go that far. I write only the salient things that happen to me during the day.

It keeps me busy, and it forces me to rest because it takes time to do it. I do it every night. It's convenient to put the cards next to me when I'm on the bed in a card file, so if in the middle of the night I think of something, it's right there. J. Edgar Hoover used to have tons of the same kind of things, tons of information. It helps me to maintain close contact with reality.

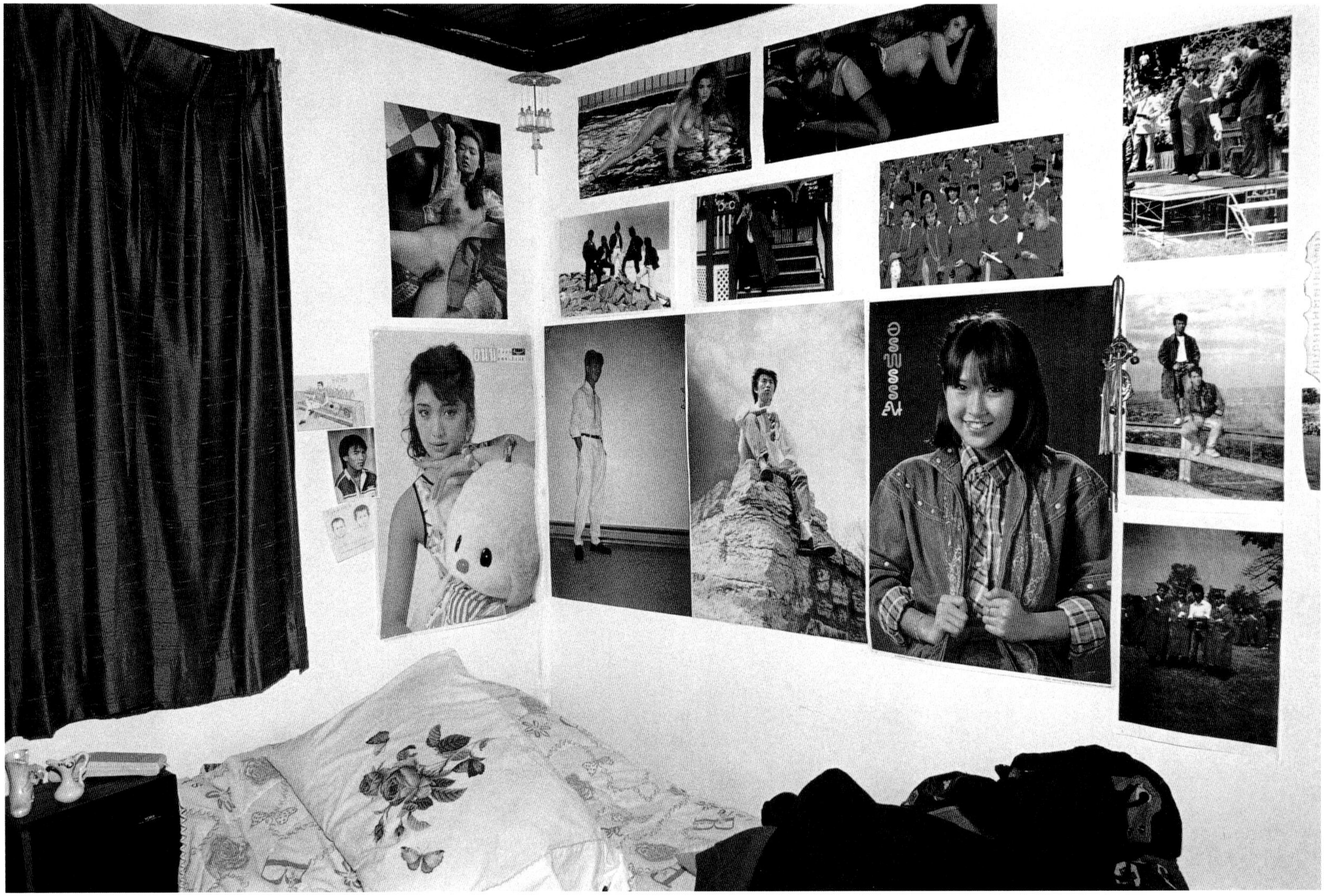

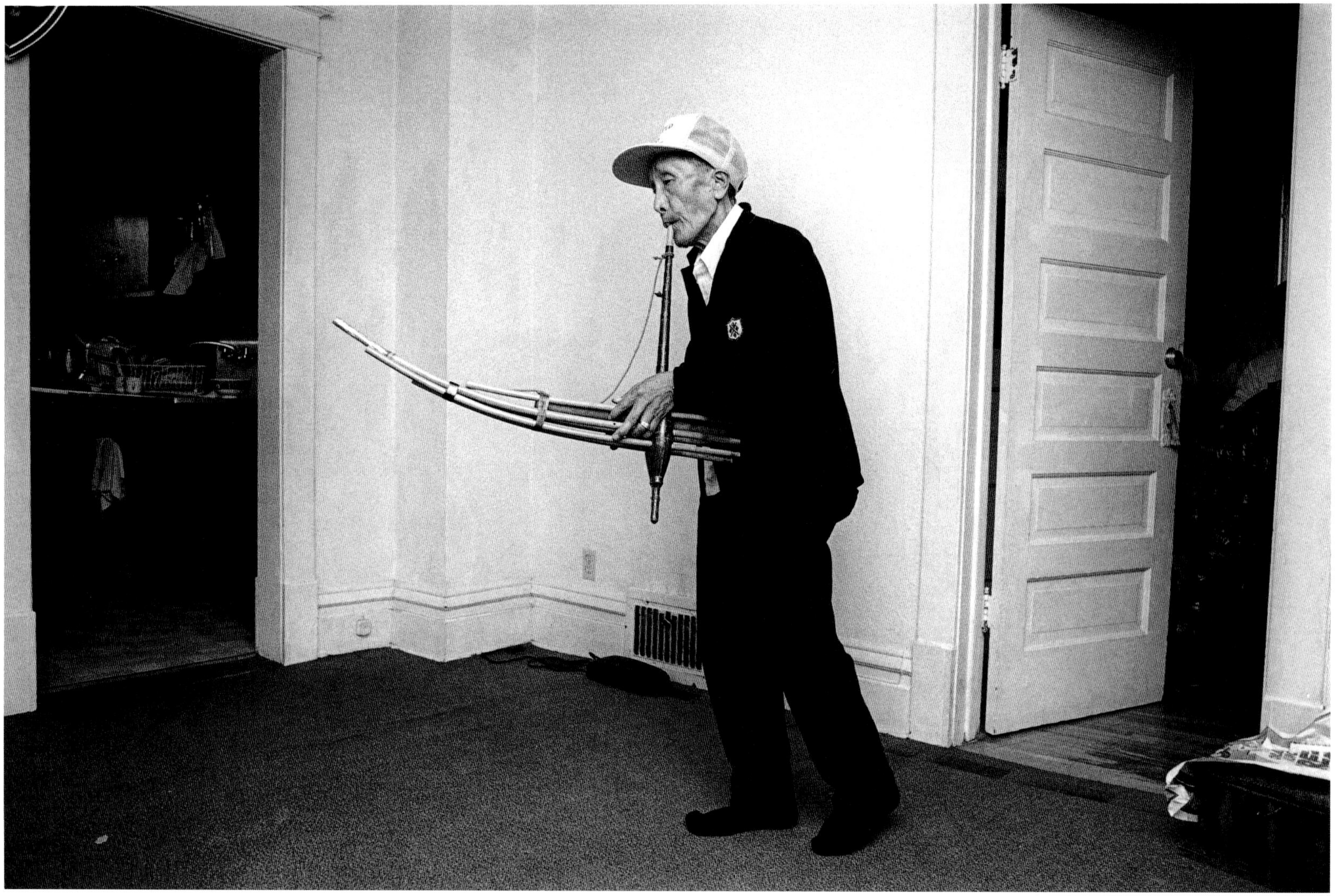

I've been playing the kheng since I was seven. I didn't have one teacher. I learned from many. It's fun for me to play. Sometimes I think about the bad things in Laos and Thailand, and I have to play the kheng.

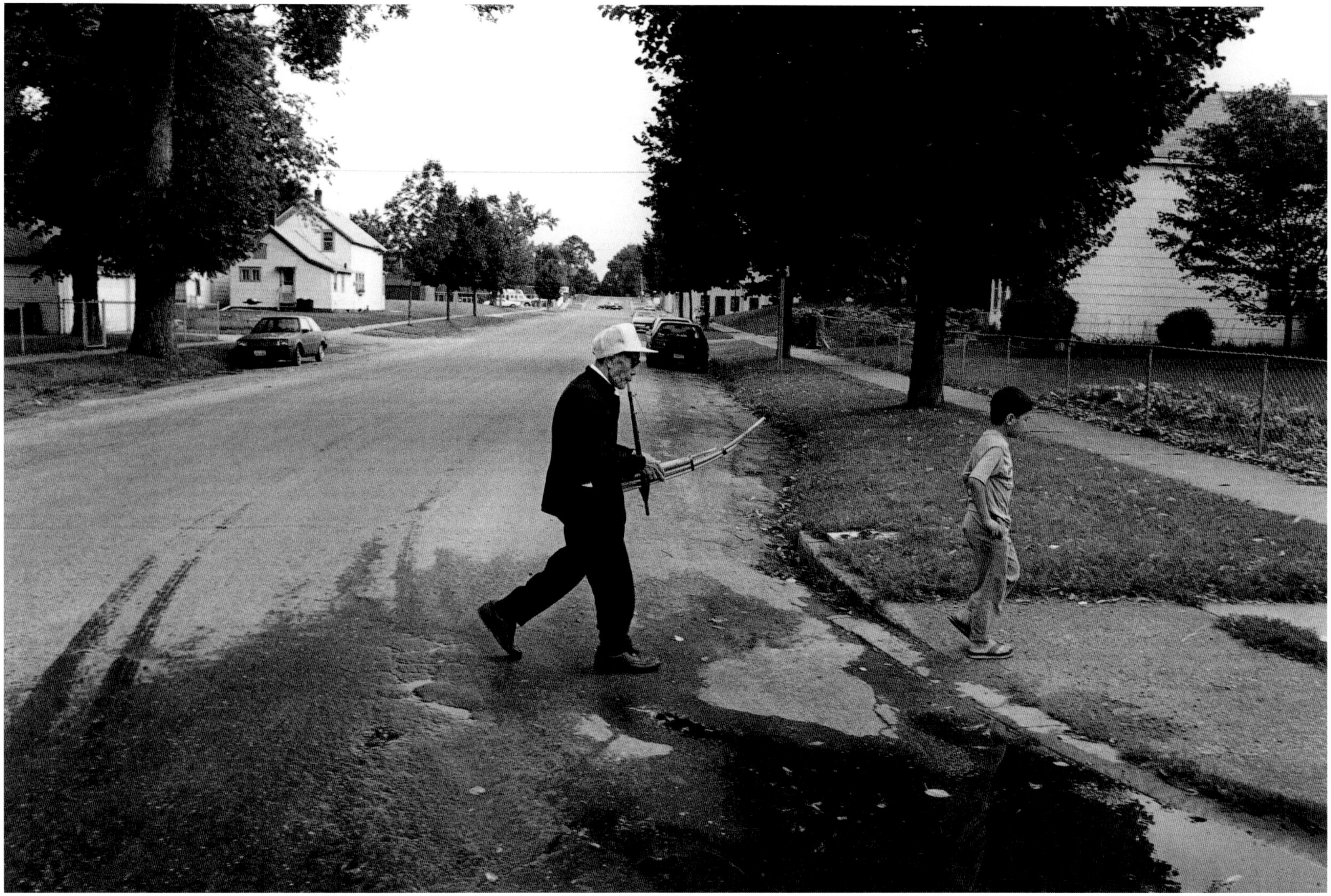

Every day, all day, all year I stay at home. I don't know how to drive a car. Nobody to take me. Sometime I lonely. I take a walk and play the kheng. I feel better.

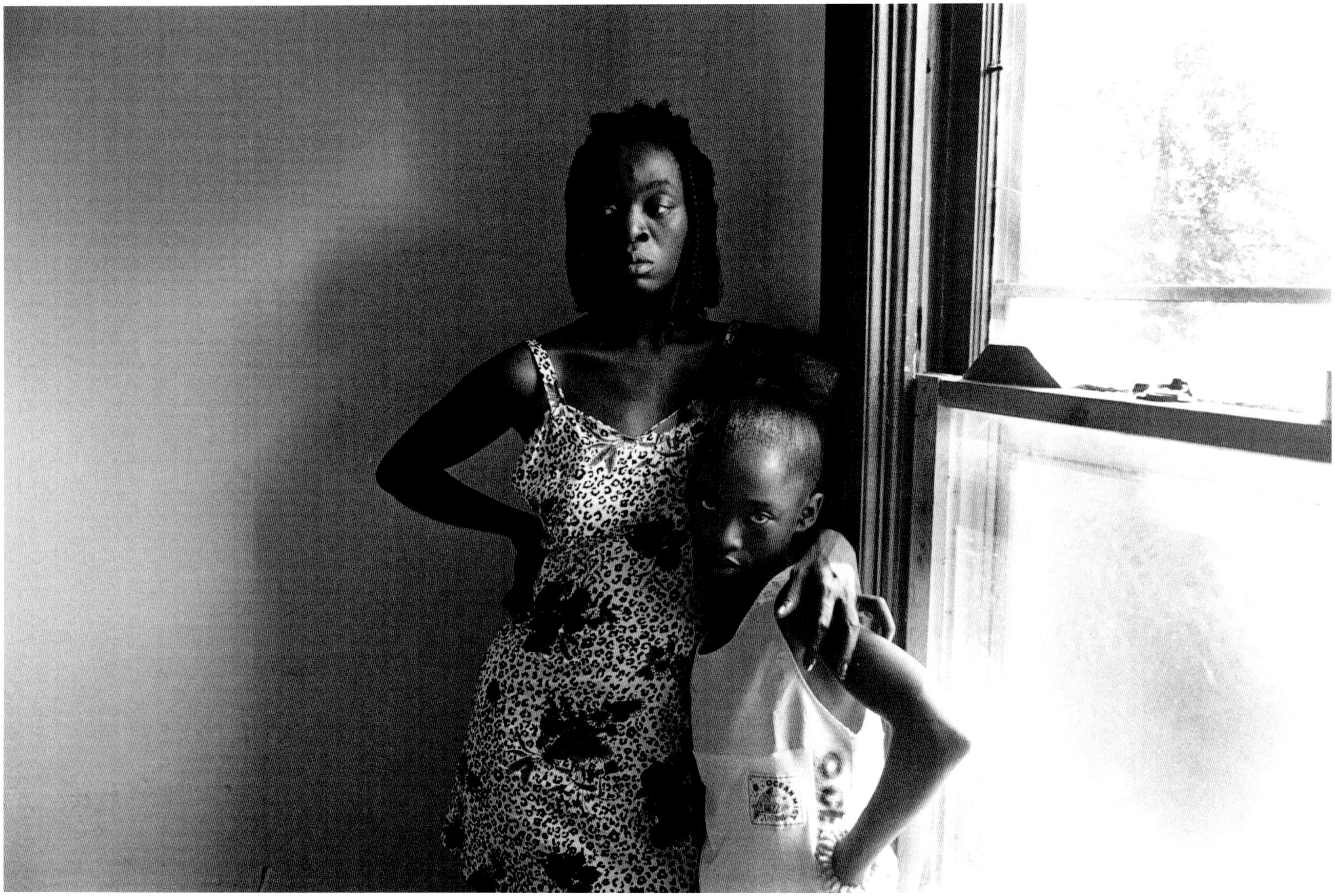

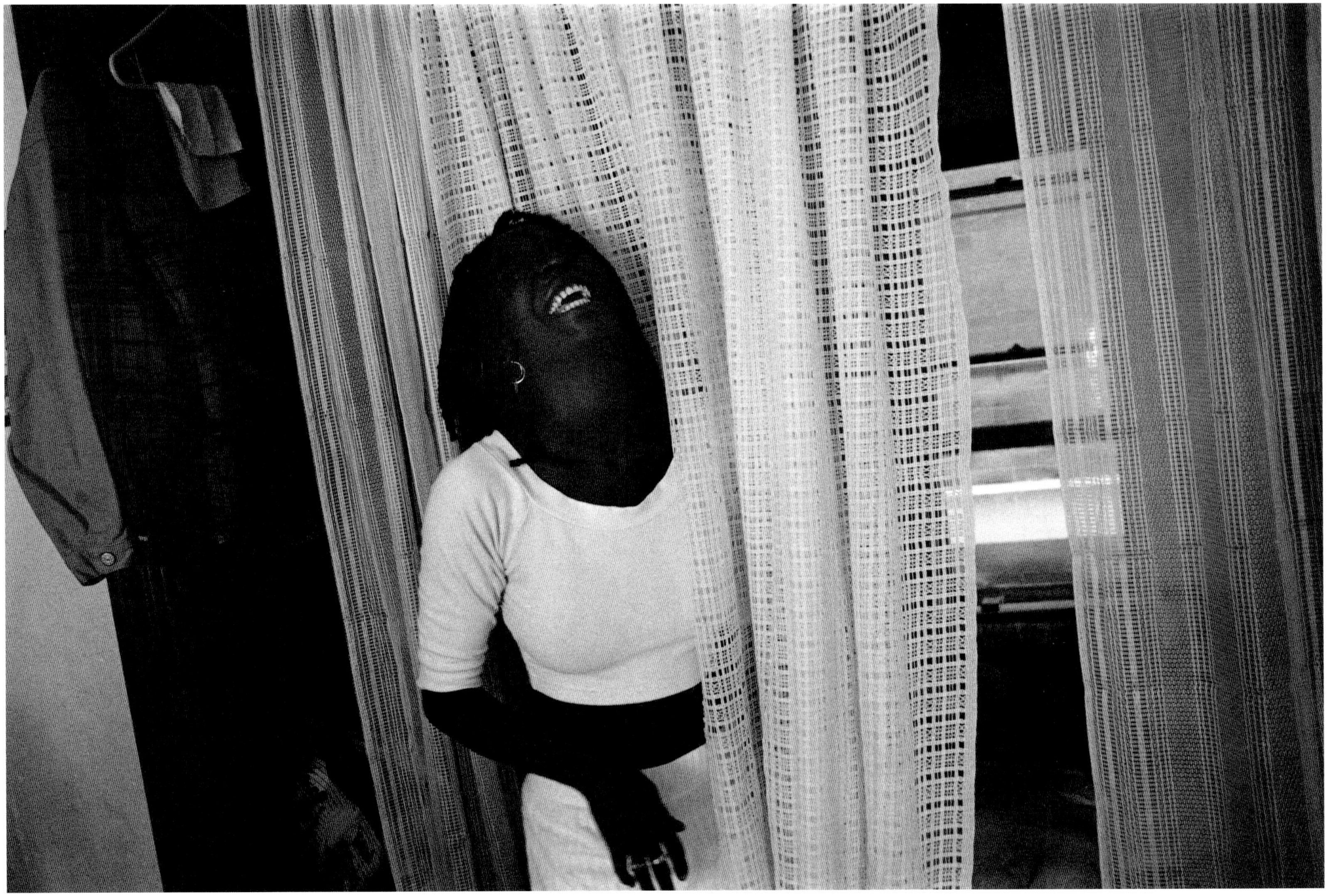

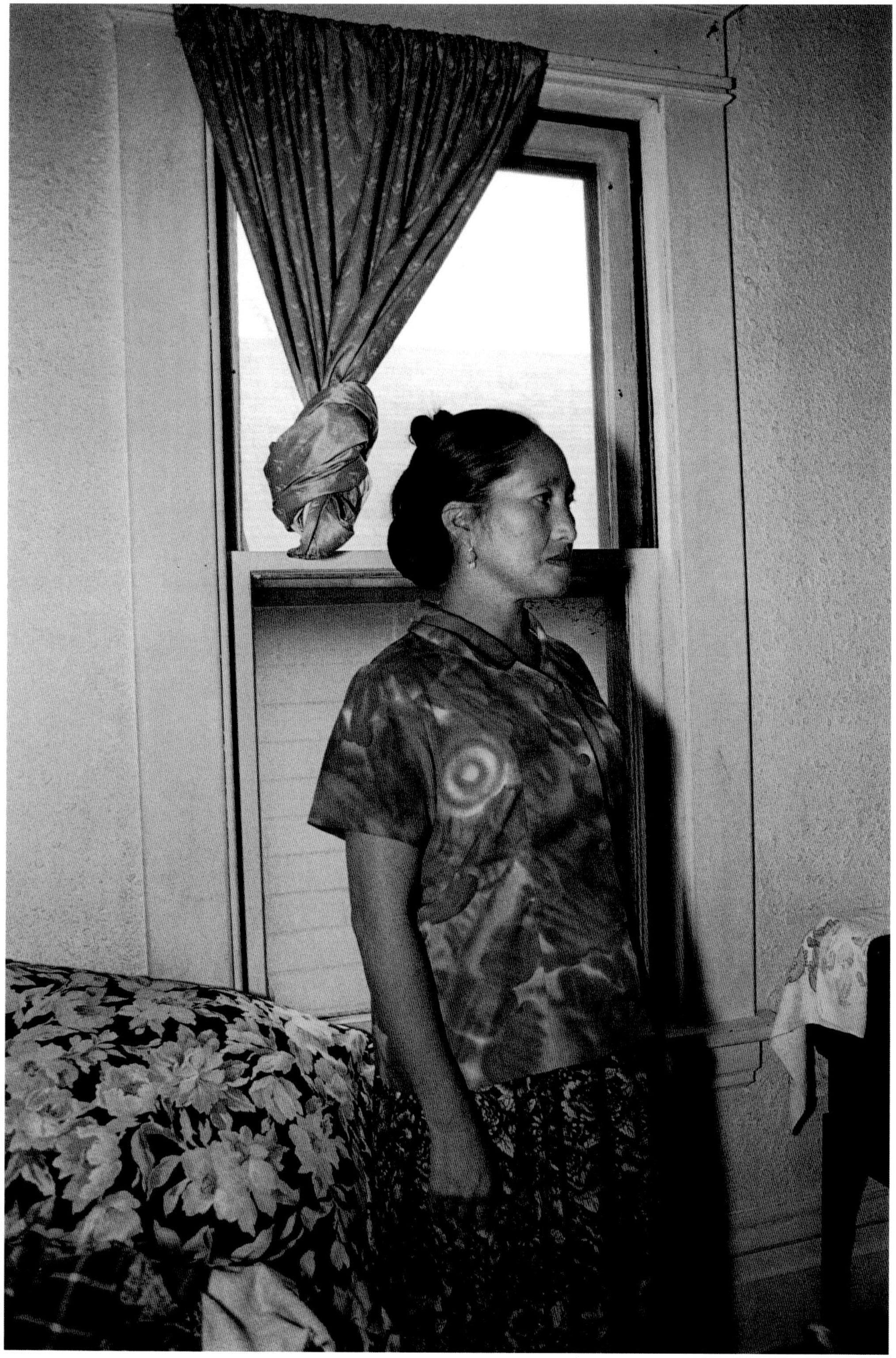

My husband and two children passed away in Thailand. We were fleeing from the communists when two of my children were shot. My husband got the rest of us to safety, but later he went back into the jungle for revenge. We never heard from him again.

I am not looking for another husband. In America they marry you a couple of days and just leave if they don't want you anymore. Same with the women. Because it's a free country. Back in Laos, both sides of the family try to discourage divorce. There's more tradition.

I could not find someone who loved me like my first husband. I don't get lonely. I'm happy without a man. It's harder in Laos if you don't have a husband to support the family. Here, you can be more independent and make your own living. But I am uneducated and have a physical problem. I got shot in the leg fleeing the communists in the jungle in Laos. If I were physically able, I could work. If I were educated, I could work. But right now I have to depend on the government.

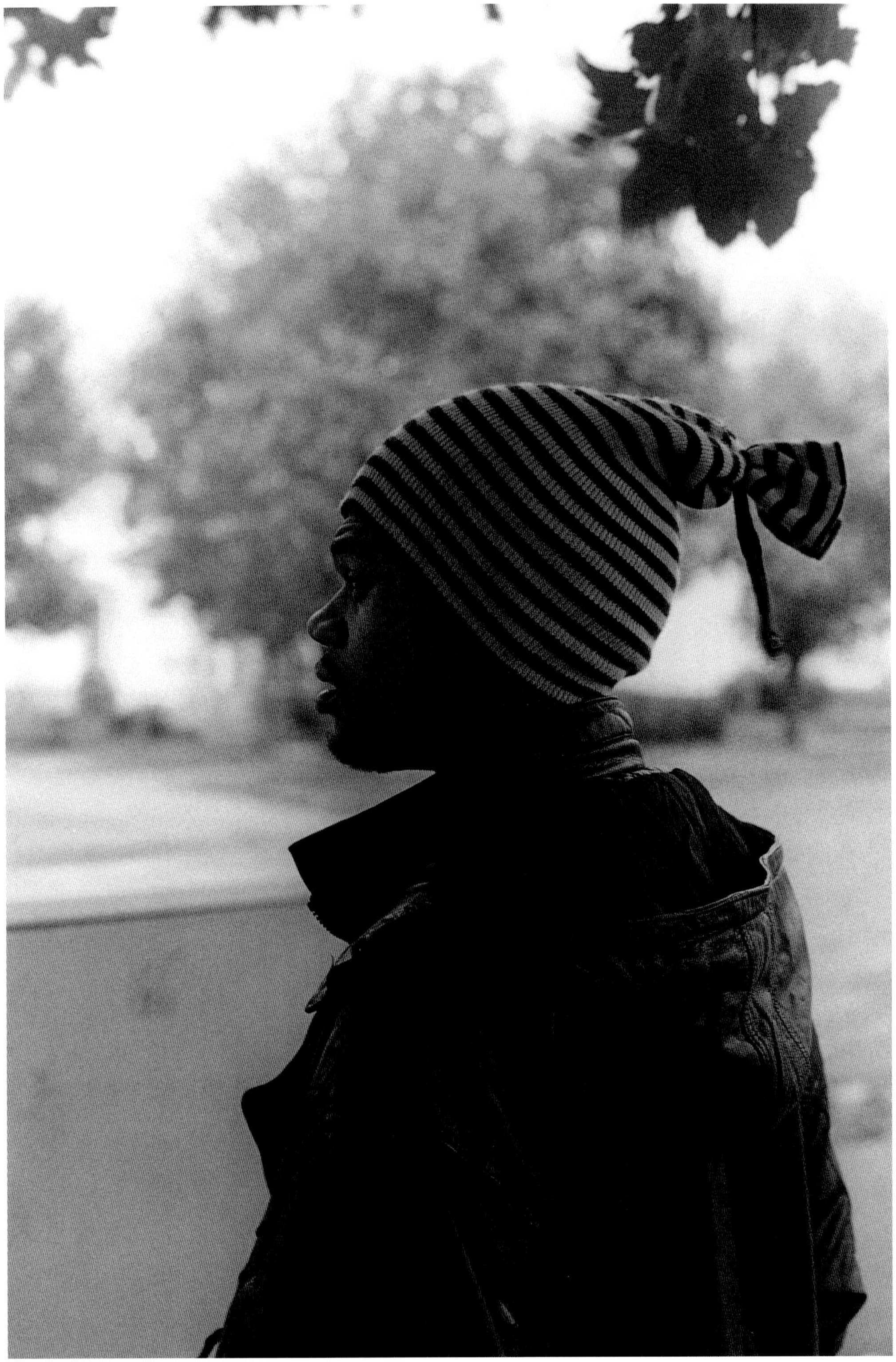

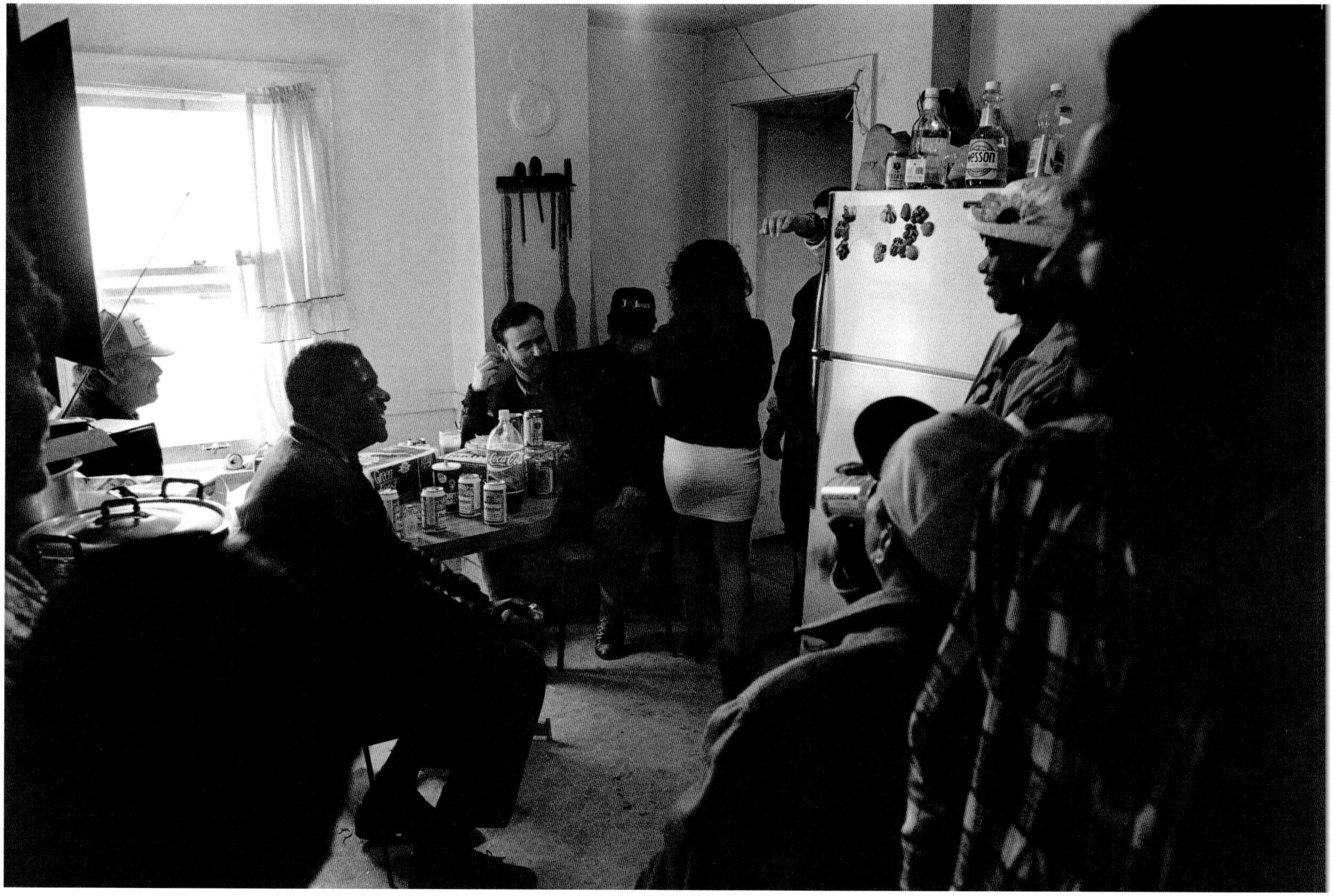

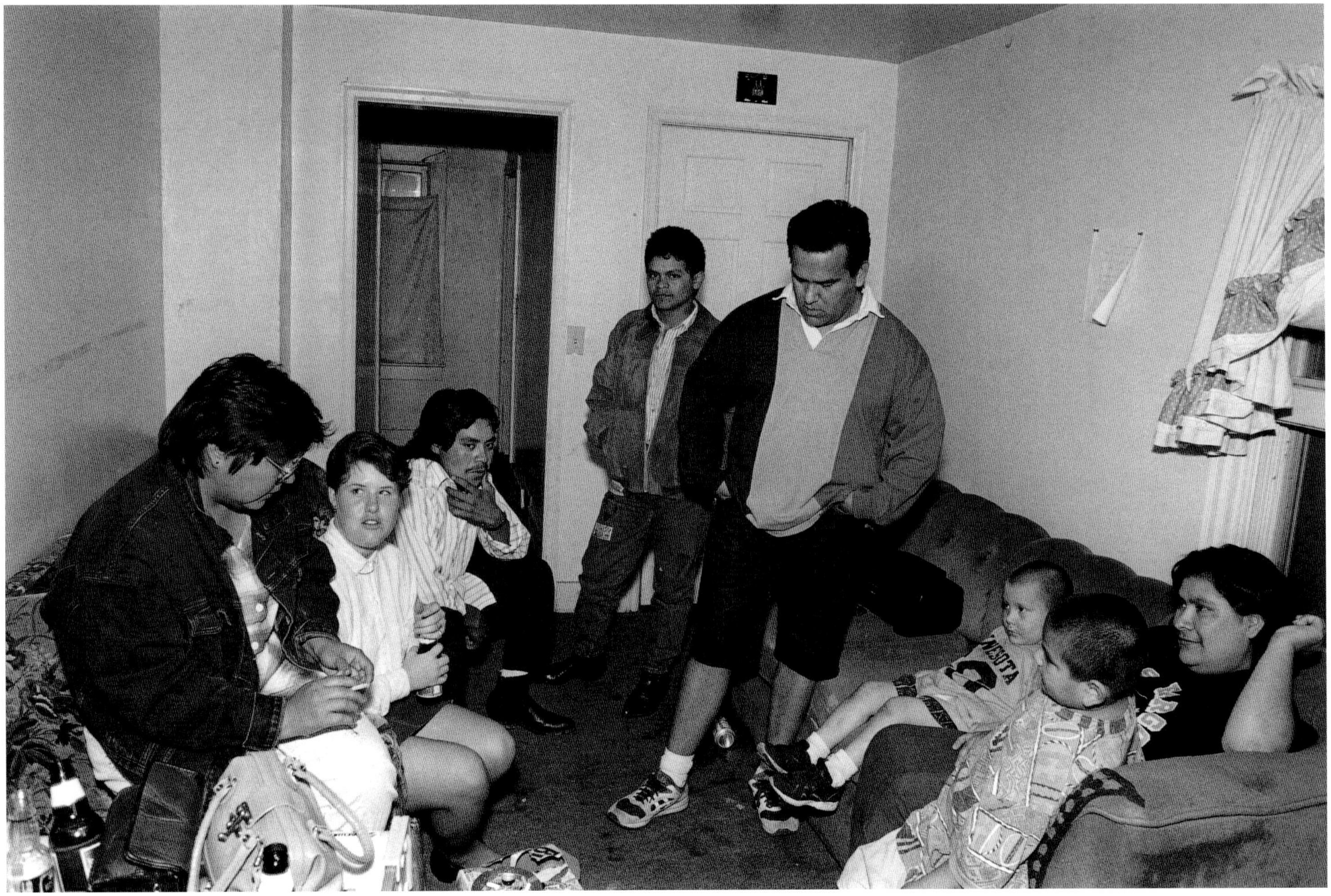

One thing that really surprised me when we got here from California was that nobody here speaks Spanish. If my wife needs to call the police, she can't. There's no one to understand her. In central L.A. the police speak Spanish. In all the stores they speak Spanish. The Anglos speak Spanish. Even the Chinos [Chinese] *speak Spanish.*

In West St. Paul [where there is a large Mexican community] *it's a little problematical because there are Mexicans from so many different places and so many different ways of living. Some play music really loud, some drink a lot. And so people are always getting in arguments and fights. So it's easier to live in Frogtown. On one side we have a Chinos* [actually Hmong]. *On the other is a Negritos* [African American]. *We like the neighborhood because it's quiet and there's no trouble at night. But we don't know many people because we don't speak English well.*

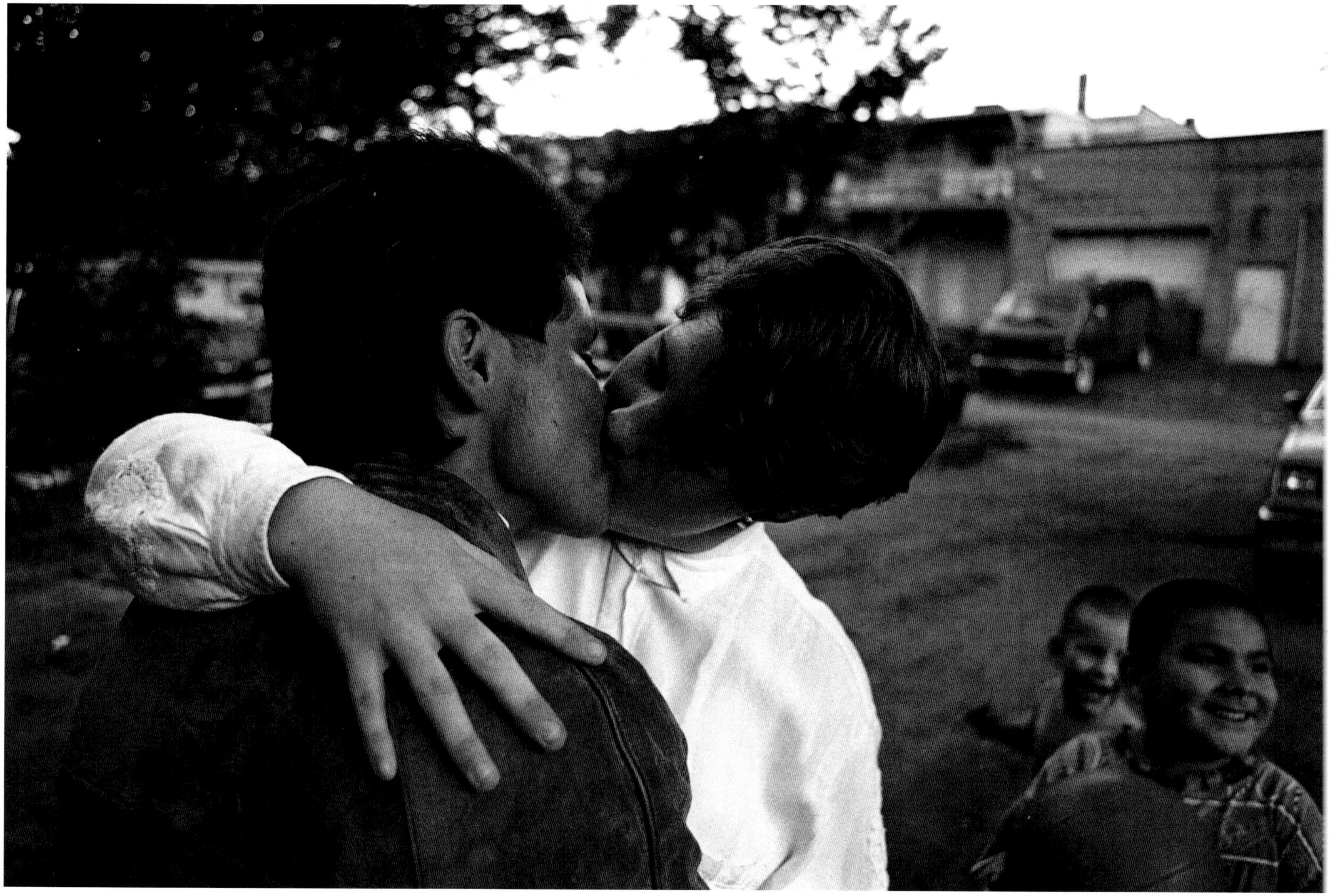

This is my first American girlfriend. We met at a party, and she asked me to go to a movie with her. I like American girls. I would like to marry an American girl because they are more pretty. I like how they act, all nice and stuff. I like Mexican girls, too. But they are different. I can't explain how.

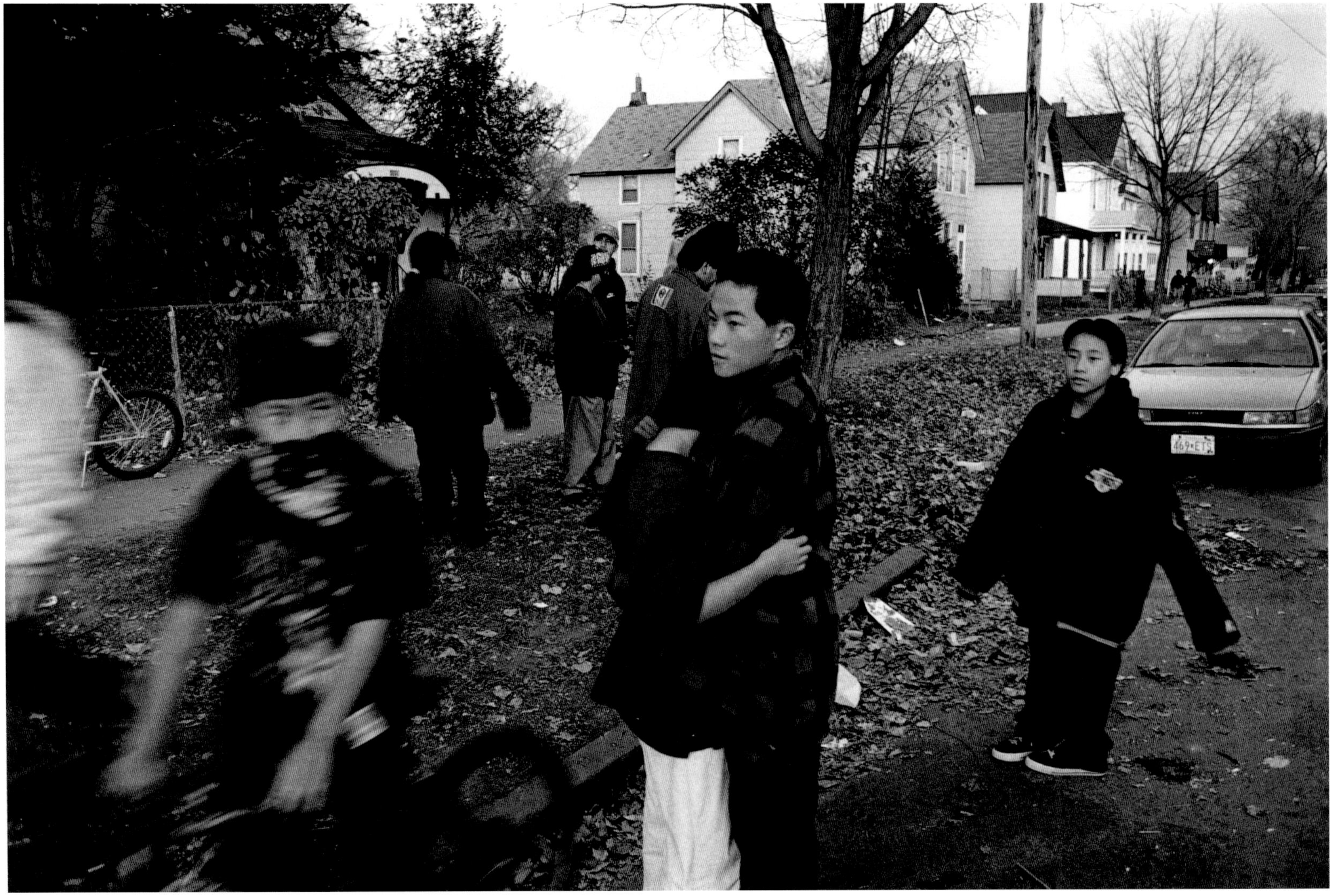

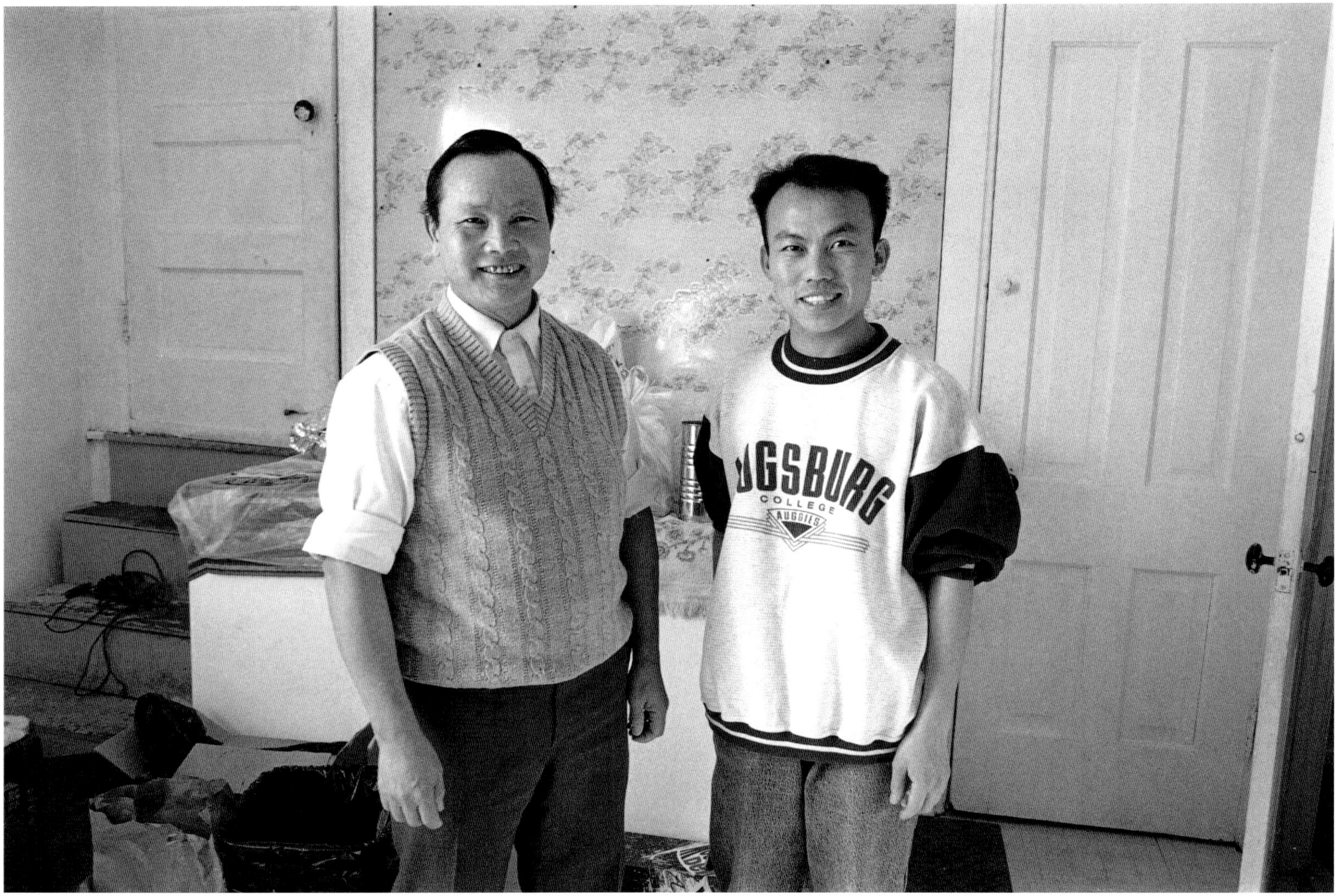

I was in a camp in Thailand for four years. Now I go to Augsburg College in Minneapolis. I'm the only one of eleven kids in the family to go to school. Everyone in the family supports me. They look up to me as the hope for their future. I feel a pressure to succeed, and so I try the best I can. I'm going to school for my whole family.

Since I was born to this earth I have never heard or seen a place called the Hmong country. Our people are spread around the world. Where we live, that's where our country is.

Sometimes we have a feeling that other people, like the native people, don't treat us as good as they are supposed to. And so we kind of feel bad. It's also hard for us to find the job we want with the education we have. And we feel bad about that.

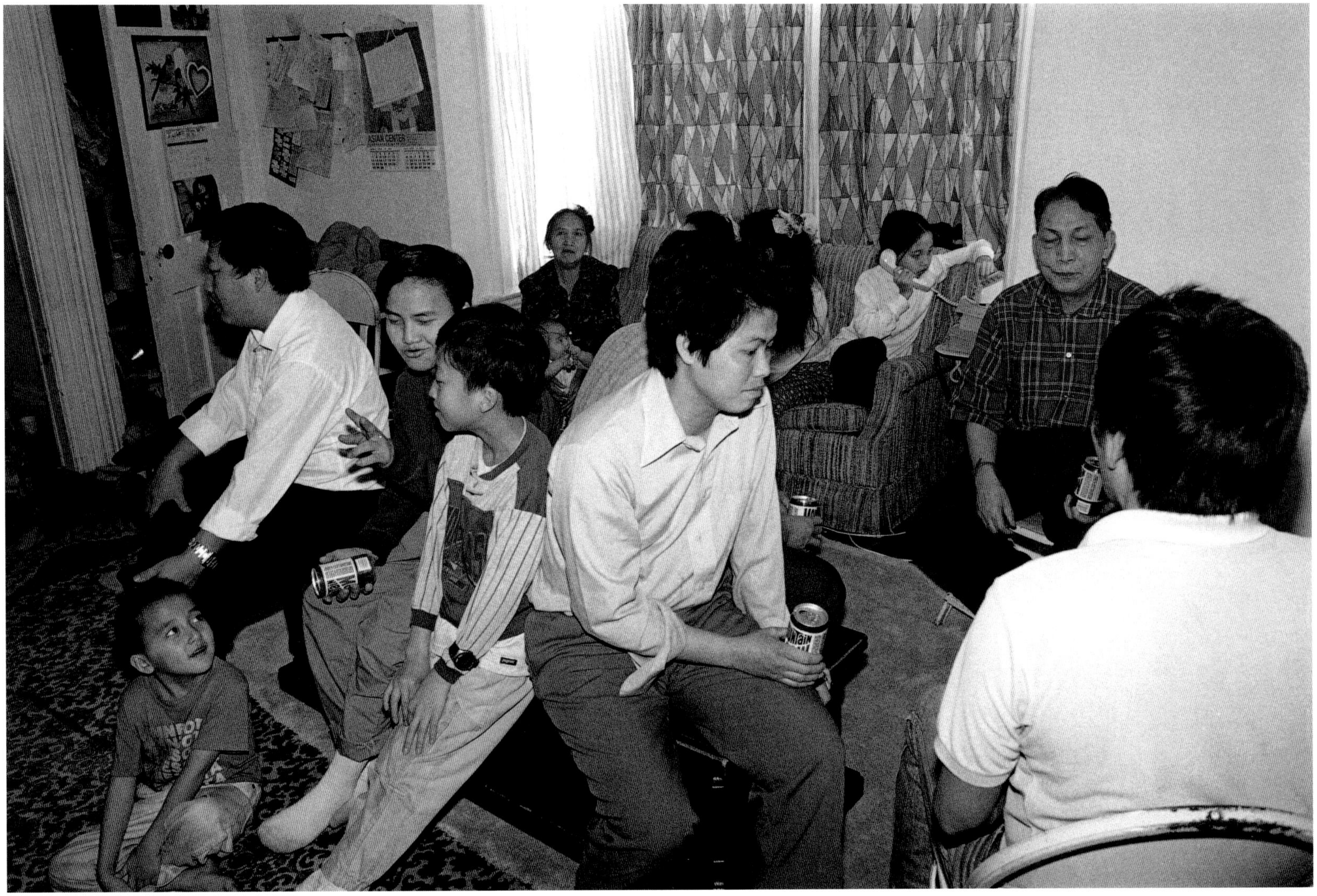
ASIAN CENTER

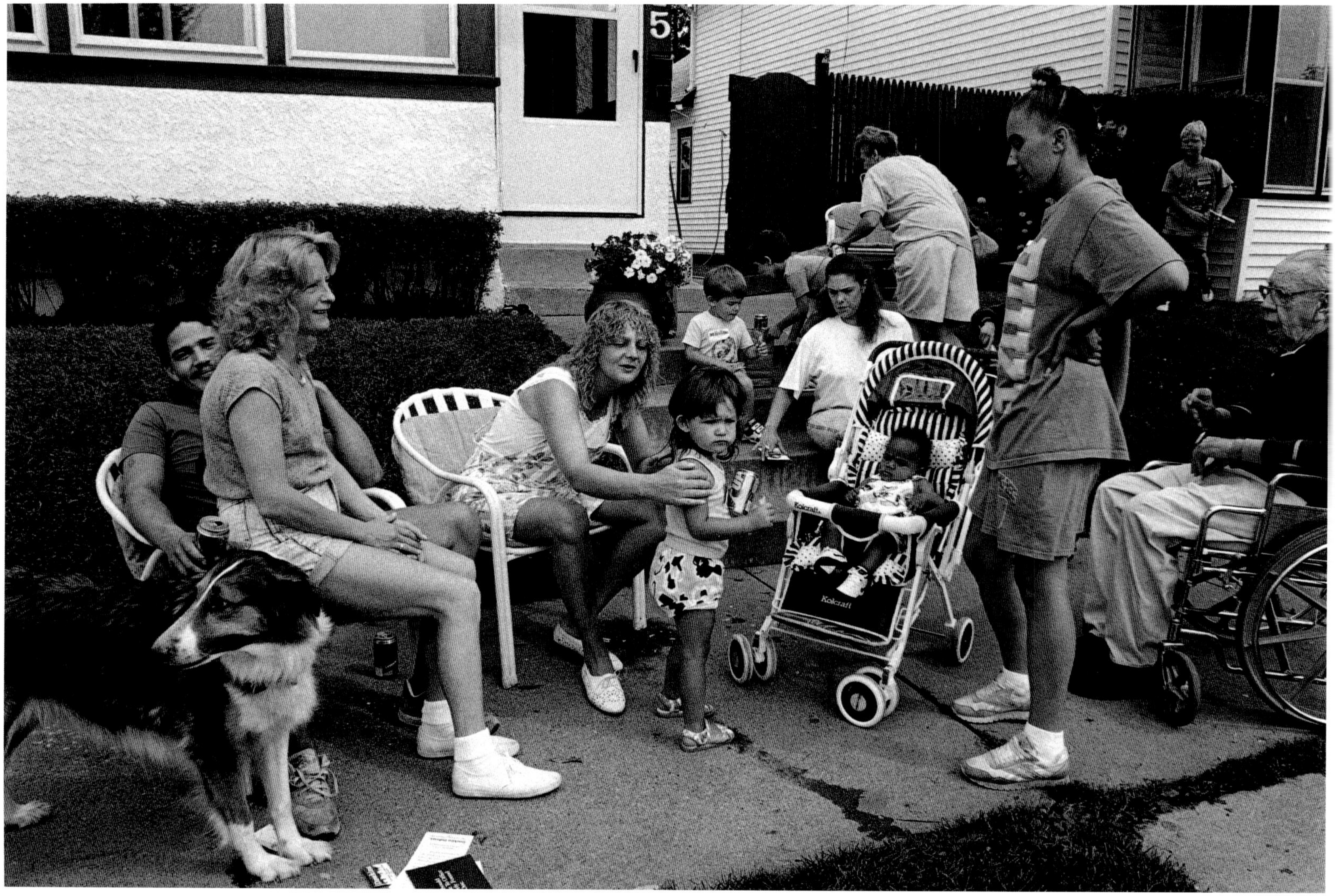
5
Kolcraft

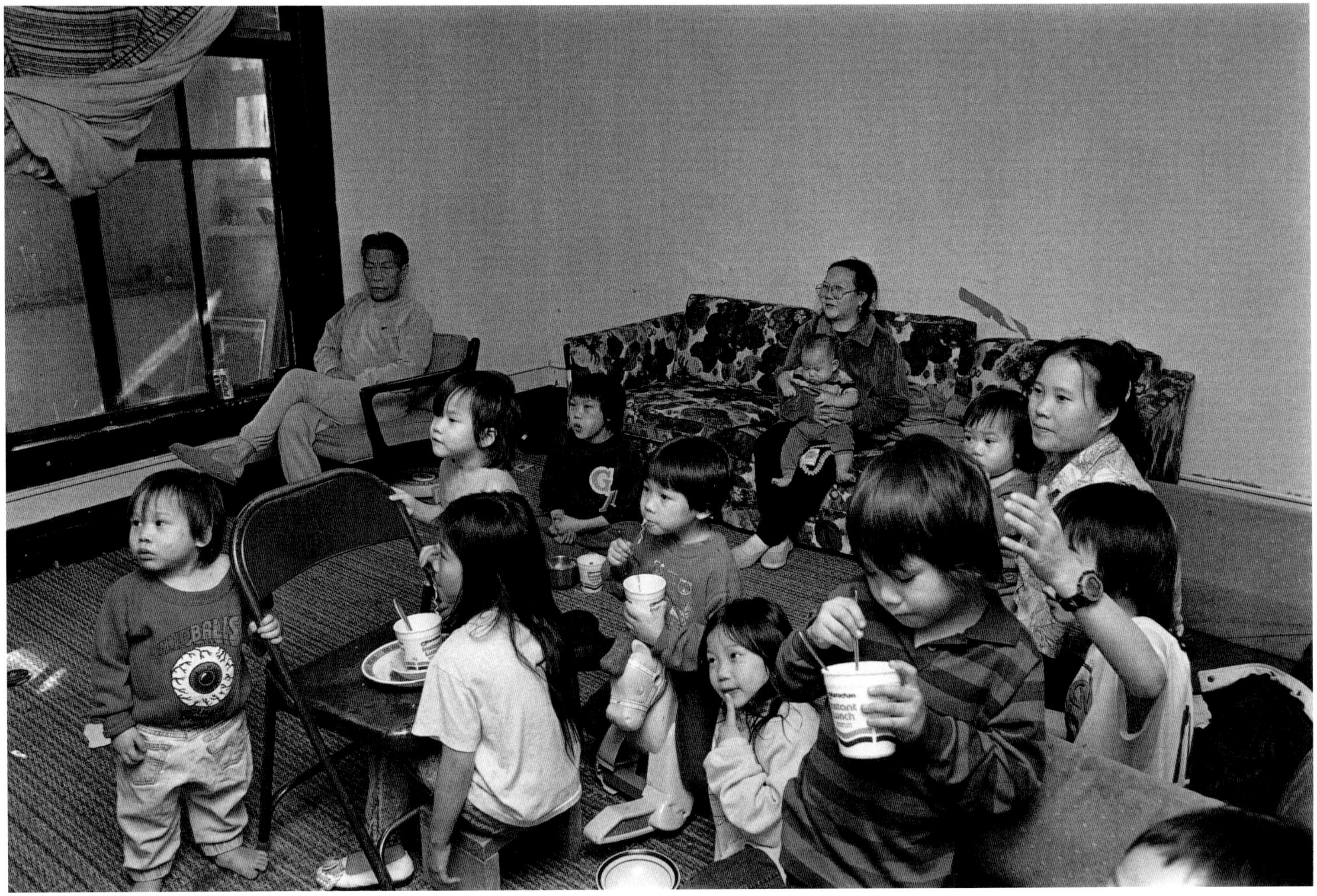

I had my first child when I was fourteen. I am twenty-five now, and I have eleven kids. I never thought I would have so many. I don't like having so many. When I was a teenager, I thought I would have only five kids. I don't know what happened. My husband helps, and the older ones help take care of the younger ones. My sister has ten kids. When she visits, she brings all her kids. The house then is too crowded.

It is hard to control all the kids sometimes, but I never feel like it is too much. Someday, when the youngest is maybe five, I would like to go back to high school. I never finished. I liked high school very much. When I go back, I would like to learn about everything.

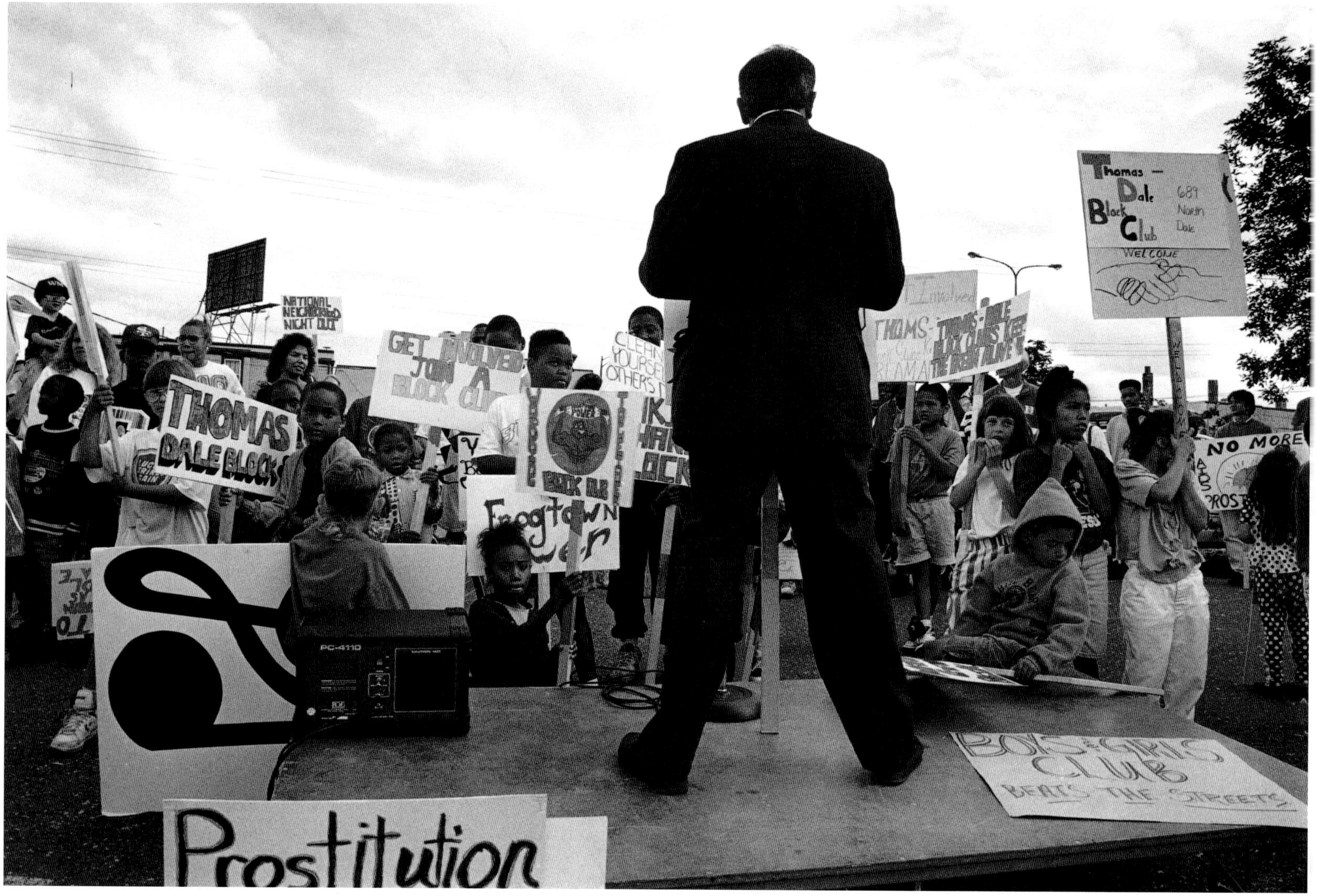
Thomas - Dale Block Club
689 North Dale
WELCOME
NATIONAL NEIGHBORHOOD NIGHT OUT
GET INVOLVED JOIN A BLOCK CLUB
THOMAS DALE BLOCK
Frogtown
NO MORE
PC-4110
BOYS & GIRLS CLUB BEATS THE STREETS
Prostitution

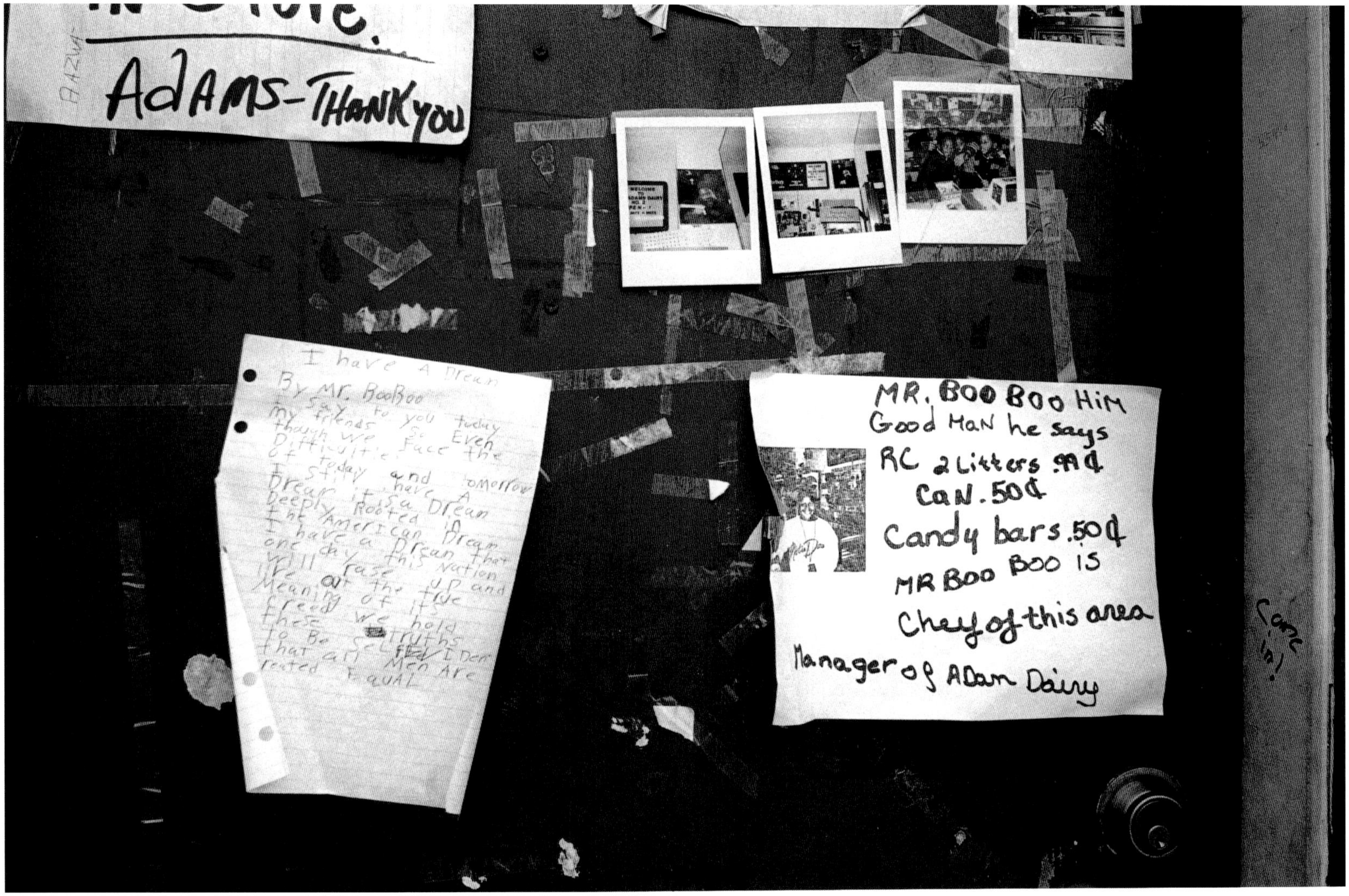
AdAMS-THANK you
I have A Dream
By MR. BooBoo
MR. BOO BOO HIM
Good MaN he says
RC 2 Litters .99¢
CaN .50¢
Candy bars .50¢
MR BOO BOO IS
Cheyof this area
Manager of ADam Dairy
Come in!

Mike (the owner of Adams Dairy) and his friend Mr. Boo Boo.

Mike: *Mr. Boo Boo, his father came into store all the time to buy groceries and cigarettes. Sometime he would work for me, sweeping and cleaning the store. Someone came into store and told me somebody shot and killed Mr. Boo Boo's father. Mr. Boo Boo crying, crying: "My dad killed, my dad killed." When I go cemetery I gave fifty dollars to buy flower. My heart cry. I told Mr. Boo Boo I buy for him clothes, I buy for him shoes.*

Anything he wants I buy for him. I take care of him because him don't have father. Me father for him. I take care of him. He take money from register—five, ten—to buy food, to buy chicken. Whatever he want, I no stop him. I treat him like my children. Him okay now.

Mr. Boo Boo: *A long time ago my dad used to work with Mike at the store. After my dad died Mike called my house and asked, do I want to work and take my dad's place? I asked my mom, and she said yeah. At first I didn't know what to do, but he taught me how to do everything.*

I watch so nobody steals. I bag bags, put pop in the coolers. I give change. I work almost everyday from six until nine. Every time I come here Mike gives me pop and stuff. I like working here a lot. It's fun.

Mike is nice. He's just like [my real father]. *A long time ago my dad and my brothers and sisters, we went on trips and stuff. Then he got shot. So everything that I did with my dad before, Mike does.*

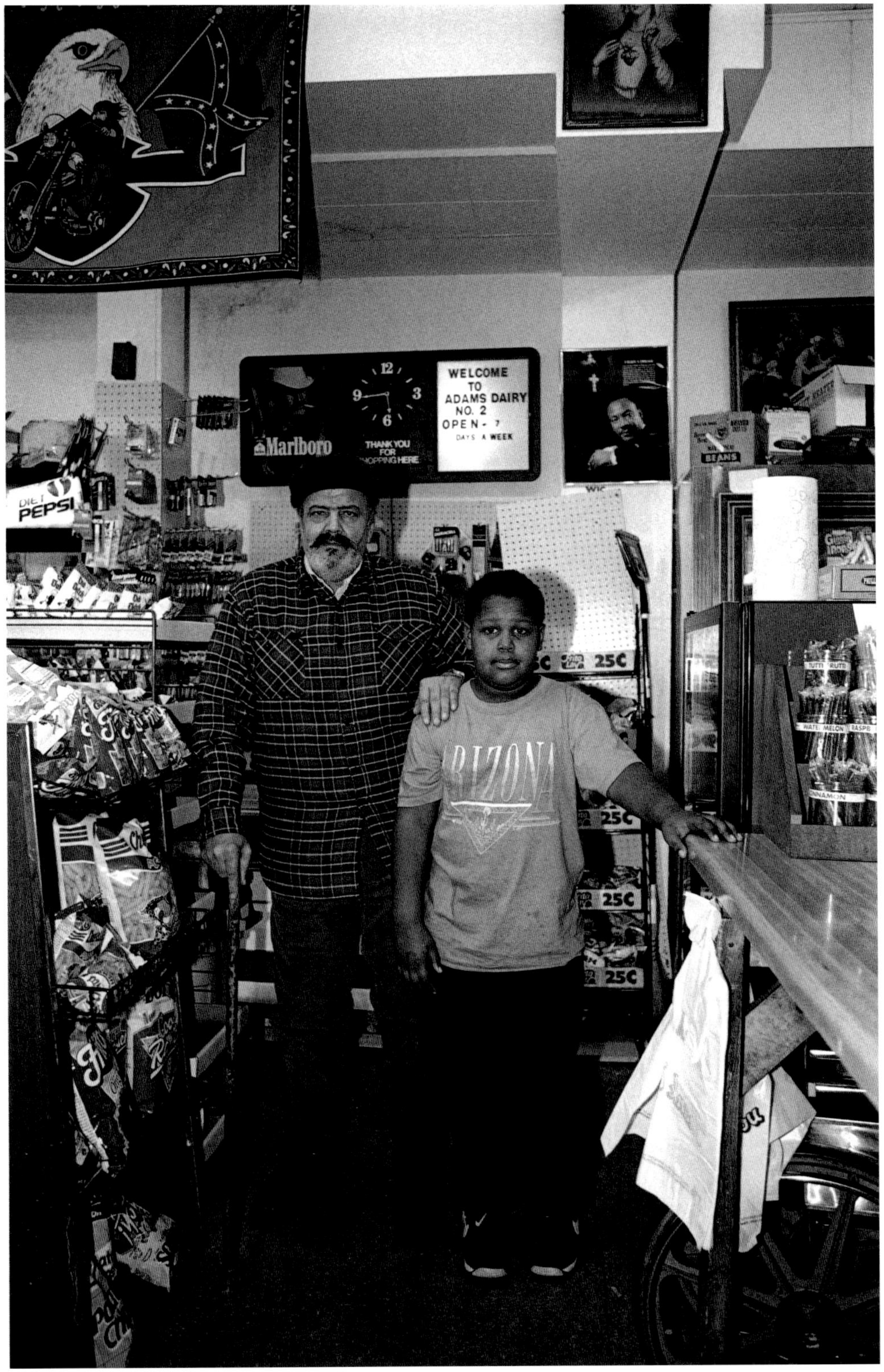
WELCOME
TO
ADAMS DAIRY
NO. 2
OPEN- 7
DAYS A WEEK
Marlboro
THANK YOU
FOR
SHOPPING HERE
DIET
PEPSI
ARIZONA
25¢

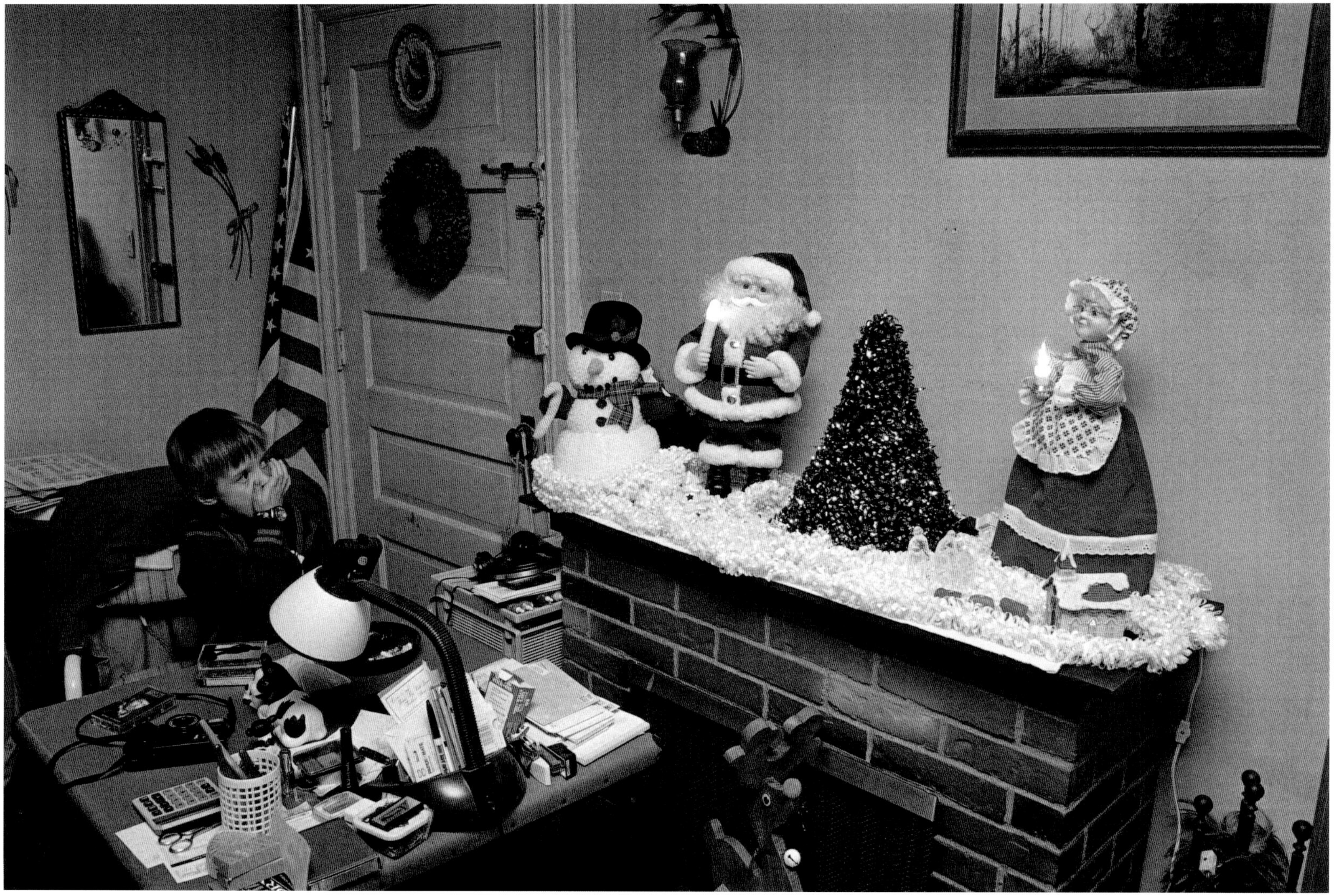

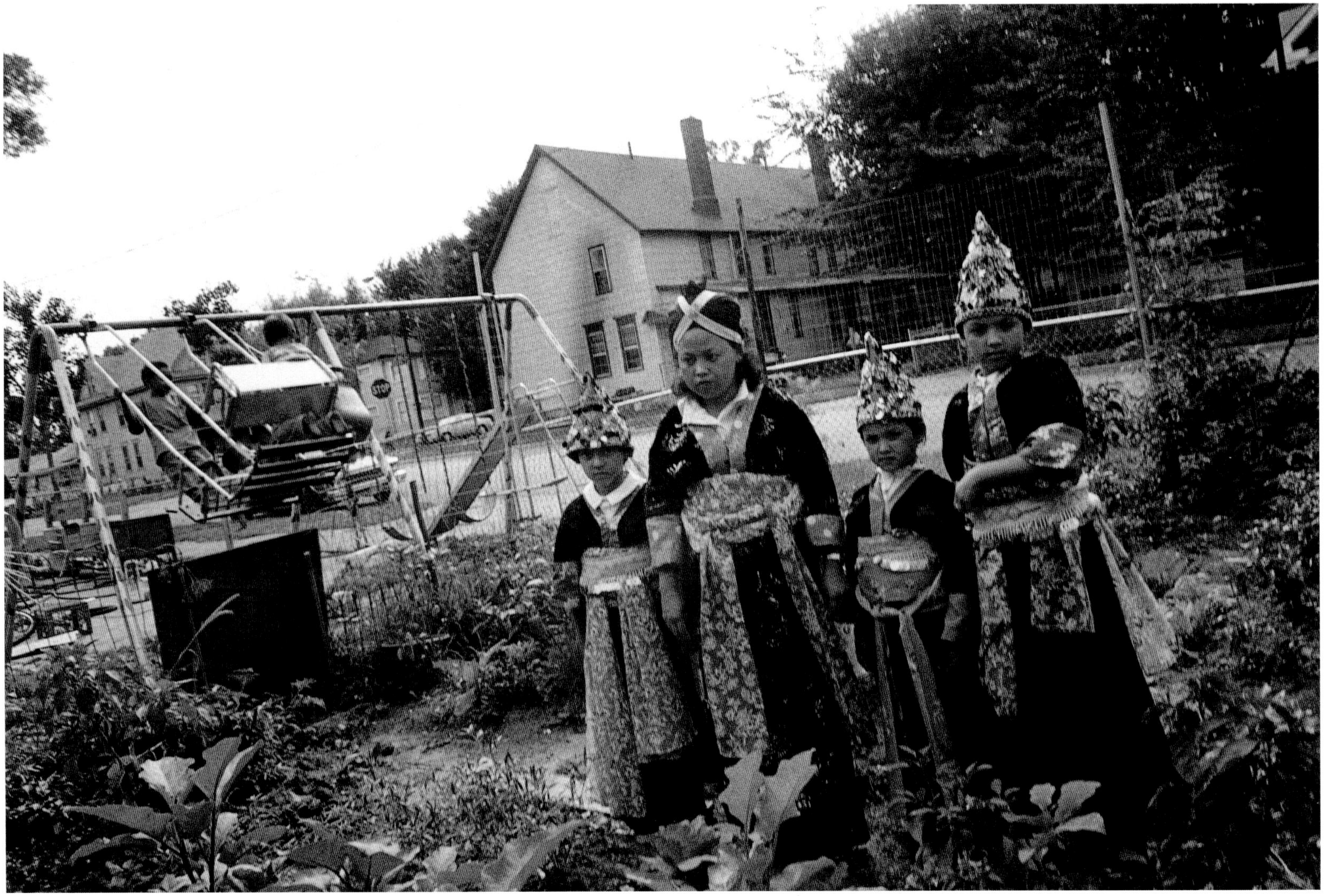

It's almost like a religious ritual for them, these clothes. Back in Laos, they wore these outfits when they were looking for a man to get married. They wear these outfits to look nice, I guess. When my wife puts her stuff away, she folds every little one as neat as can be and puts it in a suitcase and ties it up and locks it up. It's really some kind of treasure.

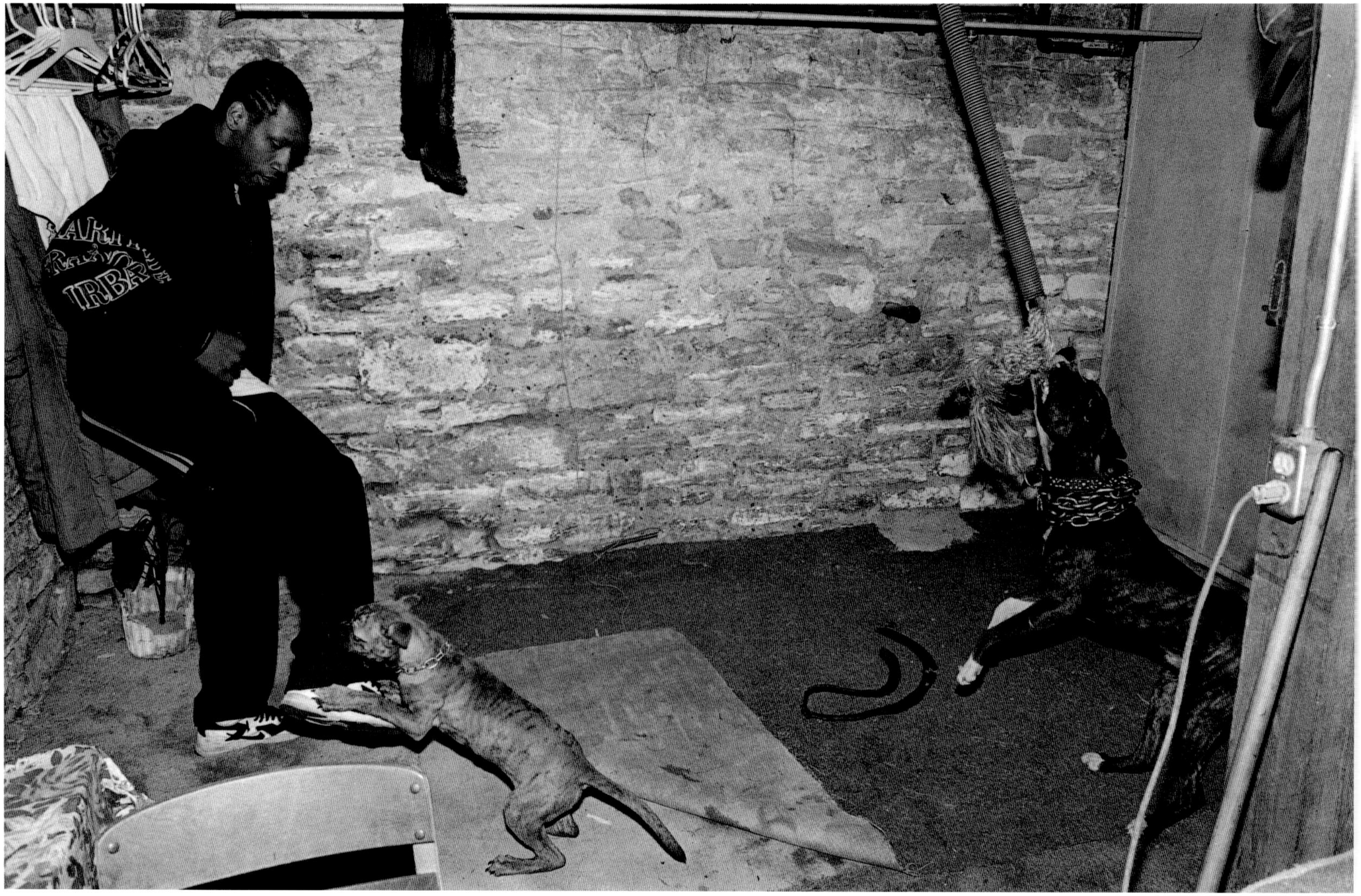

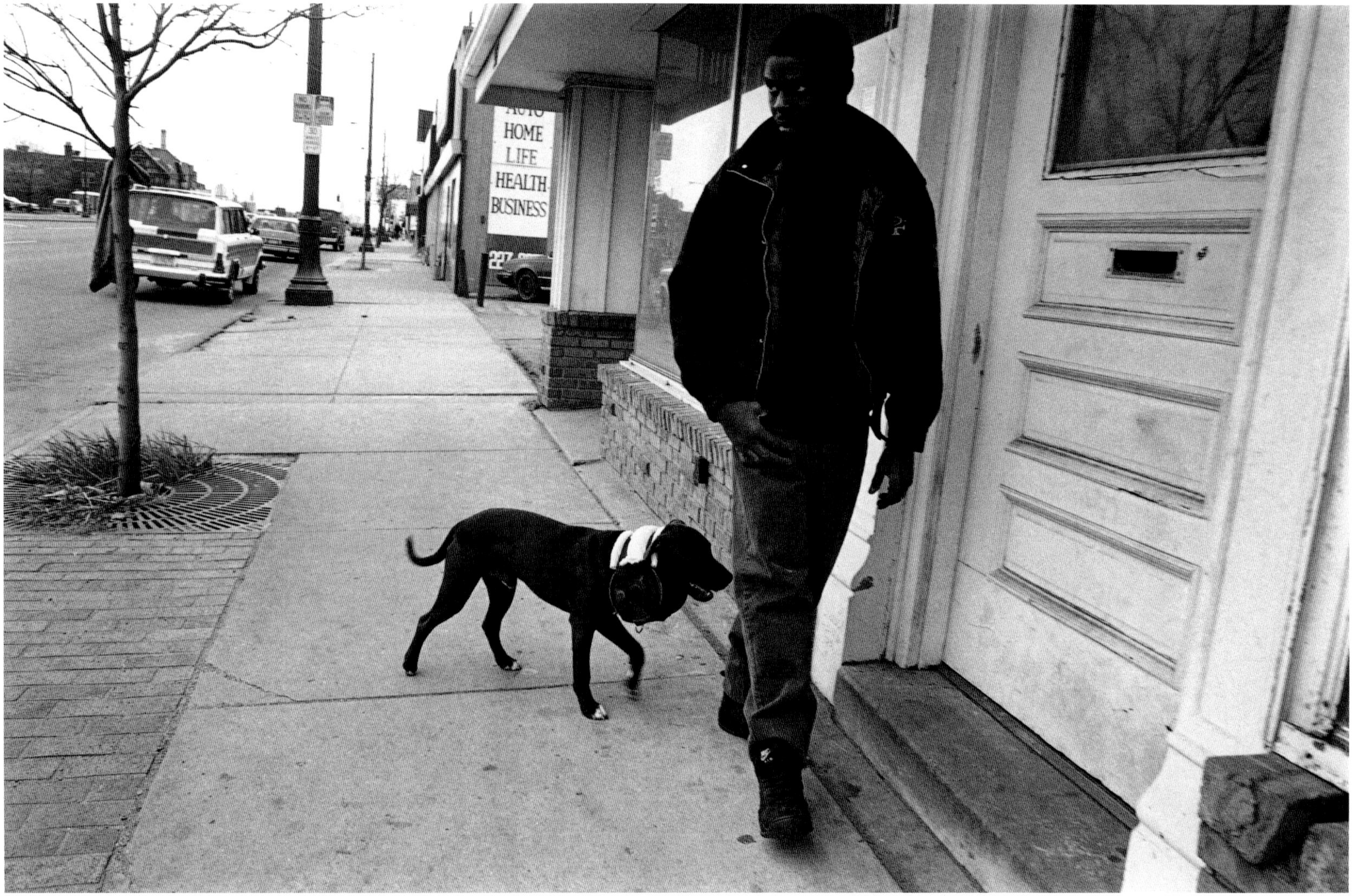

I do this to build him up. Dog gets a lot bigger this way.

It's just ten pounds now. He'll carry more.

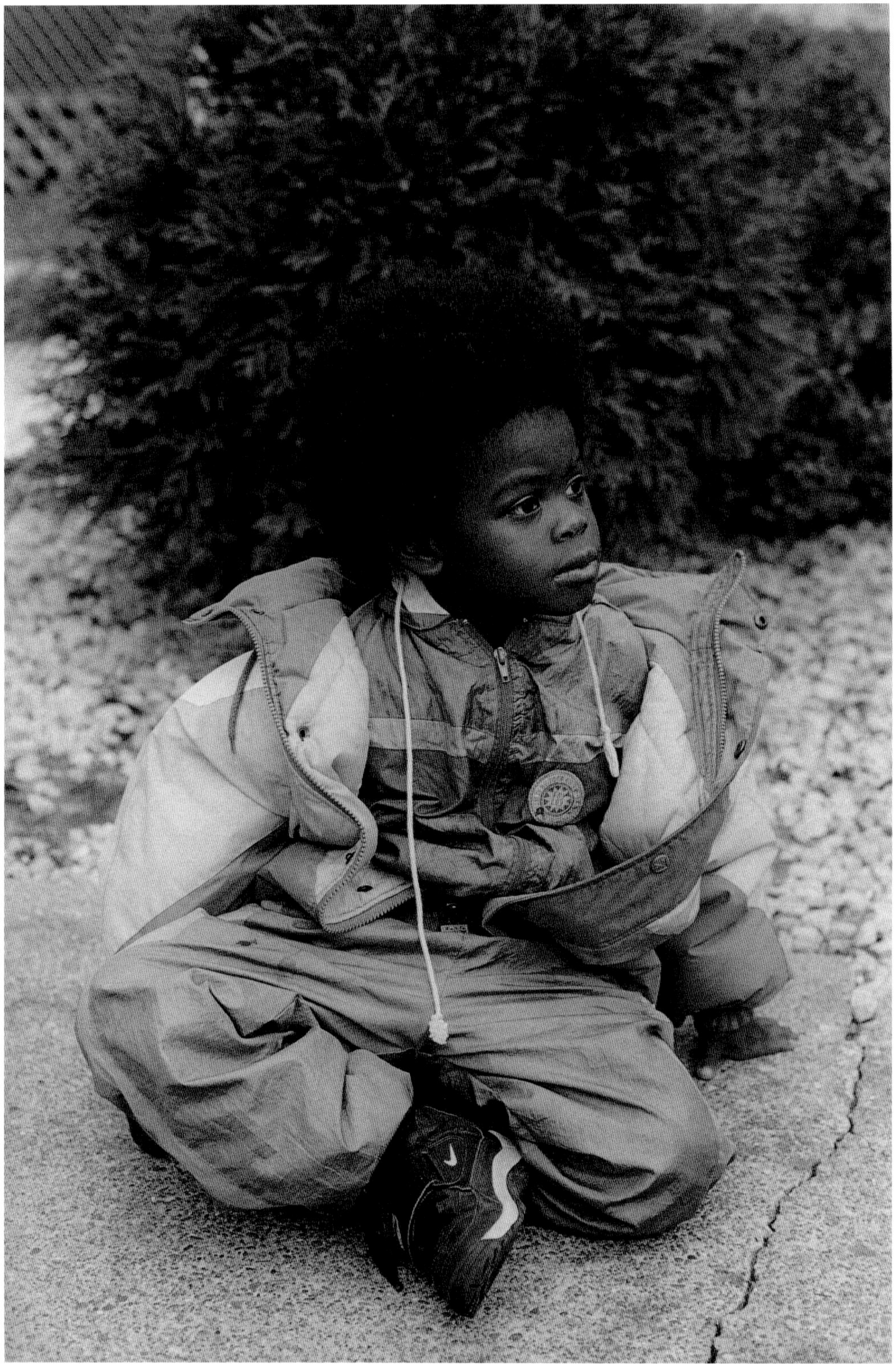

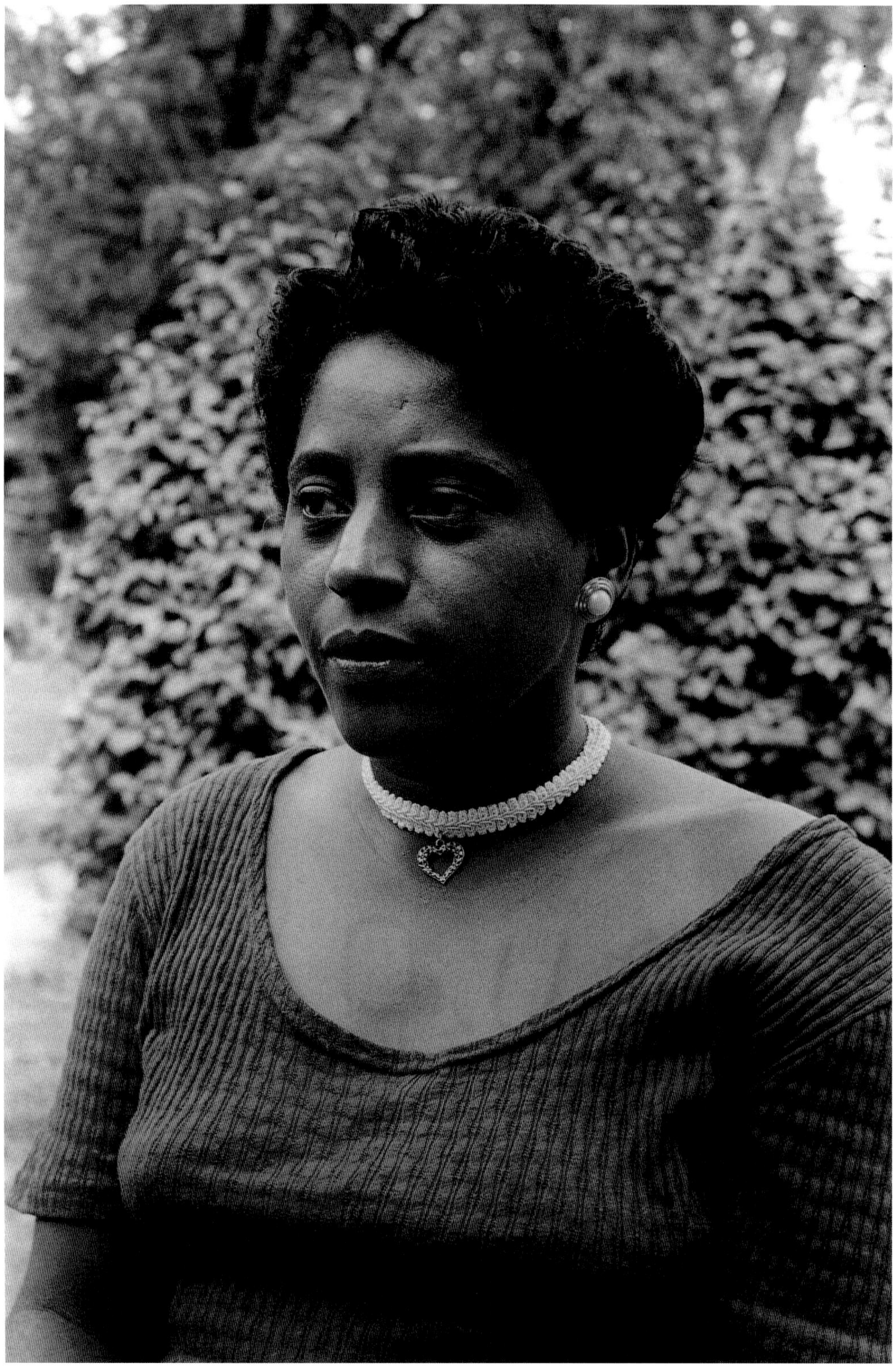

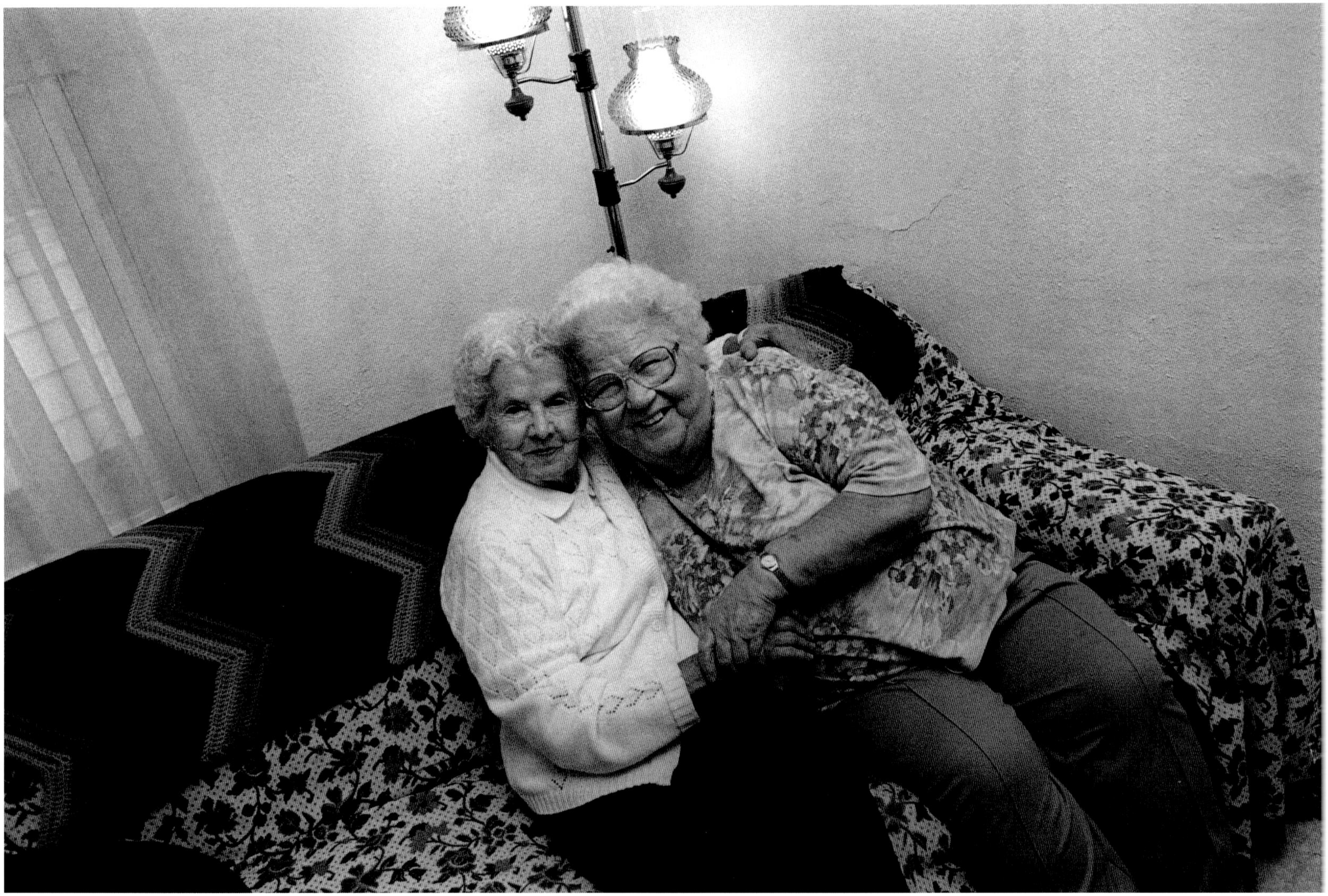

Marie (right): *I was married forty-four years. My husband died fourteen years ago. Clara was married sixty-one years when her husband died. We've lived next door to each other for seventy-three years. We've been friends all this time.*

Clara: *We never had a fight, did we? Almost every day I go over to Marie's, and we watch mass on* EWTN.

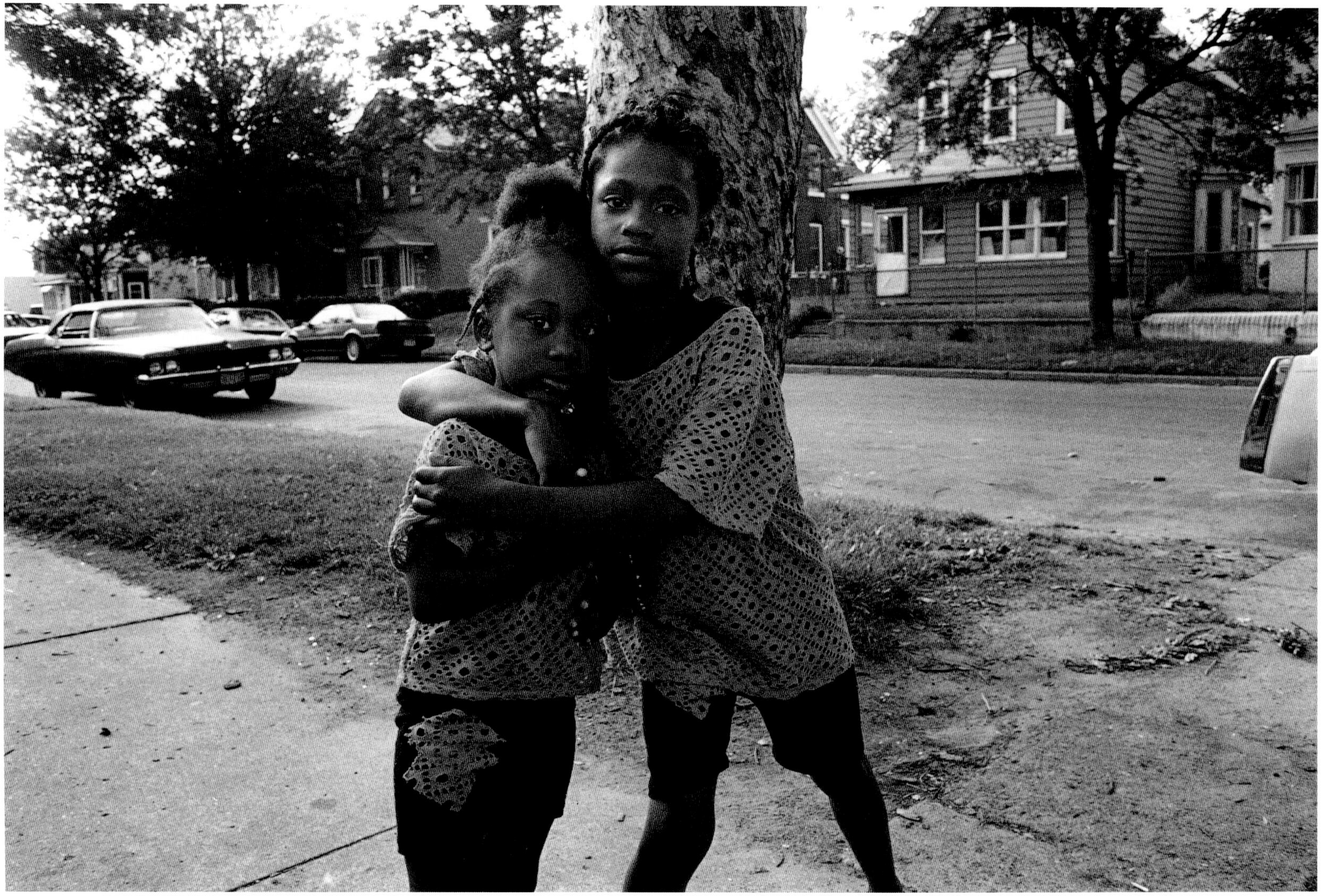

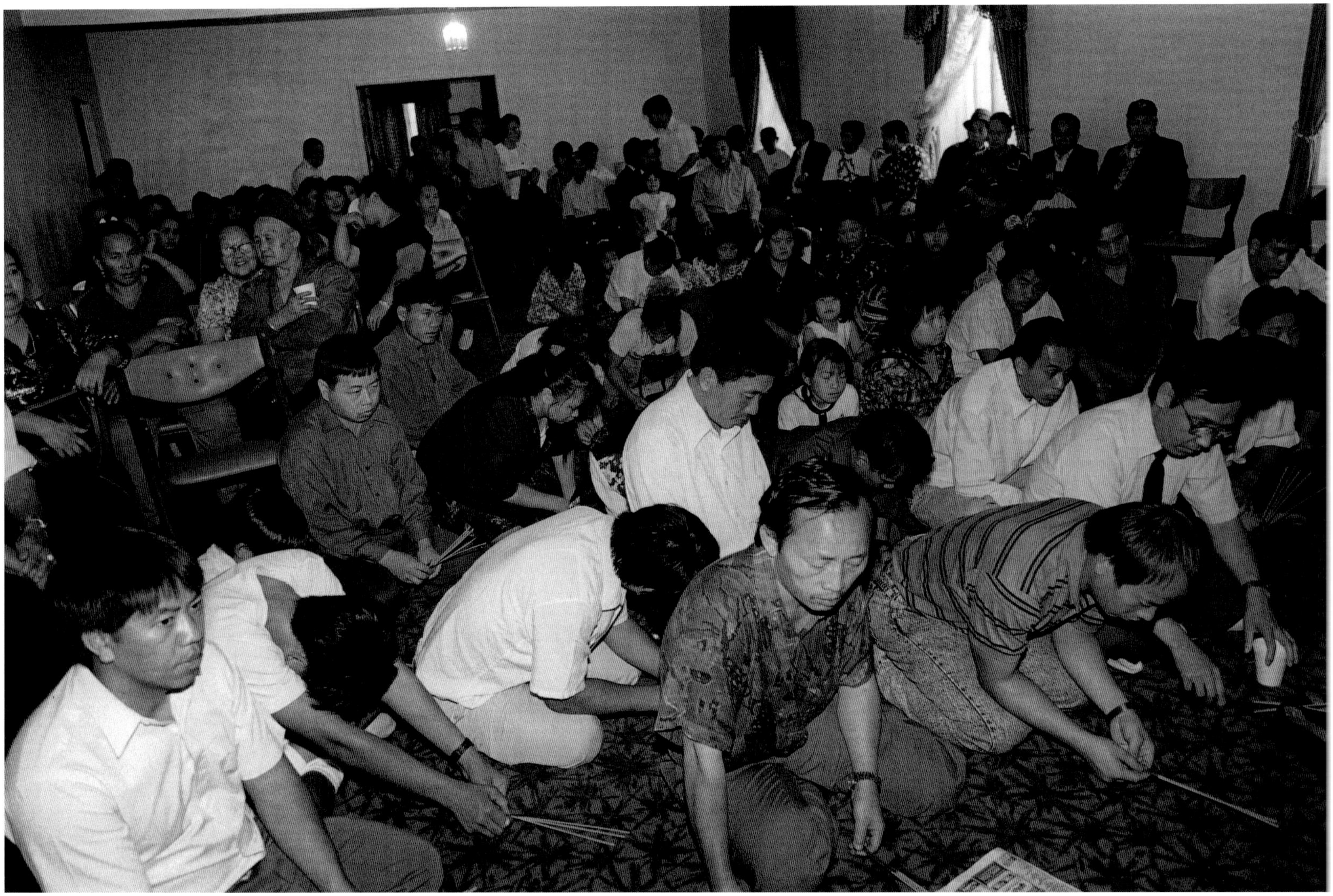

We have a beautiful traditional Hmong ceremony to celebrate the body. We stay day and night for three days. Lots of people come every day to visit the body and help the family. Many donate little gifts. All the relatives, in-laws, and cousins have to come. Most Hmong funerals are very large. Because we love each other so much. When Hmong people hear a Hmong person has passed away, then everyone comes. It doesn't matter what clan you are or if you don't know the family. It's a good time for people.

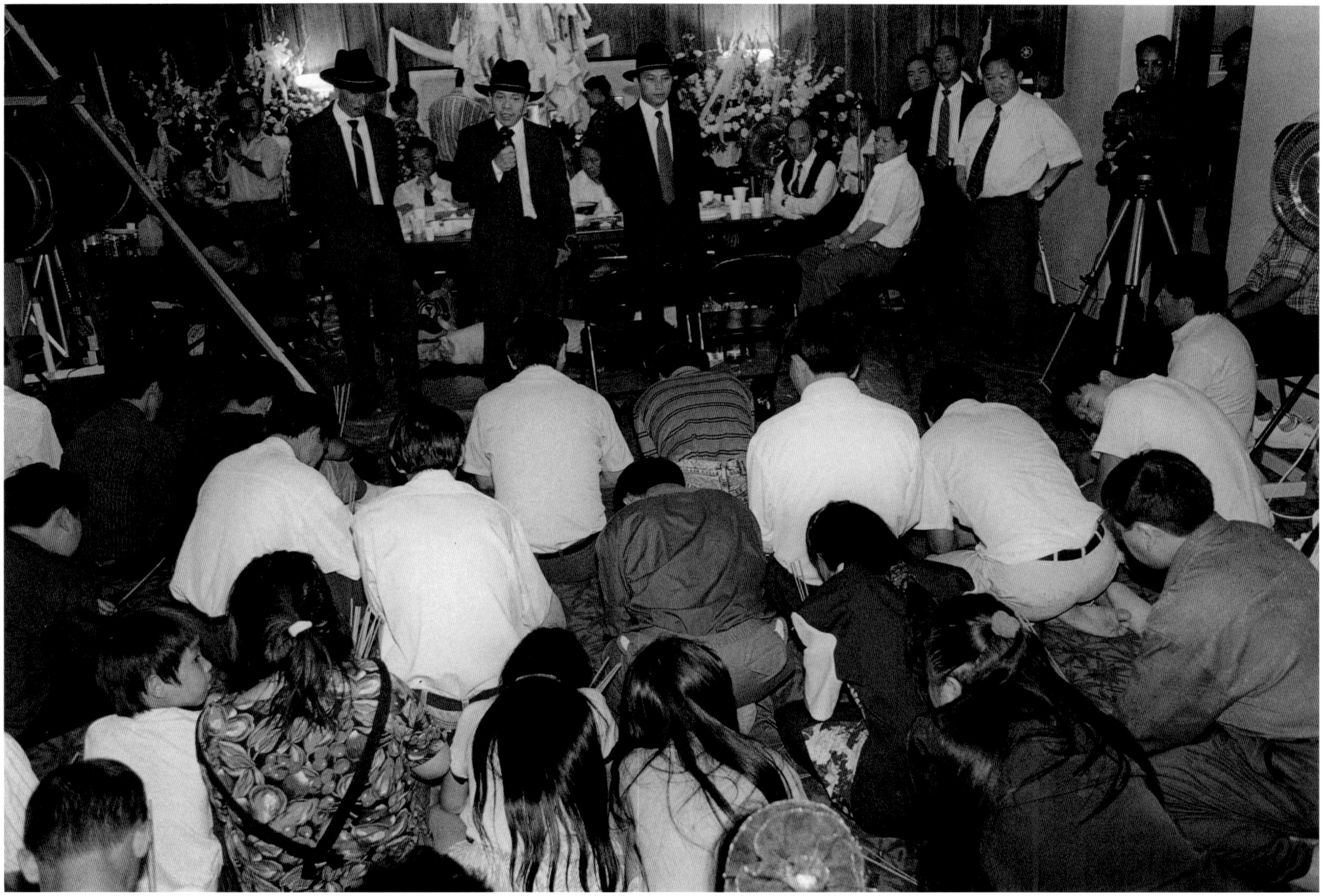

We also have very knowledgeable and educated people of the Hmong culture as masters of ceremonies. They say special words to the children and the family so they can have a long life and good future.

My uncle had cancer. But before the cancer he had an ulcer. During the war in Laos, when he was fighting in the jungle, they did not have good food to eat. Many times the soldiers would have to eat leaves. That's why he got an ulcer. When he came to this country his bad ulcer became a cancer. He was forty-six years old.

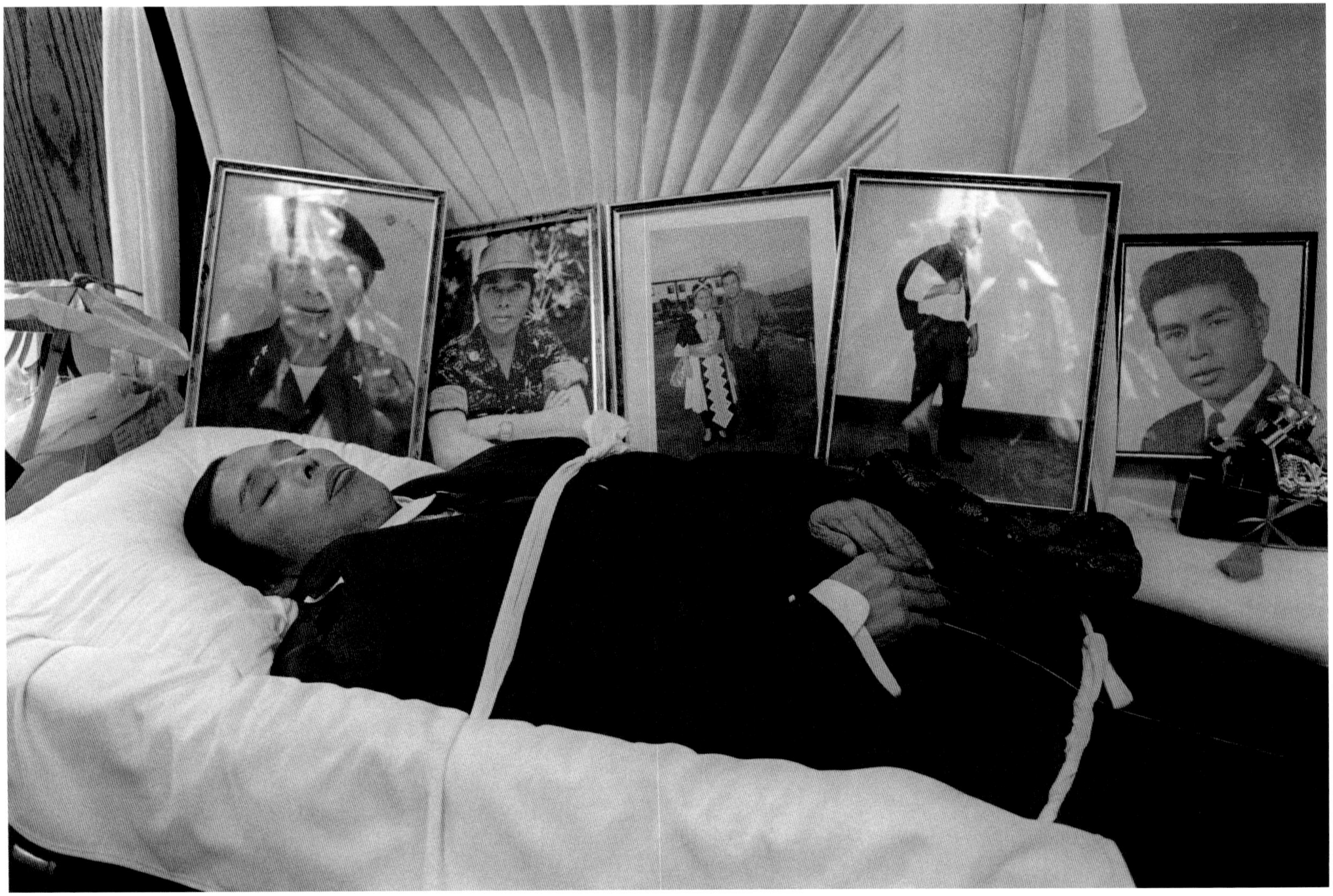

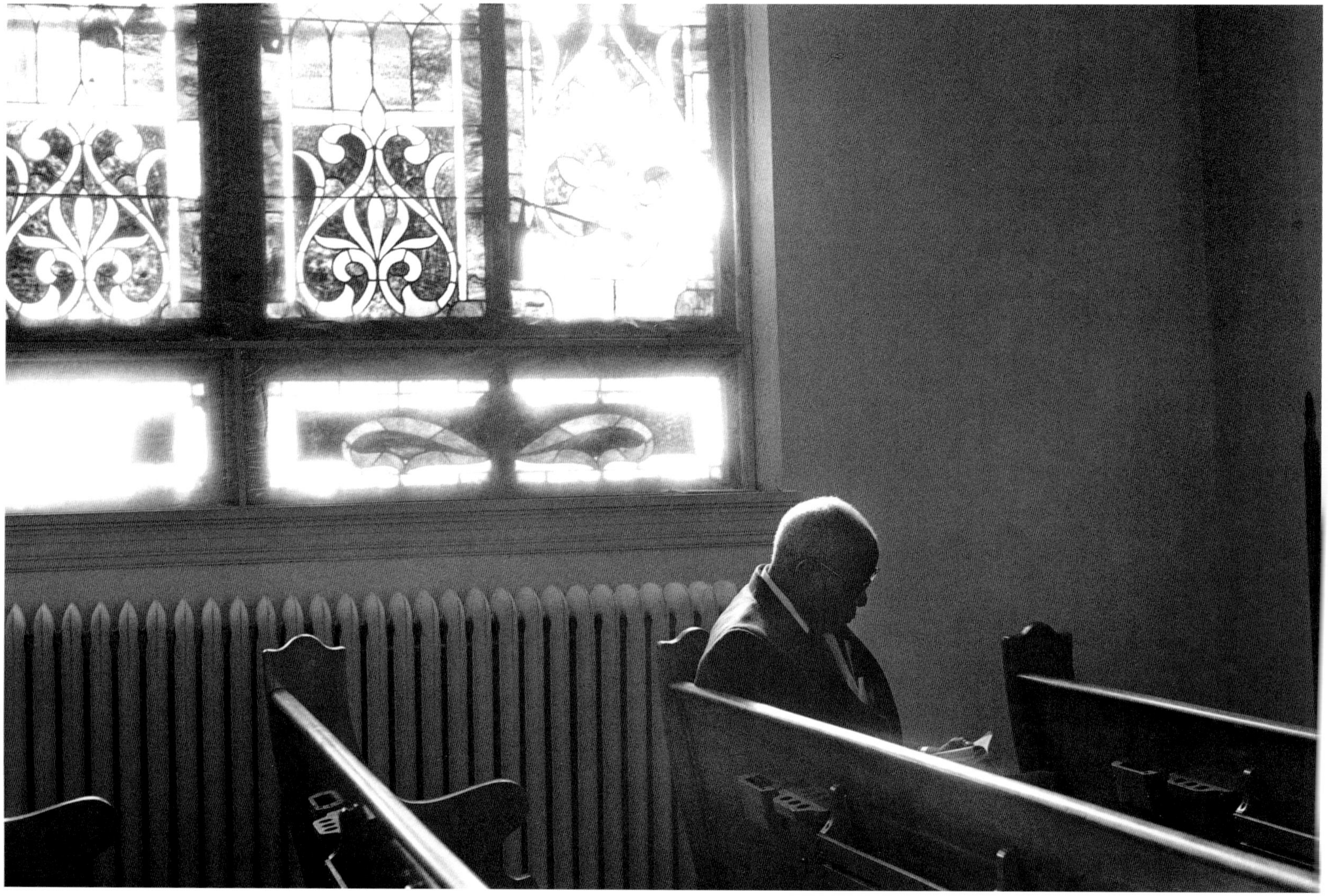

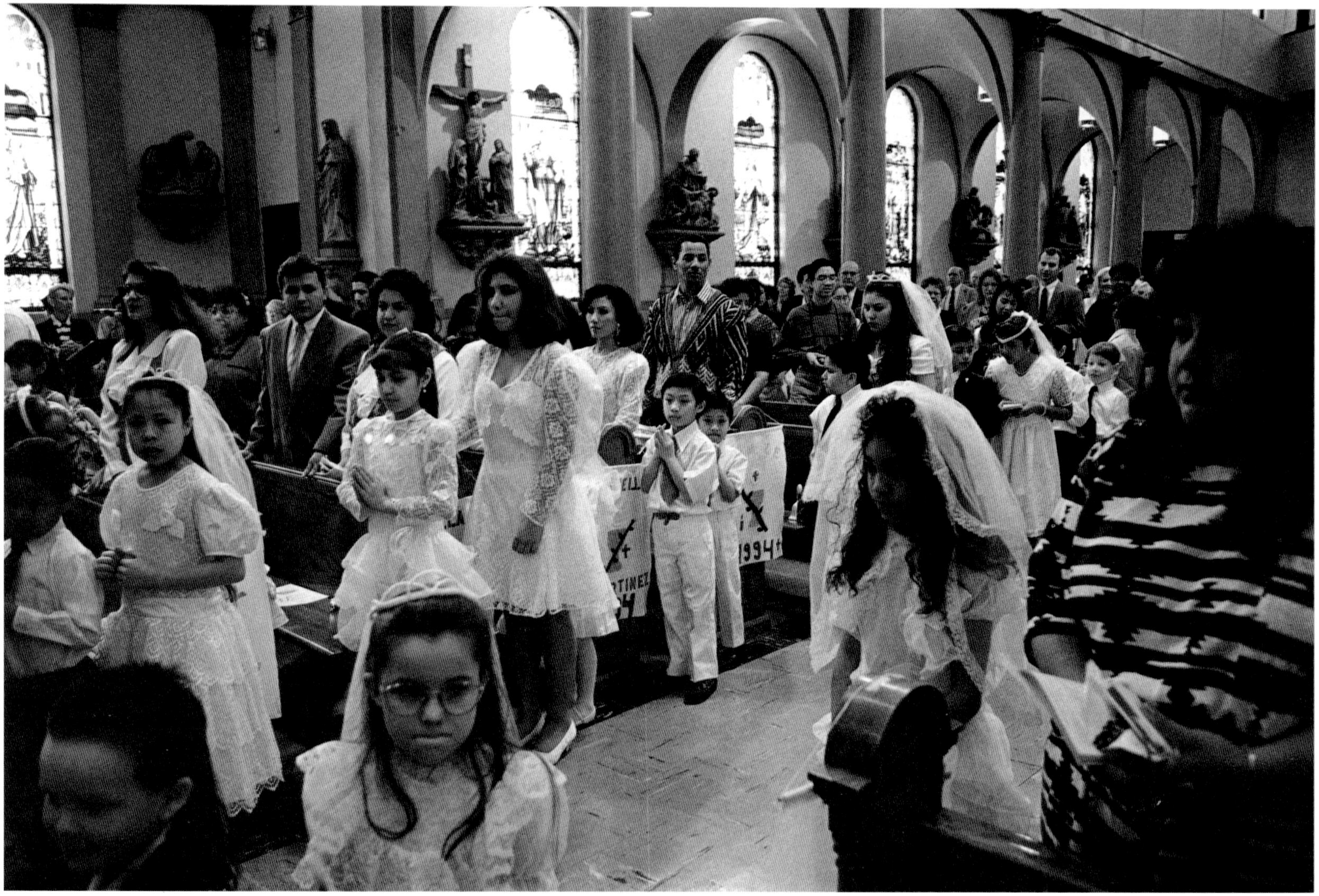

For a while we had the Scripture readings in Spanish also, but that group got too small. Our Hispanics surface when there is a need. Like First Communion. Last year we had our biggest communion class. There were fourteen Hispanic kids, nine Vietnamese, one black child, and two white kids. And one of the white kids was Polish.

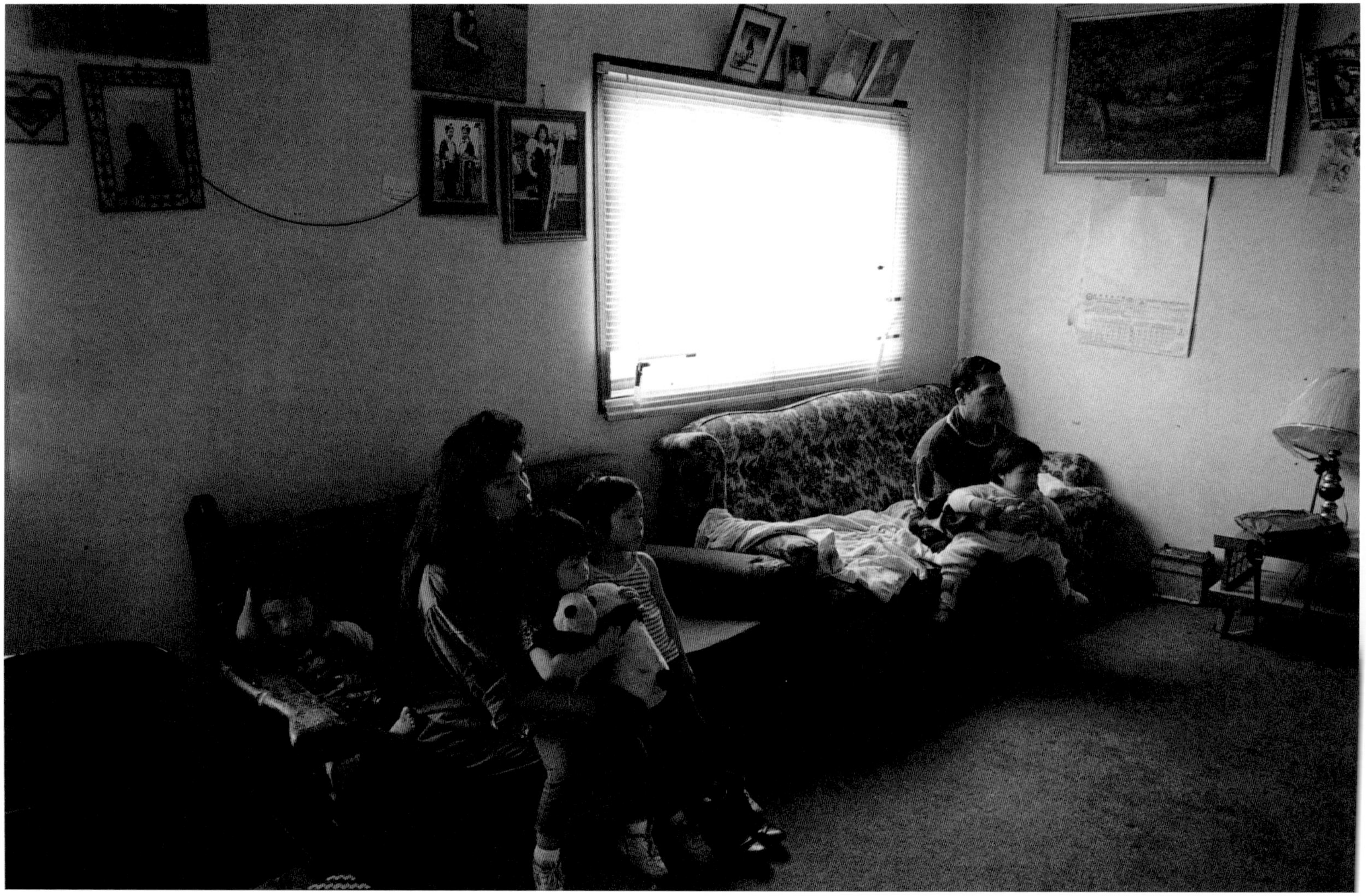

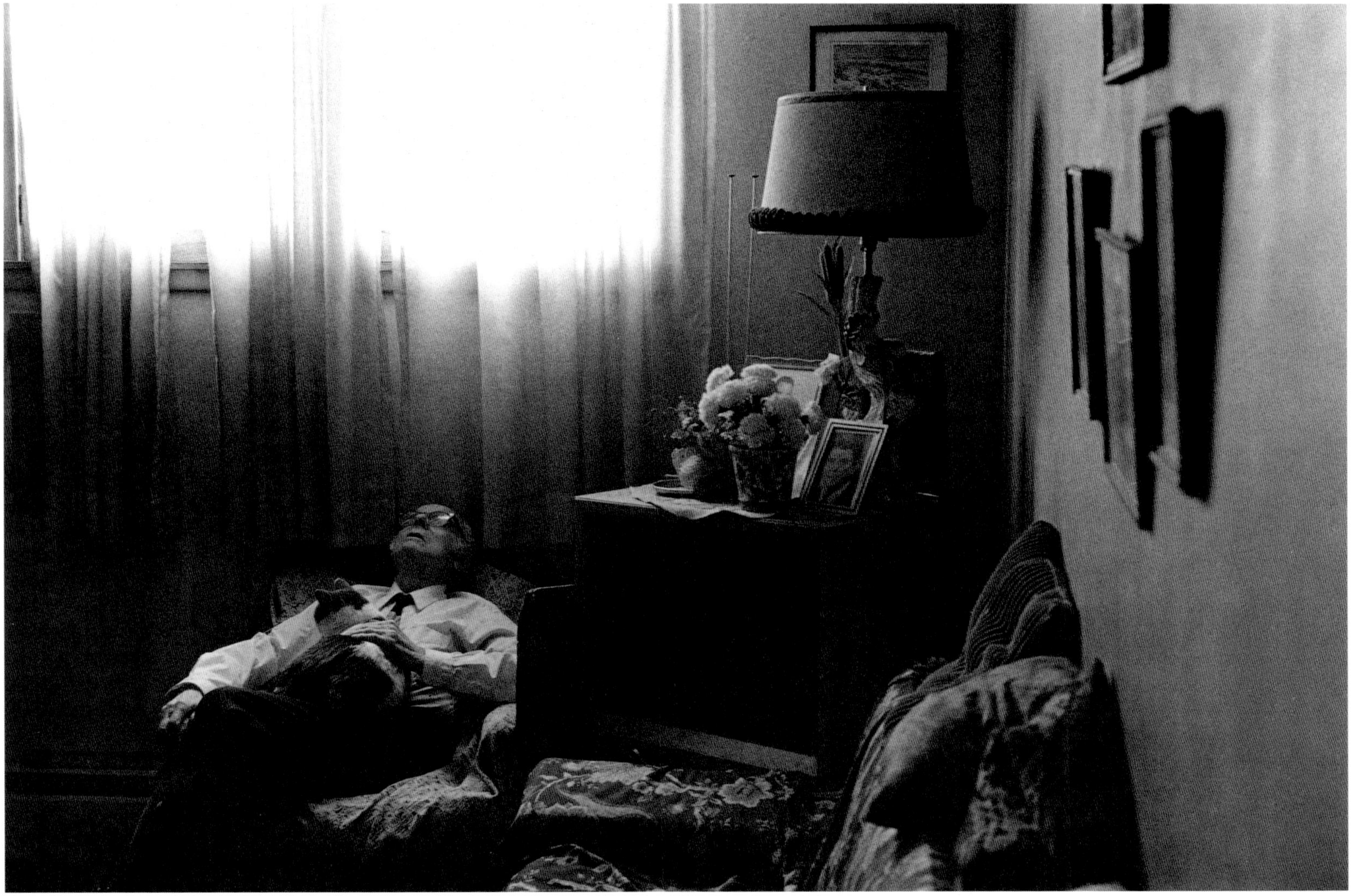

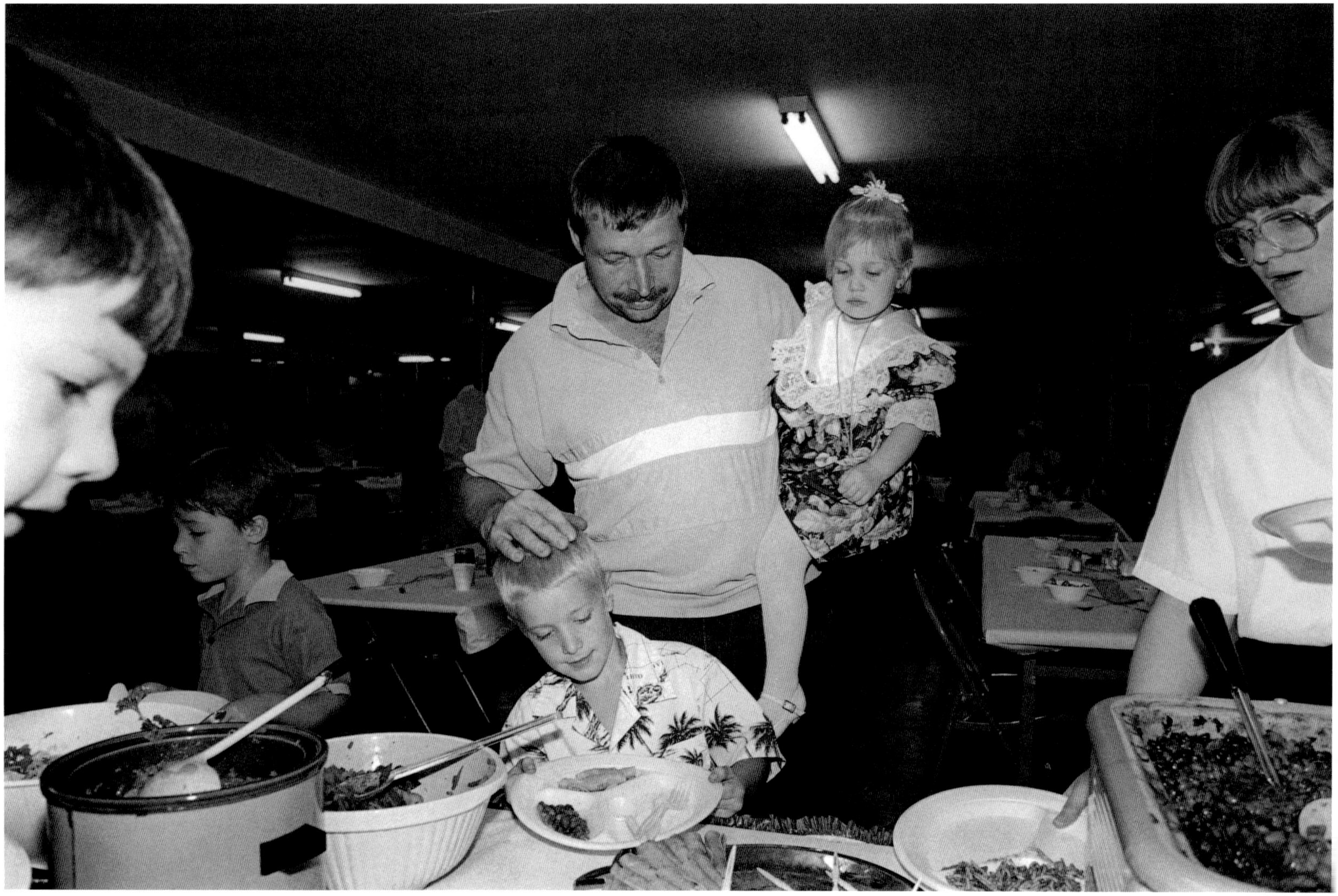

Here's a good story that typifies the multicultural experience. The parish is strong on doing dinners, but a lot of the Vietnamese didn't really care for sauerkraut and pork roast. It's not their tradition. So we tried a potluck picnic. And of course they didn't have a notion of what potluck meant. So they pooled some money, and two or three families made four hundred eggrolls. Of course, what was gone first? The eggrolls.

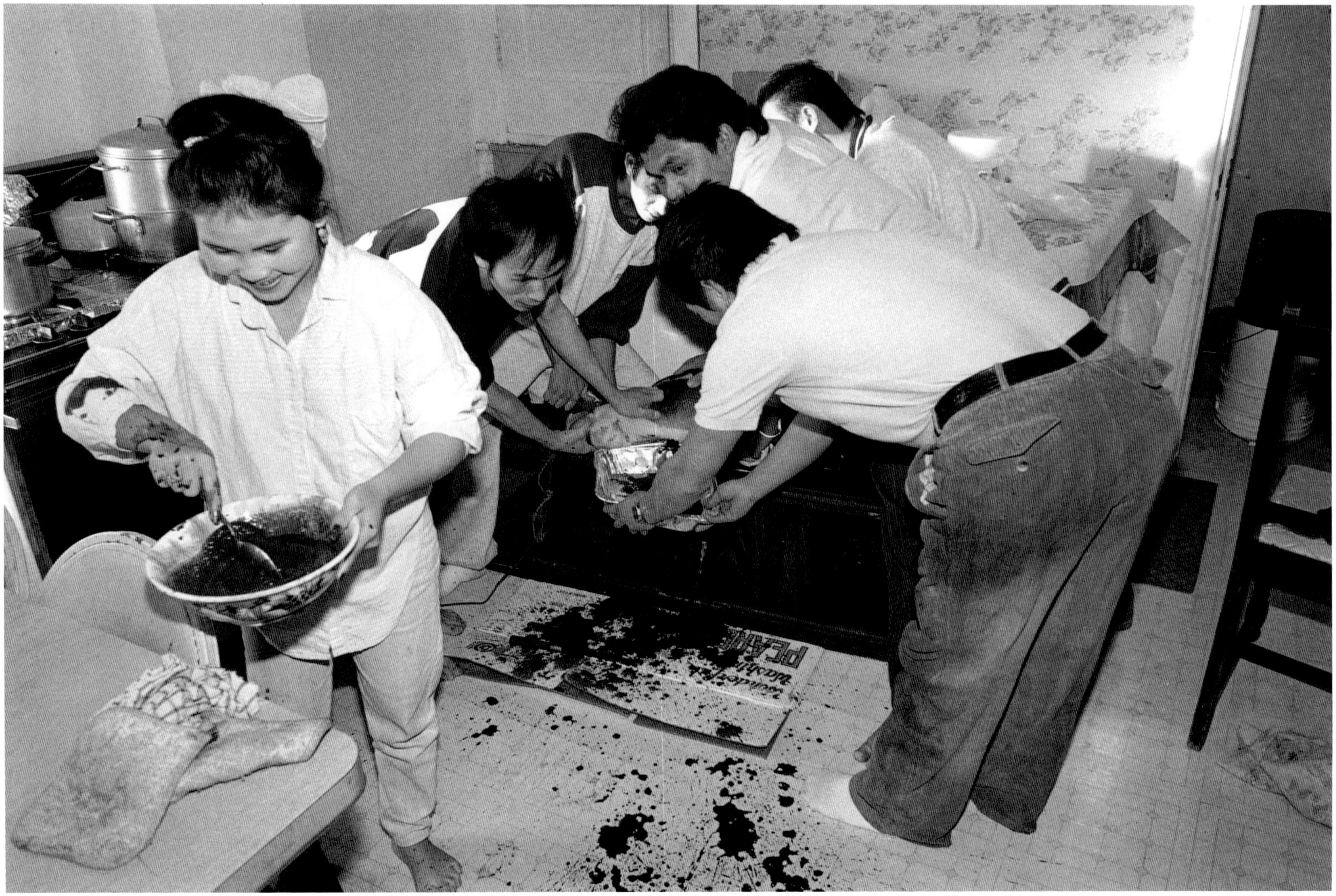

We let the blood sit so it becomes hard, like Jell-O. We mix it with different dishes and meat for special occasions. One traditional dish we mix with internal organs. Blood makes food taste better and look better.

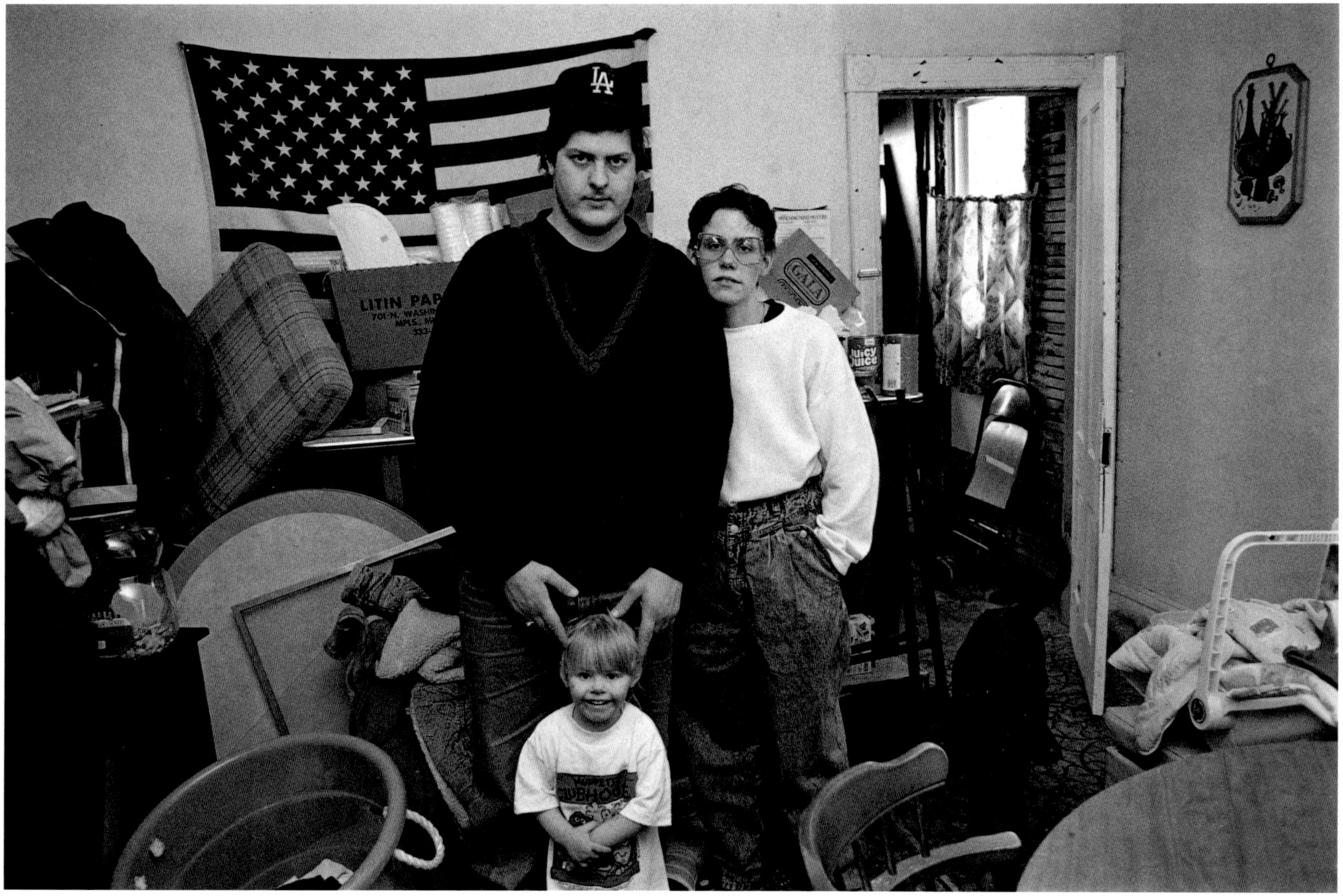

It's not like Highland Park [a middle-class St. Paul neighborhood], *where rich people live and everybody goes to cocktail parties. The only cocktail party we can afford to go to is White Castle. They're all lawyers and doctors up there making all this money. We're just peons down here trying to make ends meet.*

It's like they put all the nationalities and different personalities in one area and called it Frogtown. Like a test to see how they would get along with each other and live with each other. On this block we got Hispanic, we got Laos, we got white, we got black, we got everything here. The neighborhood is basically what you want to make it. If you want a lousy neighborhood or be a troublemaker, then that's the way it's going to be. Or you can have a positive attitude and say, "I'm going to visit my neighbor next door, and I don't care if his color is green."

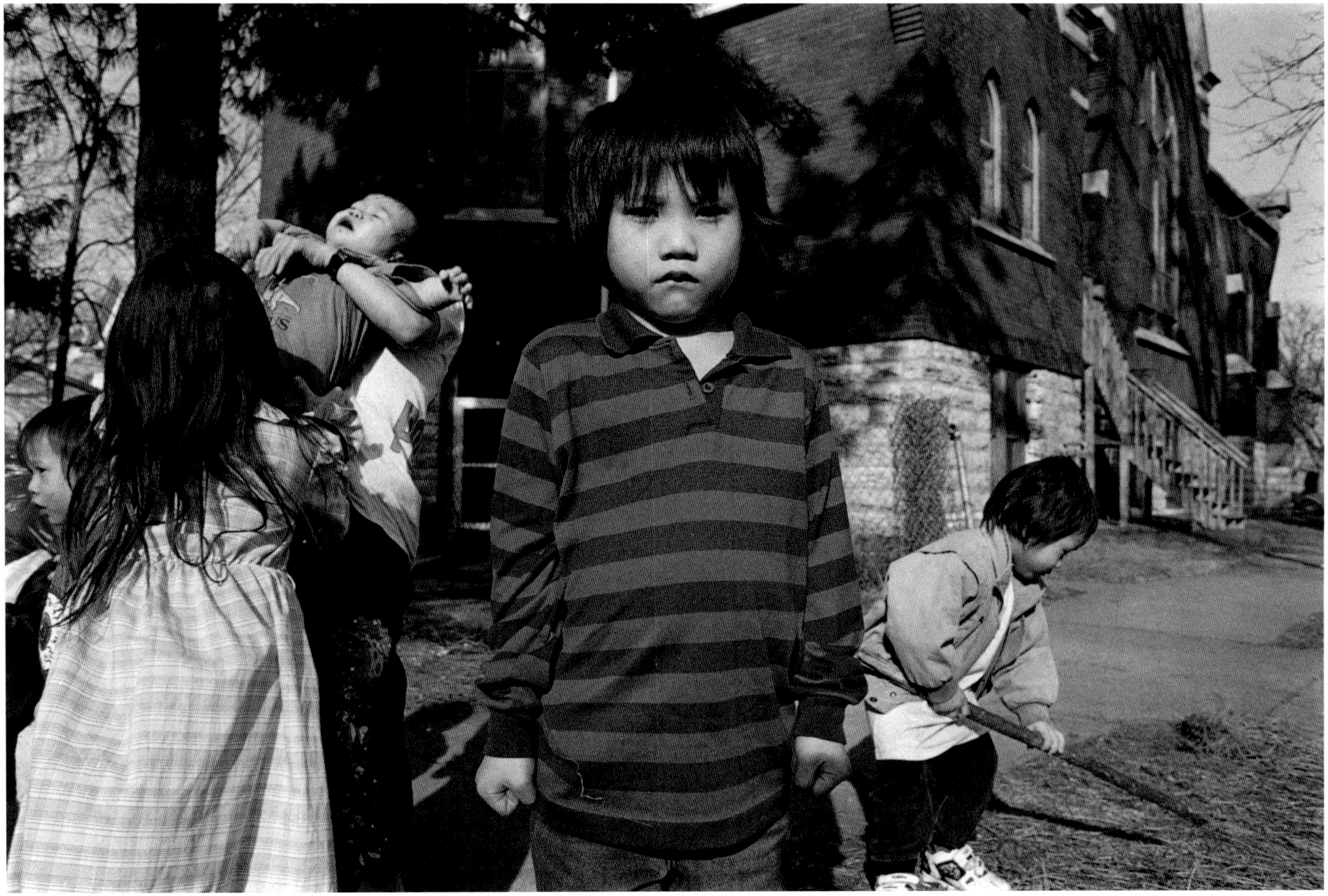

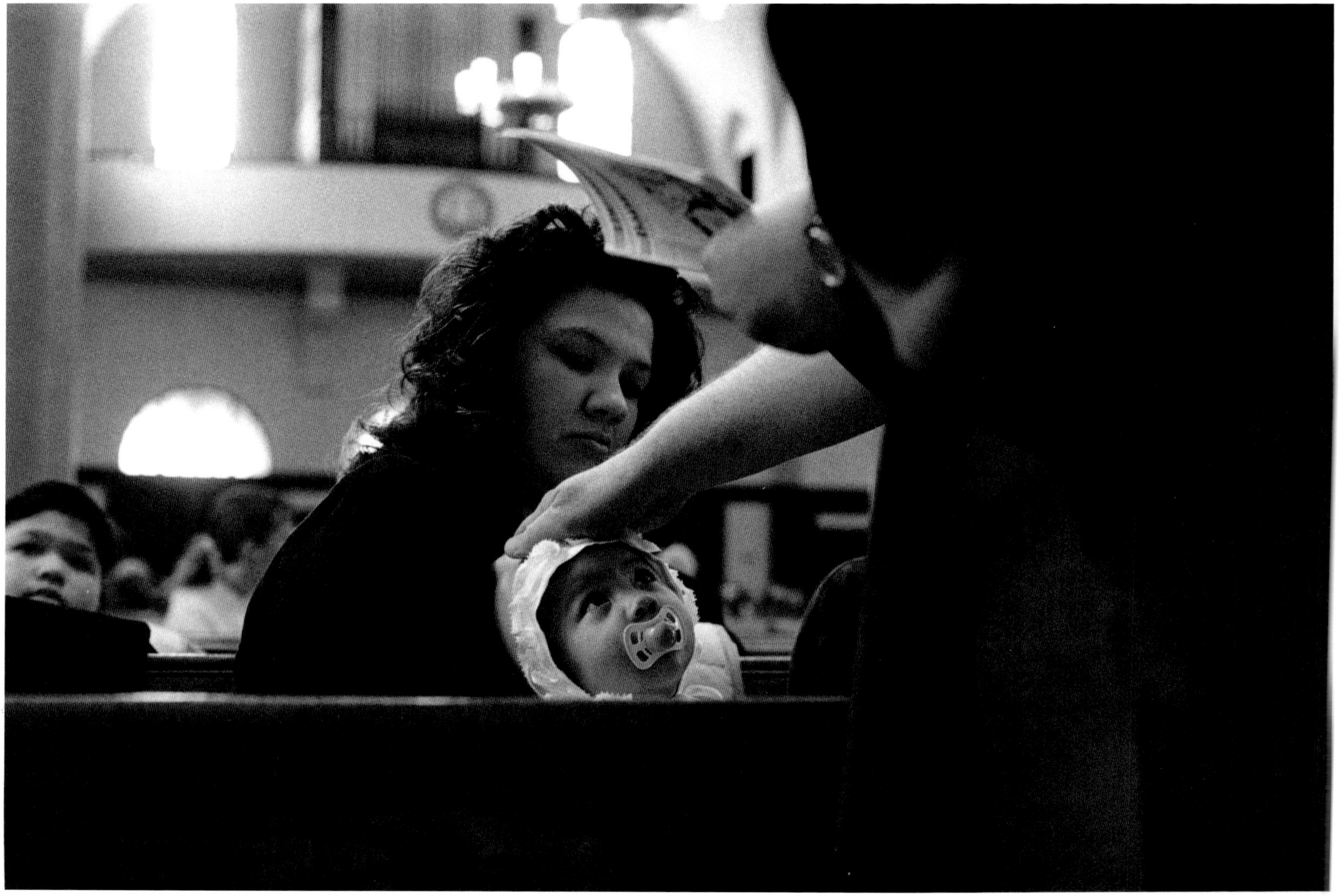

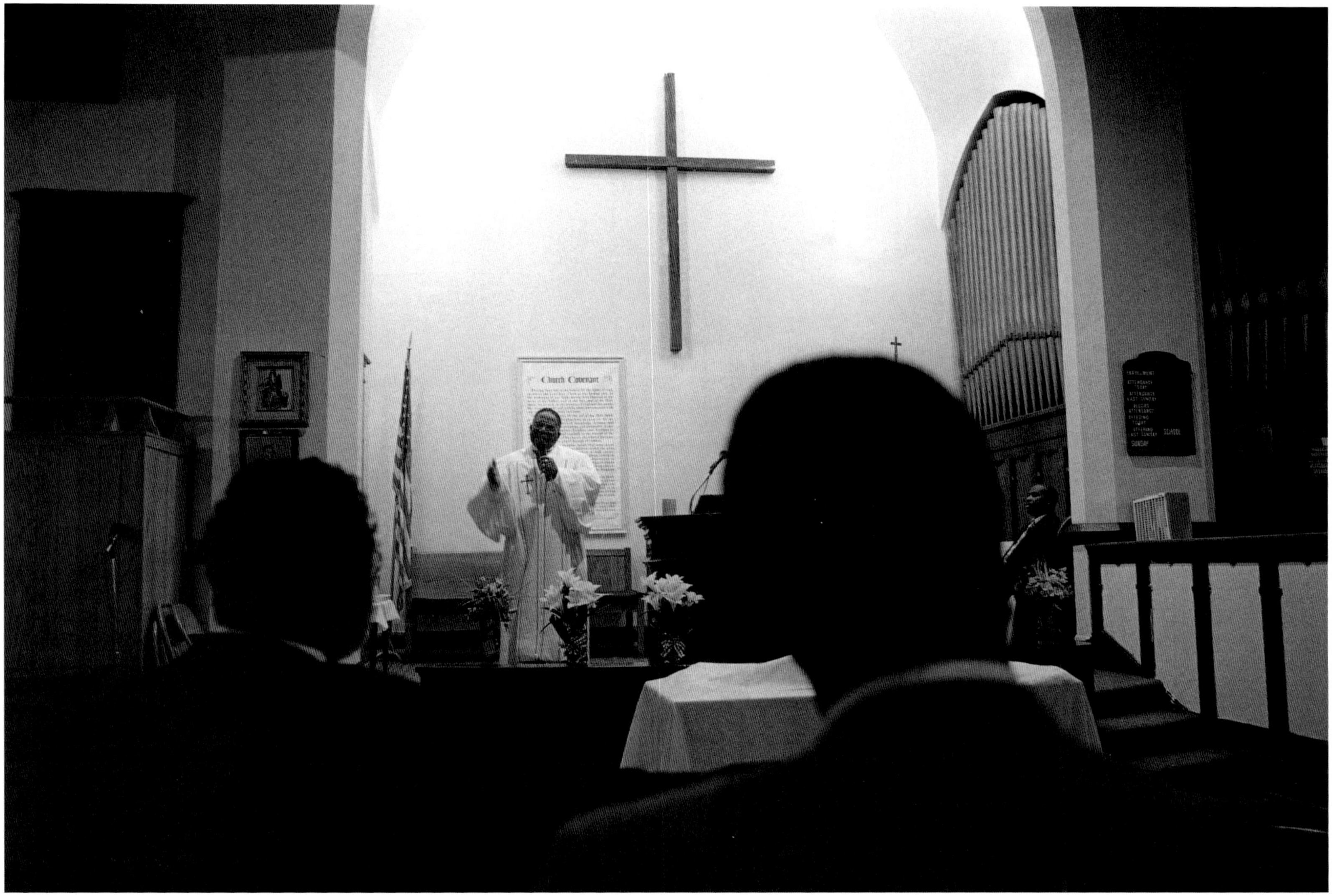
Church Covenant
SCHOOL
SUNDAY

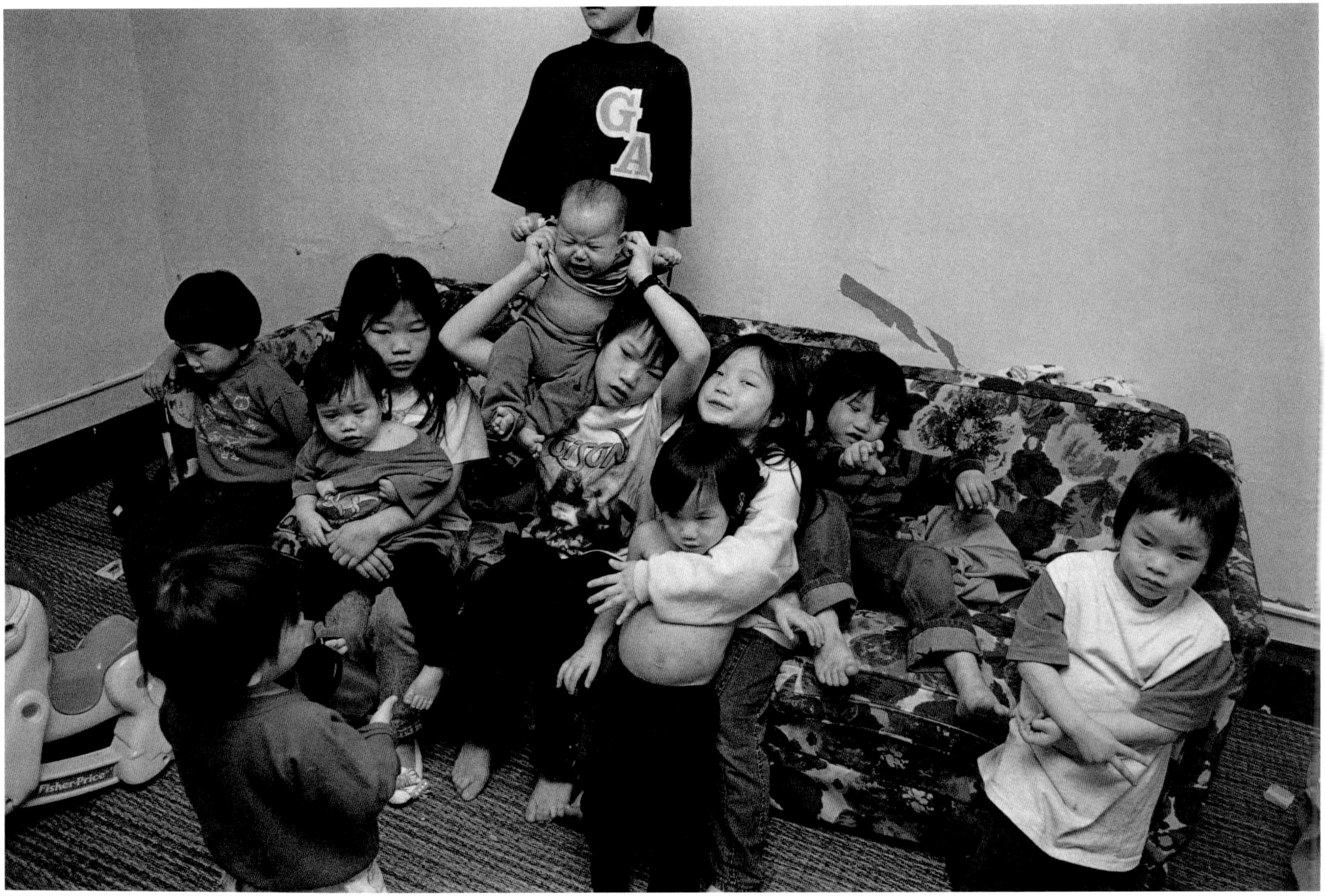
GA
Fisher-Price

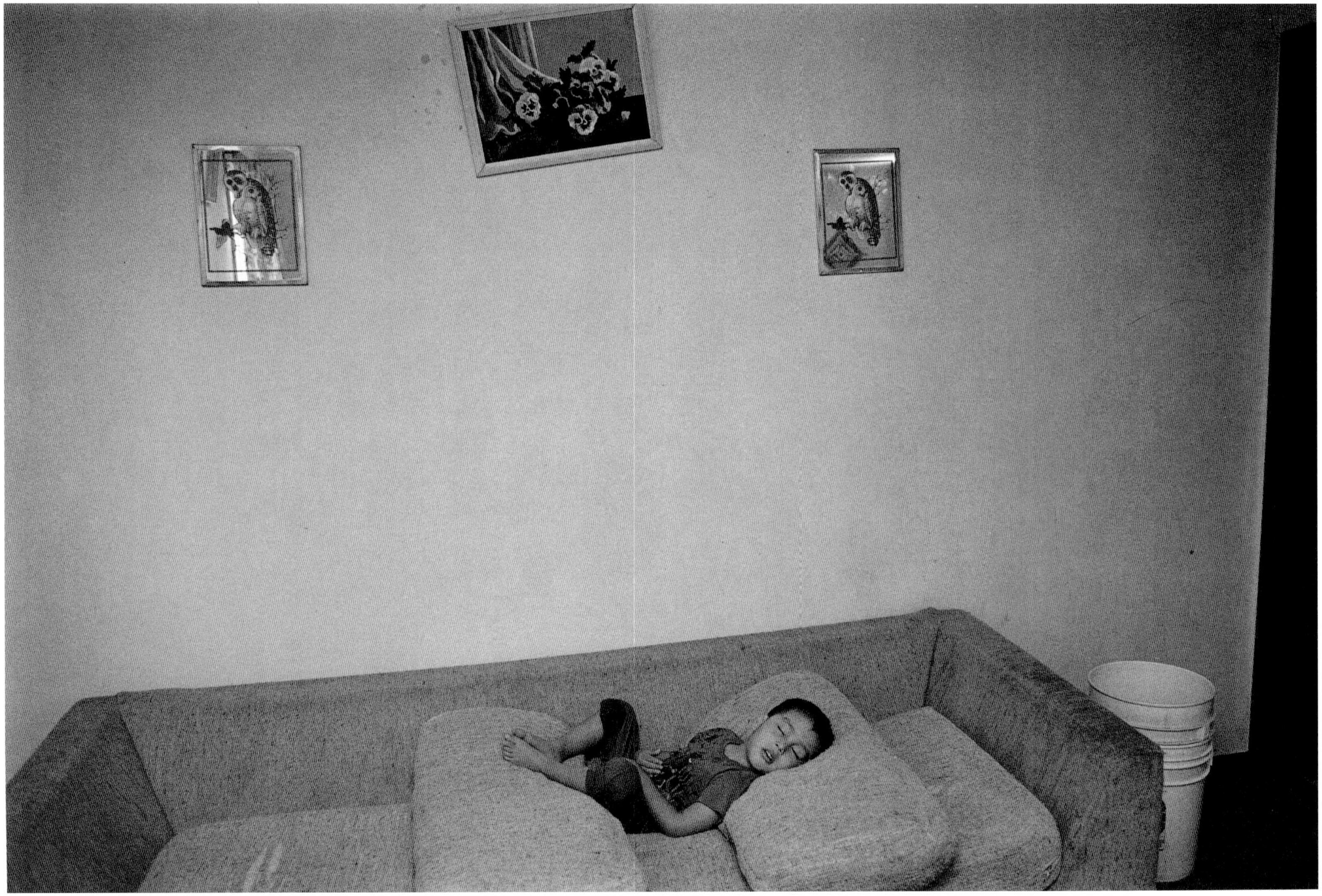

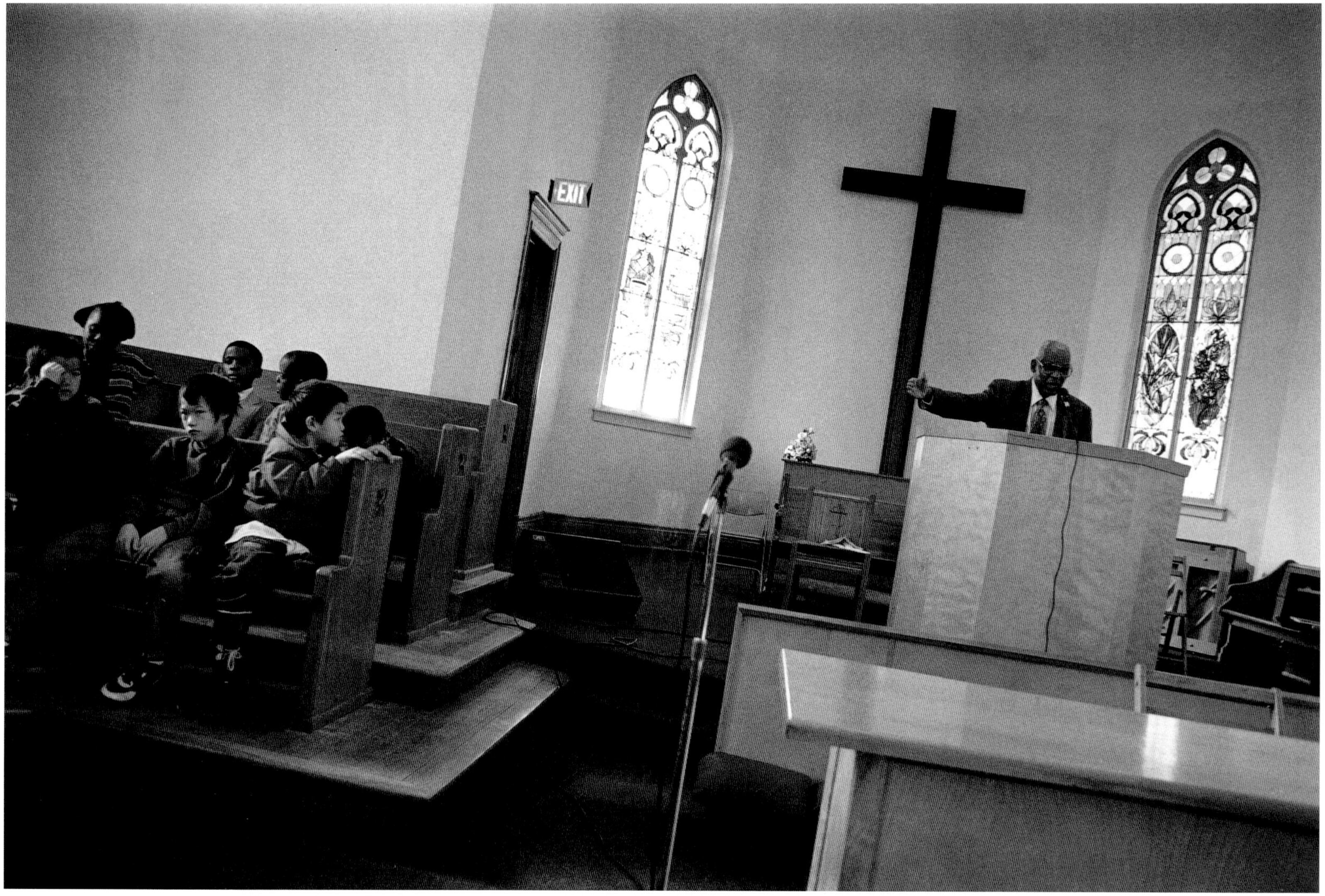
EXIT

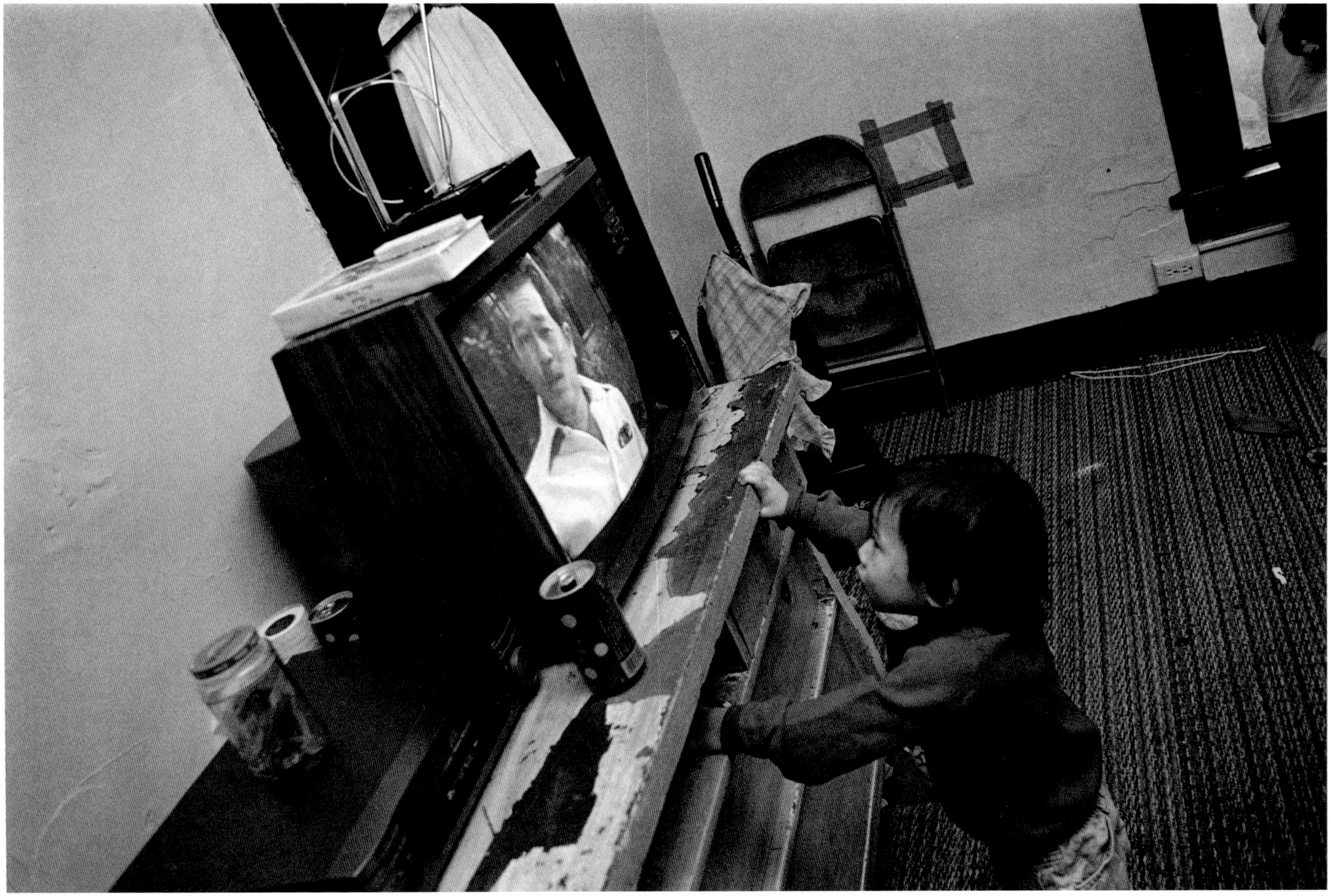

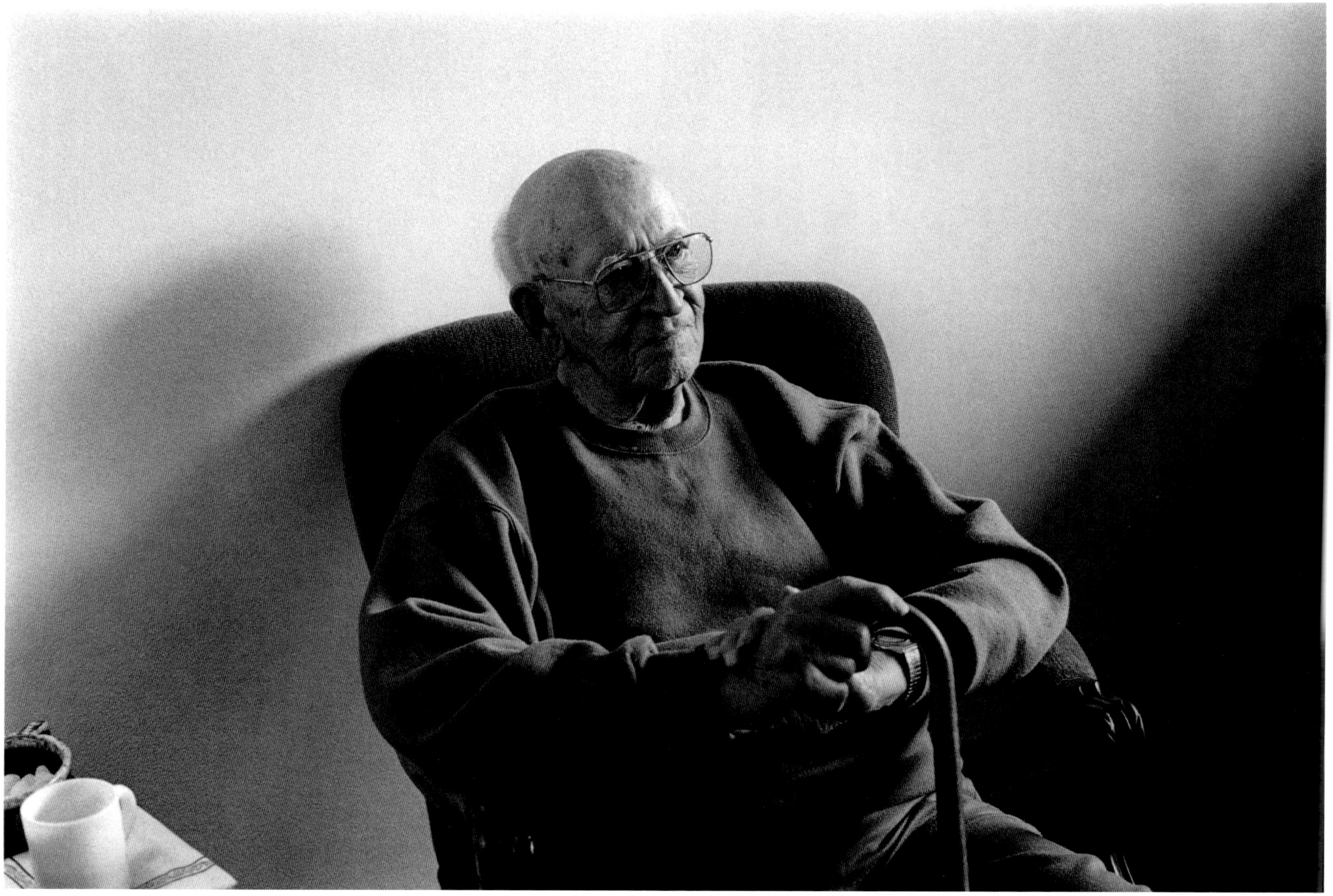

I'm 101 now. My father was an engineer on the Great Northern Railroad. I worked for the Burlington Northern most of my life. My dad built the house on Thomas in 1909, and we've been living there ever since.

I had an ordinary life, like any other fellow. Just like my neighbors. That was all there was to it. Nothing exciting, nothing troublesome, or anything like that. Like I say, we got along nice in the neighborhood with the people.

I had a cabin on Sturgeon Lake. Did a lot of fishing in that lake. But I haven't been fishing for a long time. Ever since my wife passed away in 1981. It kind of changes your whole life after that, you know. You're alone. You're not popular anymore. It's not a very happy life after that.

I got married when I come out of the Army. Just like any other fellow. He meets a girl, you know. Likes her pretty well, and the first thing you know you decide on getting married and you go on with your life. I still miss her. I guess that's natural.

We had no children. My wife, she couldn't have any. Sometimes I wish that we did have a couple of kids. But I wasn't lucky enough.

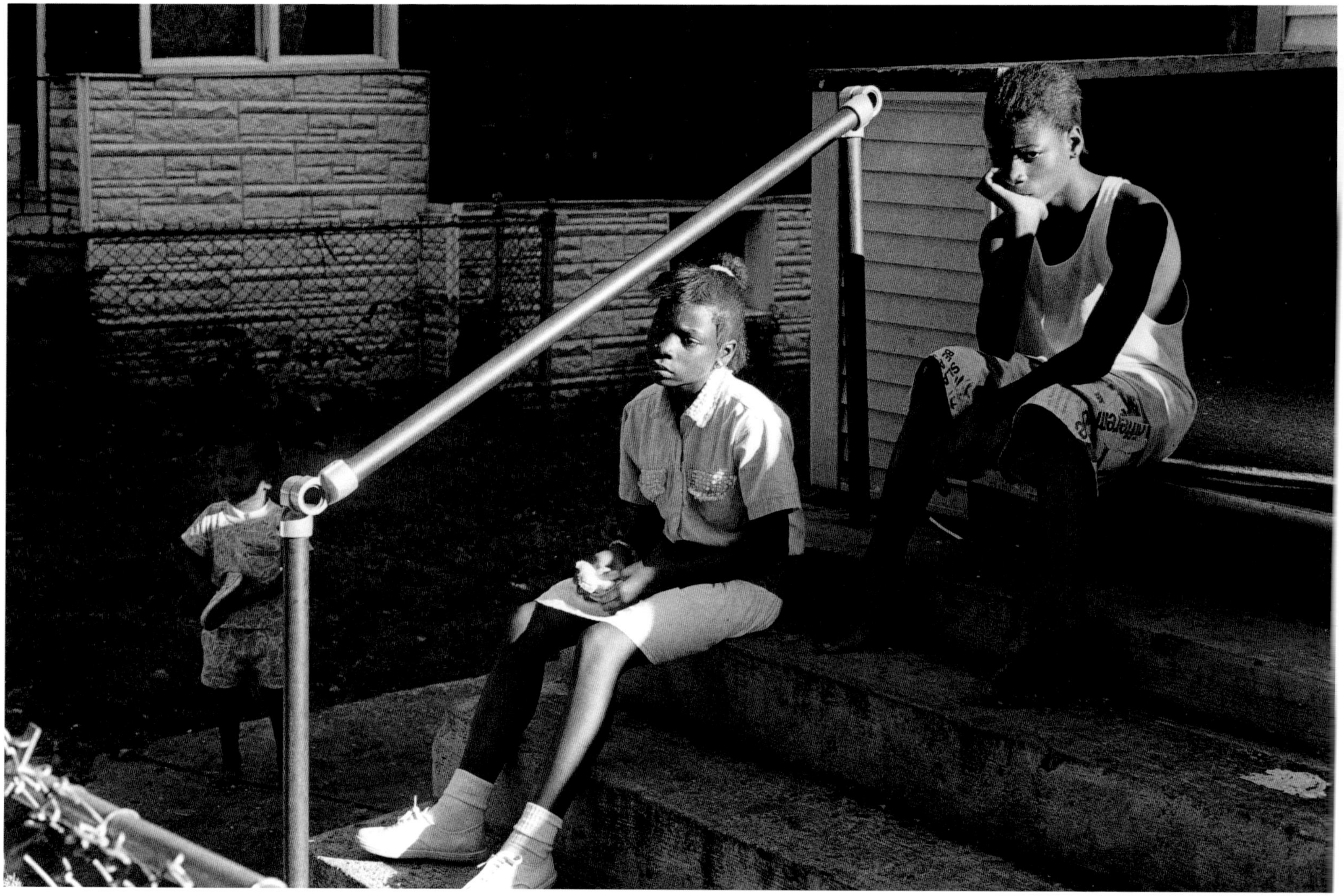

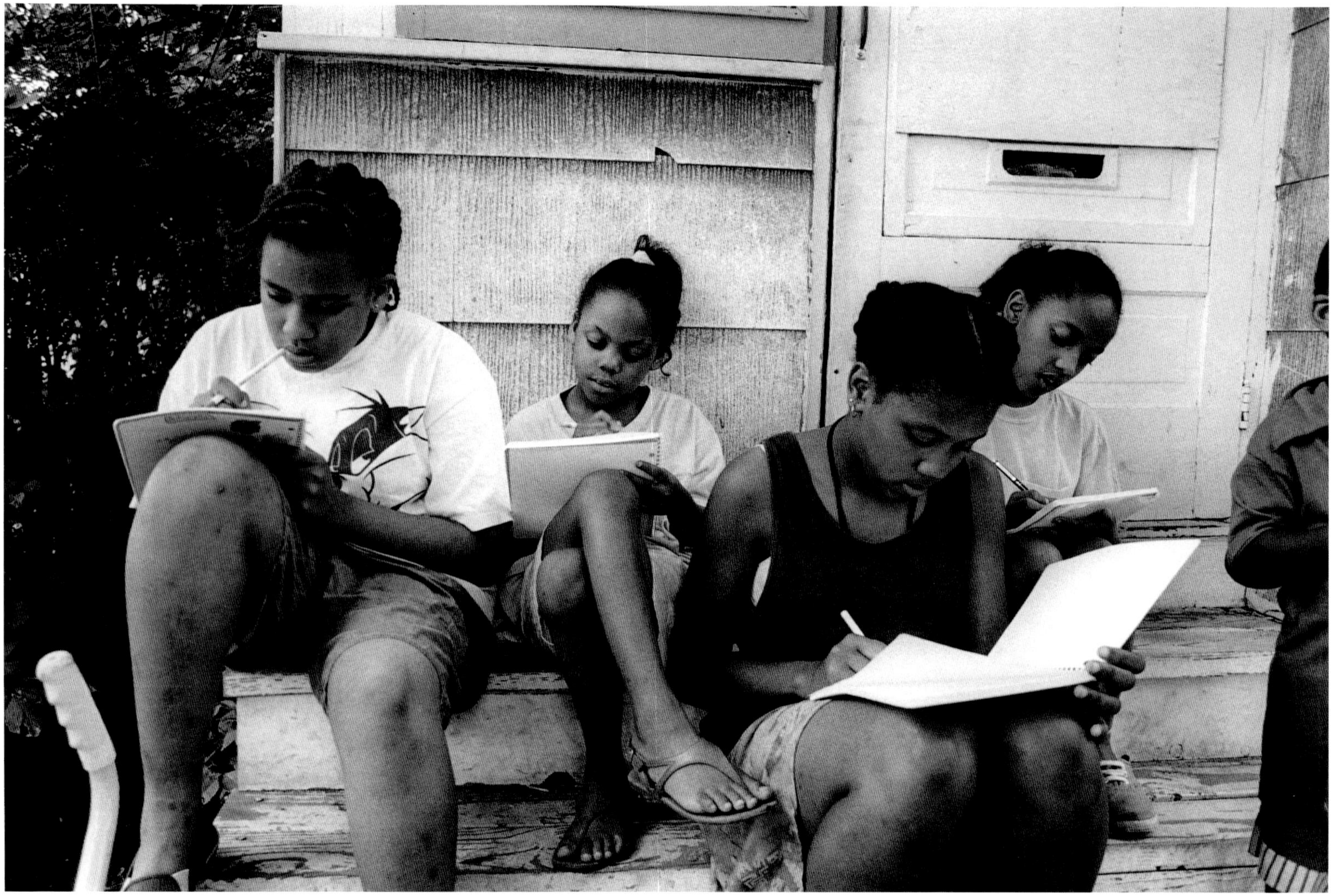

We've lived in Frogtown most of our life. It's really loud. There are a lot of kids running around throwing up gang signs and that kind of stuff. It's dumb. It makes me scared because you don't know. When I'm walking up the street and someone says something to me and I say something wrong, they might take it the wrong way.

Sometimes if you make a face or do something with your fingers, they think it's a gang sign or something. It's really violent. One time there was a car that crashed into a building across the street. Then my friend's dad, he was shot. There's a lot of arguing going on. Fights and all that. Someday I hope we move out of Frogtown. Like by Minnehaha and Snelling [about a mile west]. *It's nicer over there.*

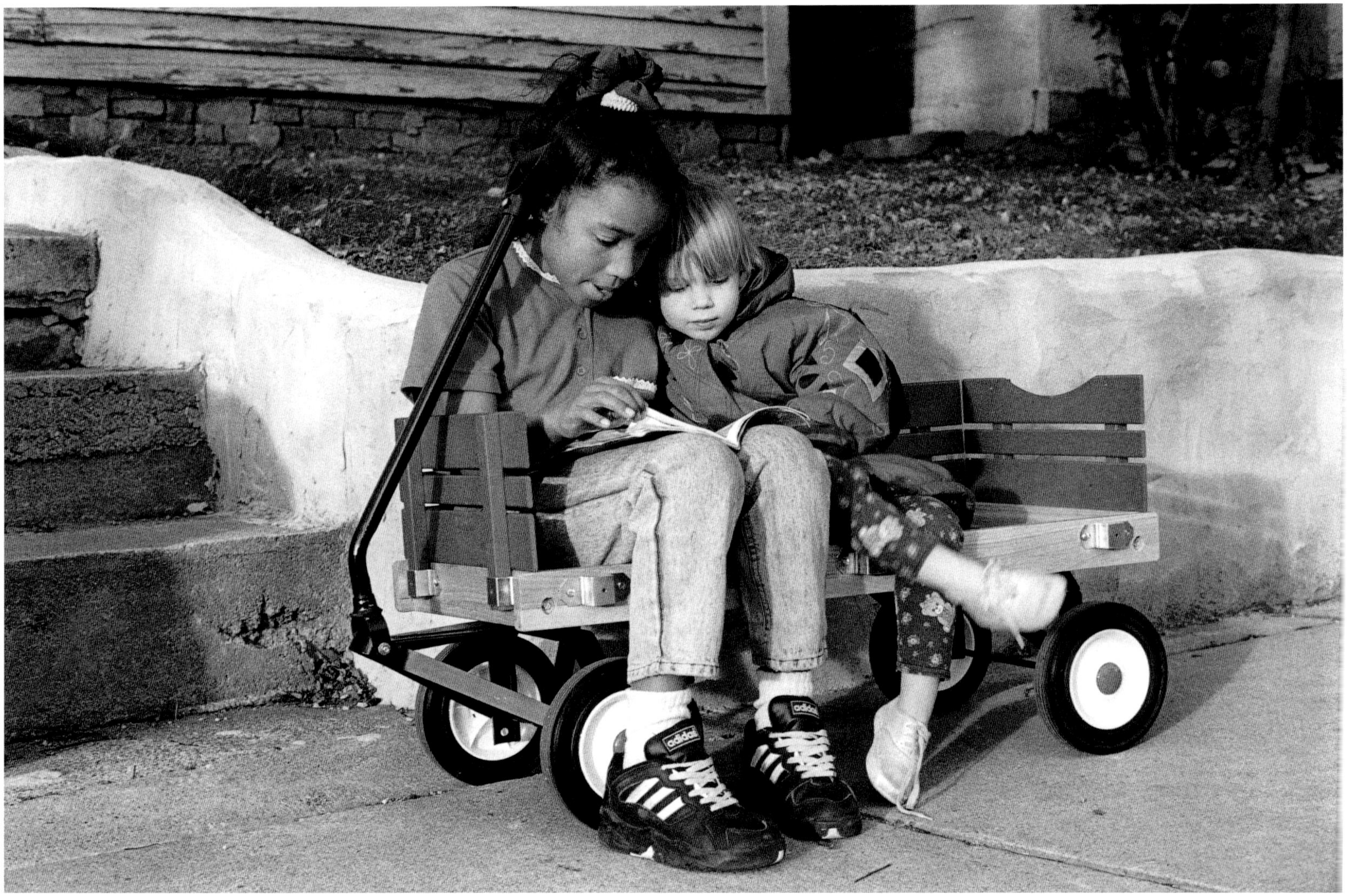

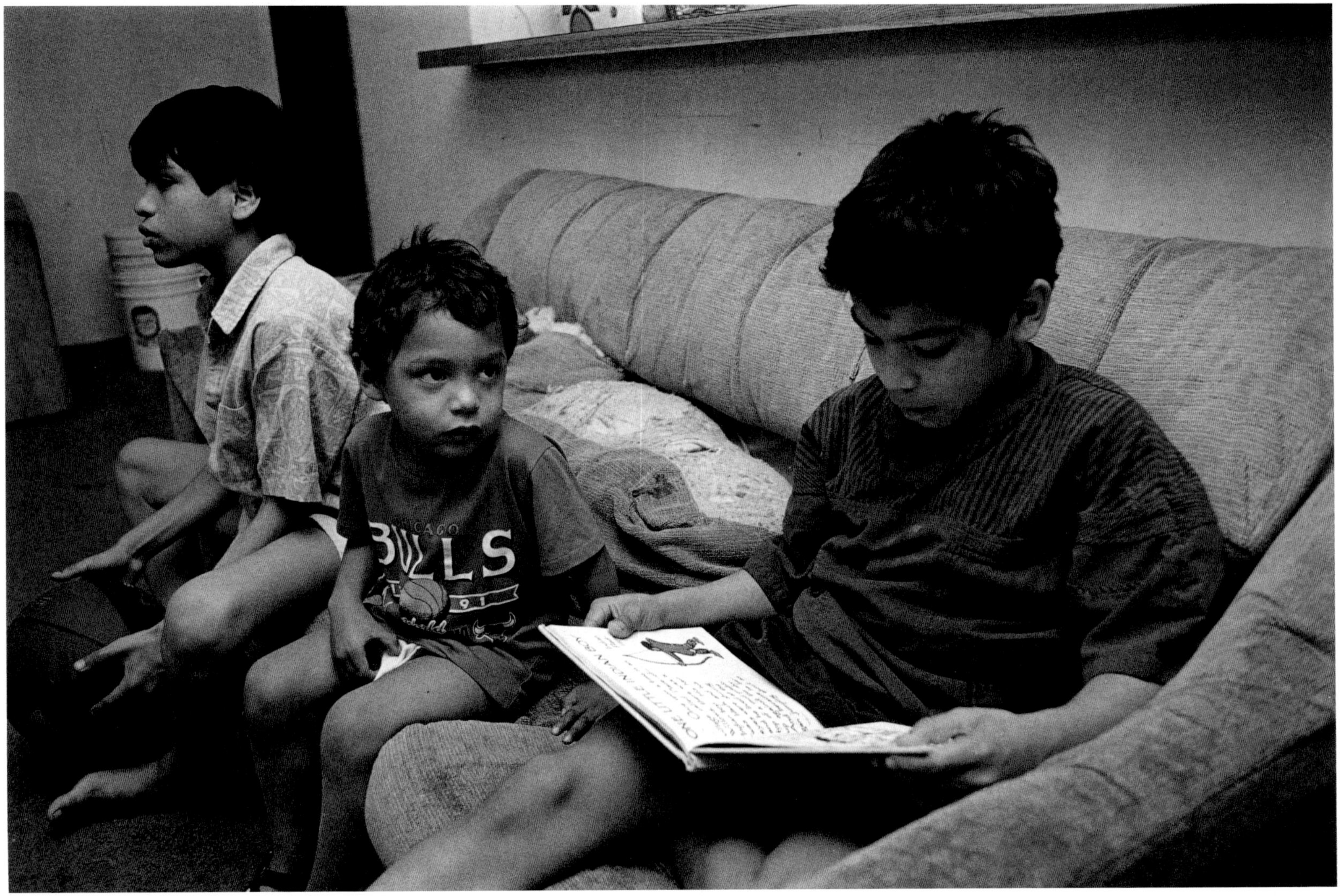
BULLS

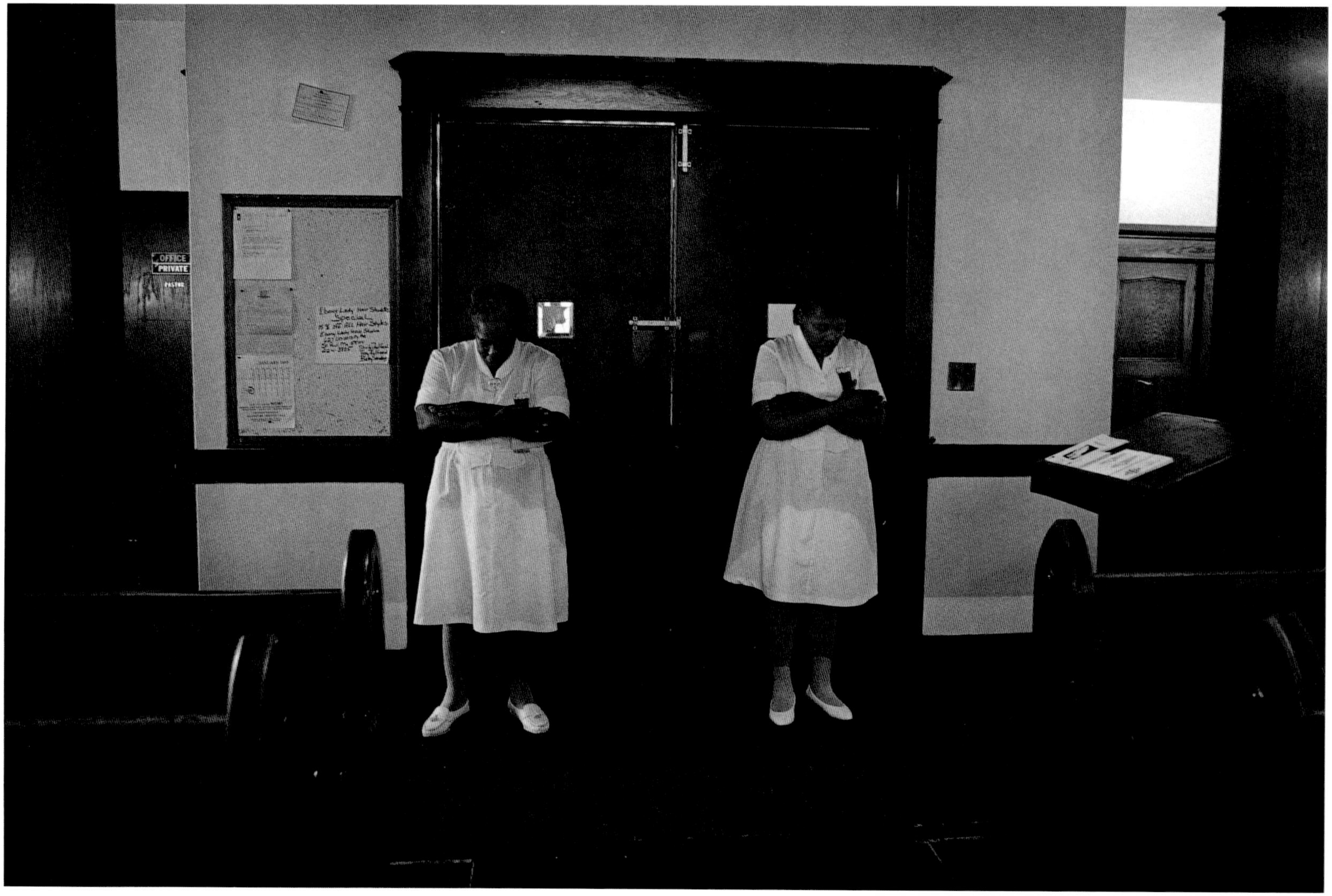
OFFICE
PRIVATE

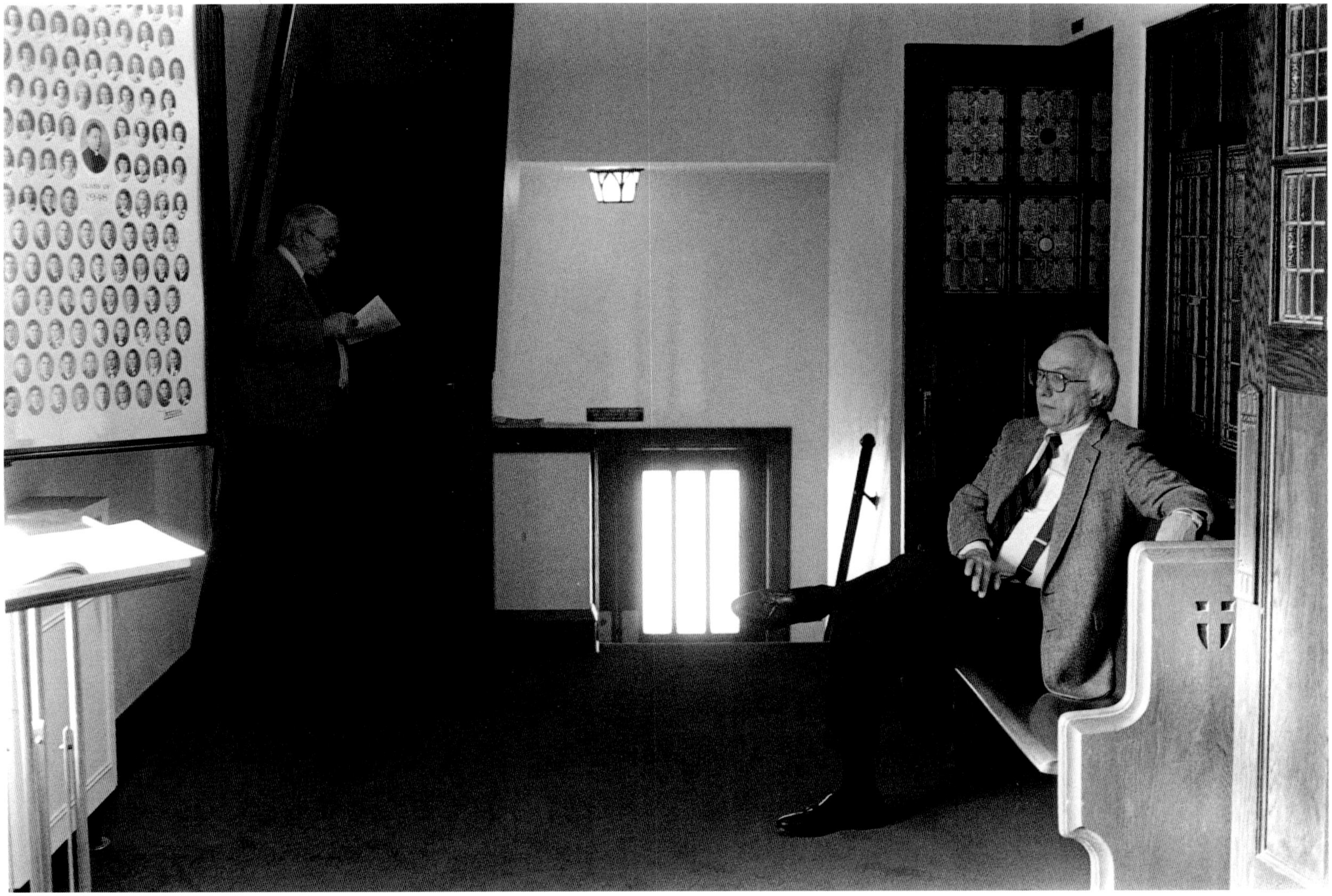

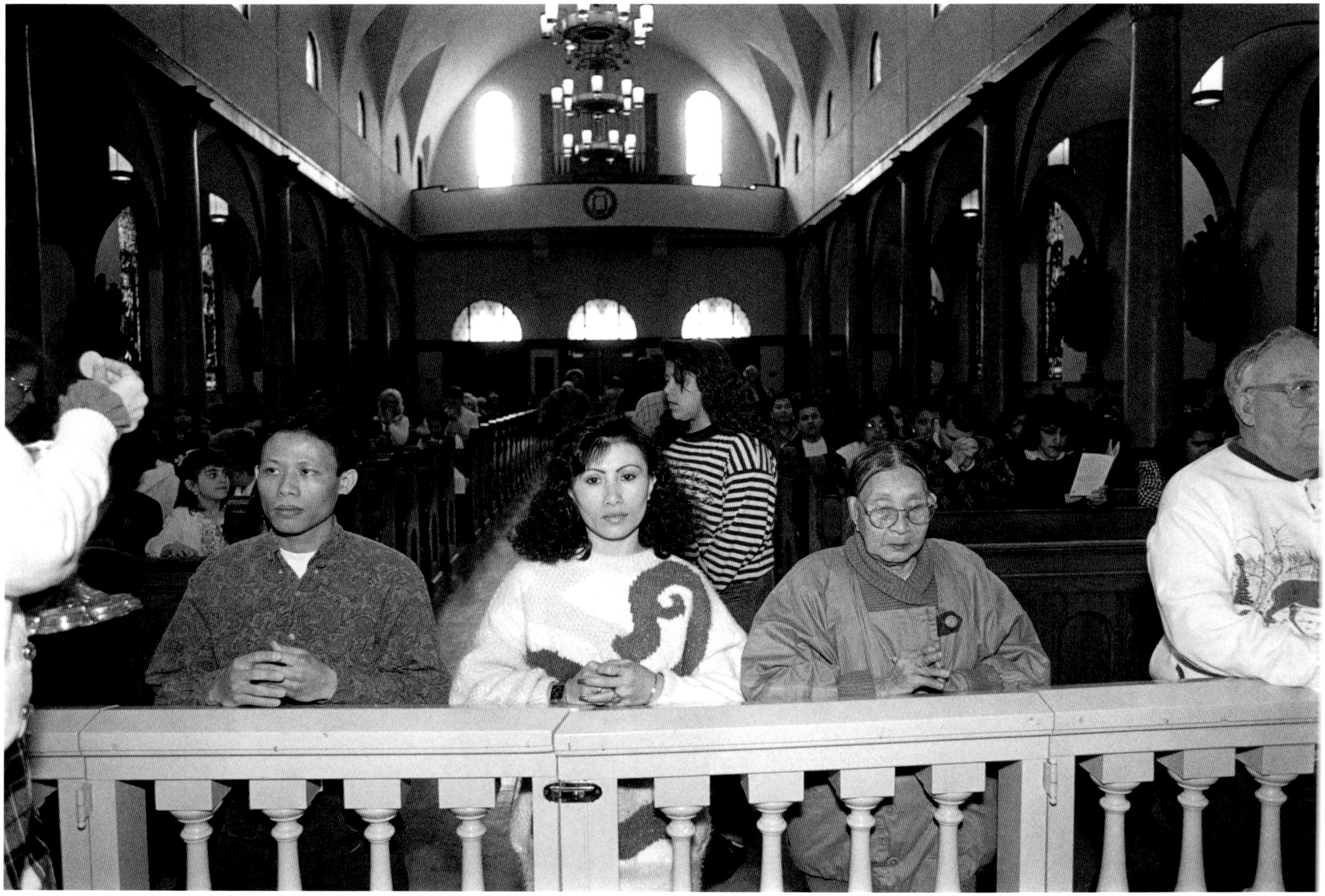

When you're trying to do something interculturally like this, there's a struggle. Some of our older members find it difficult. Why all this attention to the Vietnamese? One said it so well. Last year at Easter she said, "Father, that was a wonderful celebration. Of course, we won't have to do that next year." I said, "Well, why not?" "Because they will have been here a year. They'll know English by then." I said, "How long did we have mass in Polish for your grandparents and for your parents. How many years?" It's a time of change. A time of testing. Where is our faith? Is it all cultural, or is it bigger than that?

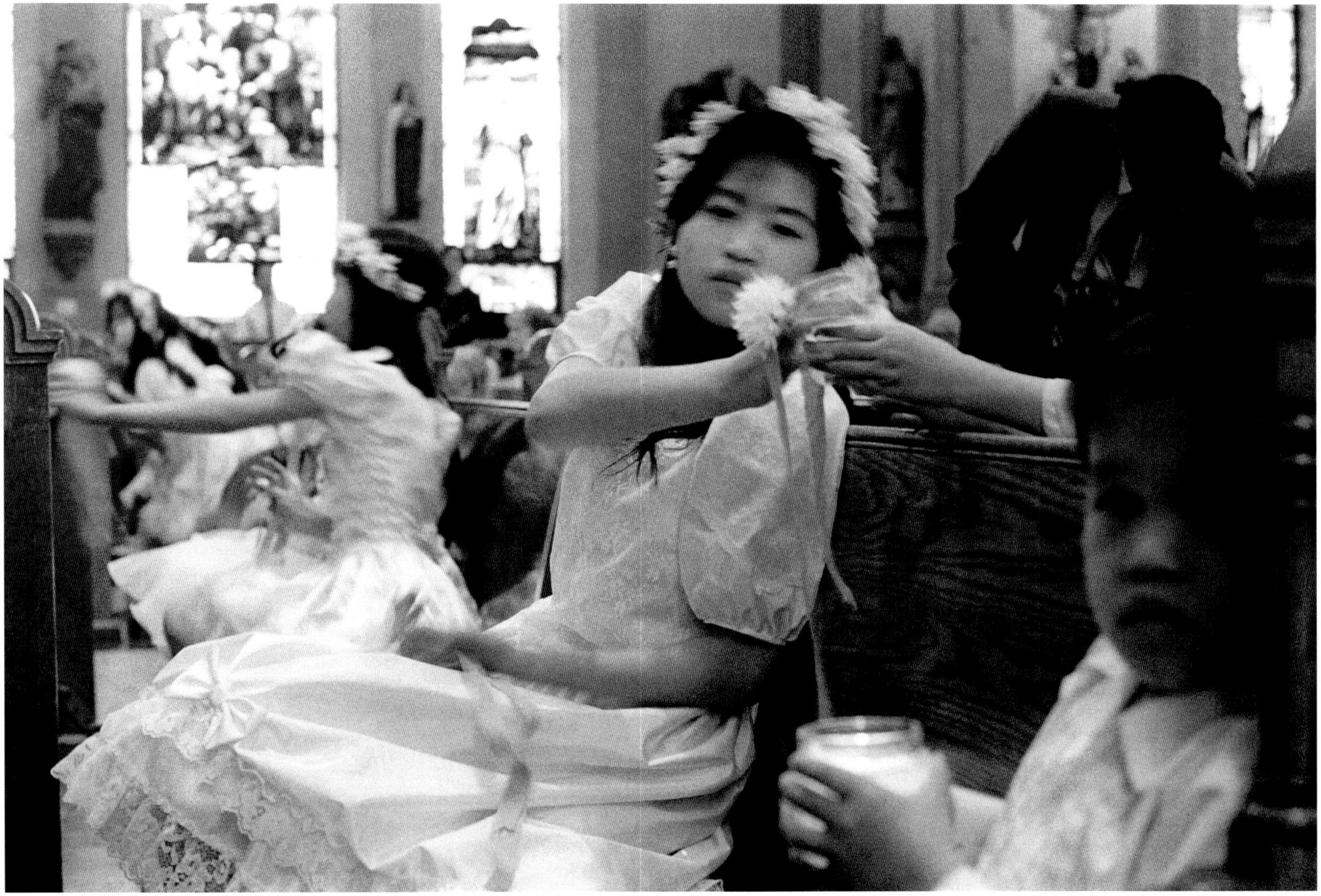

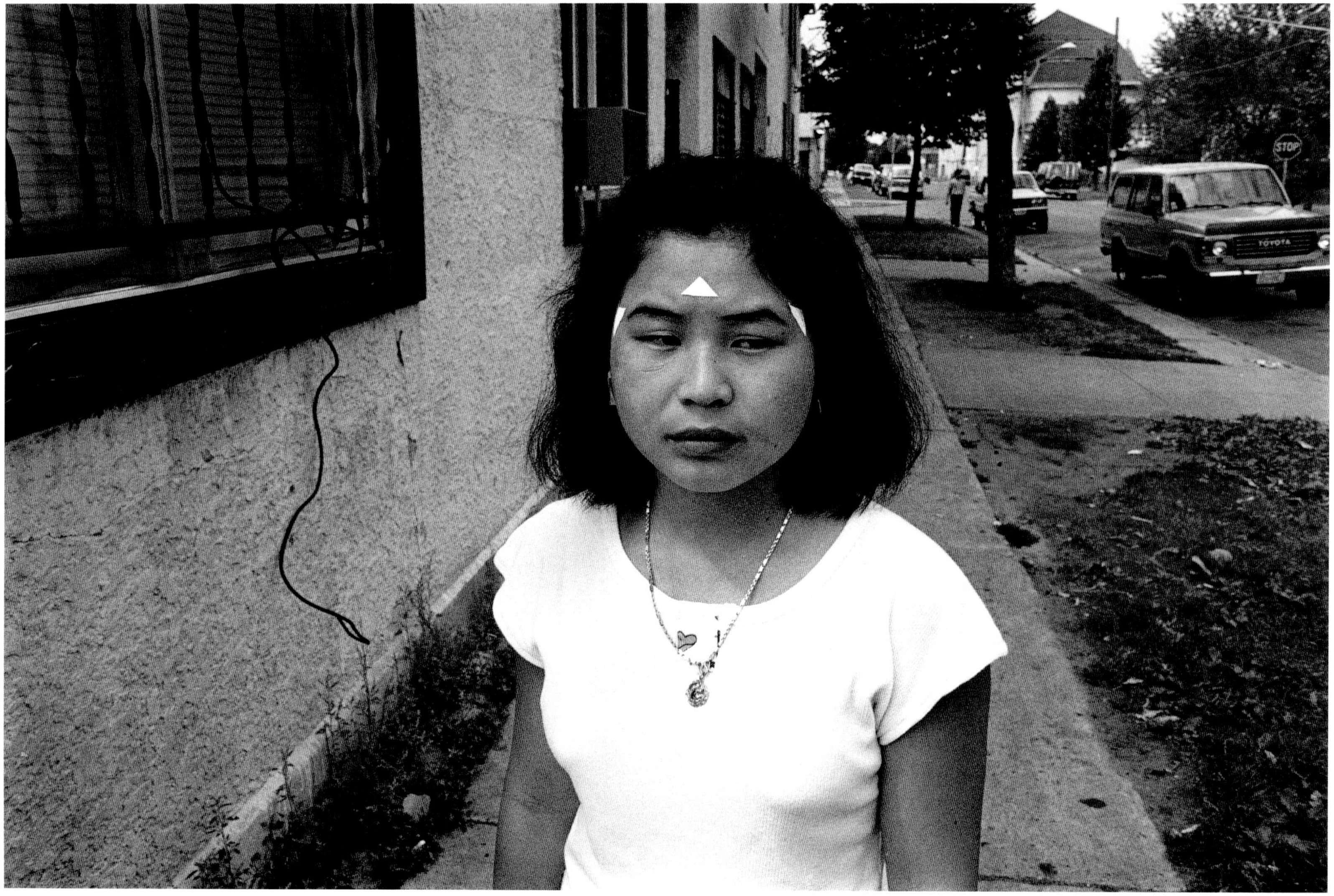

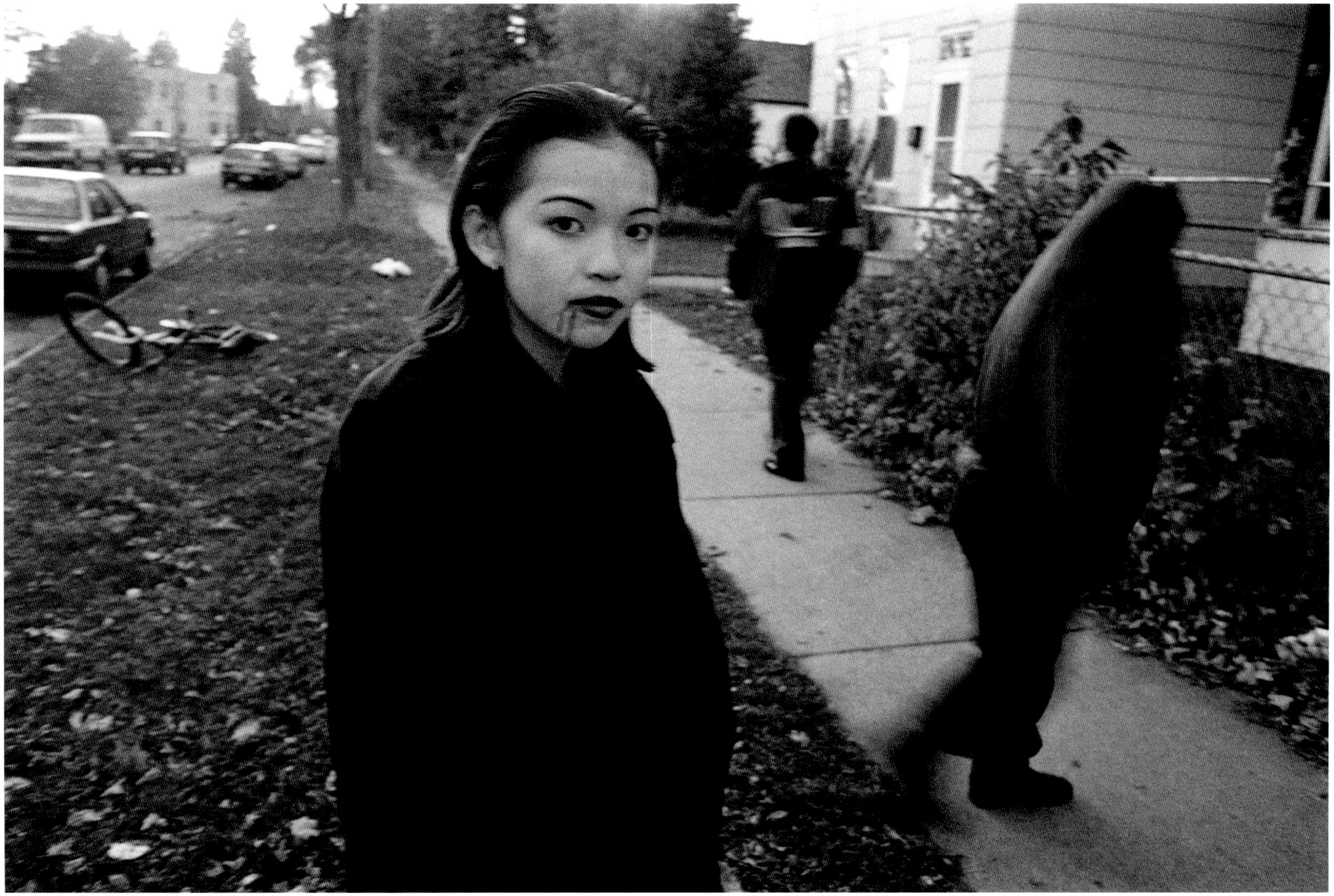

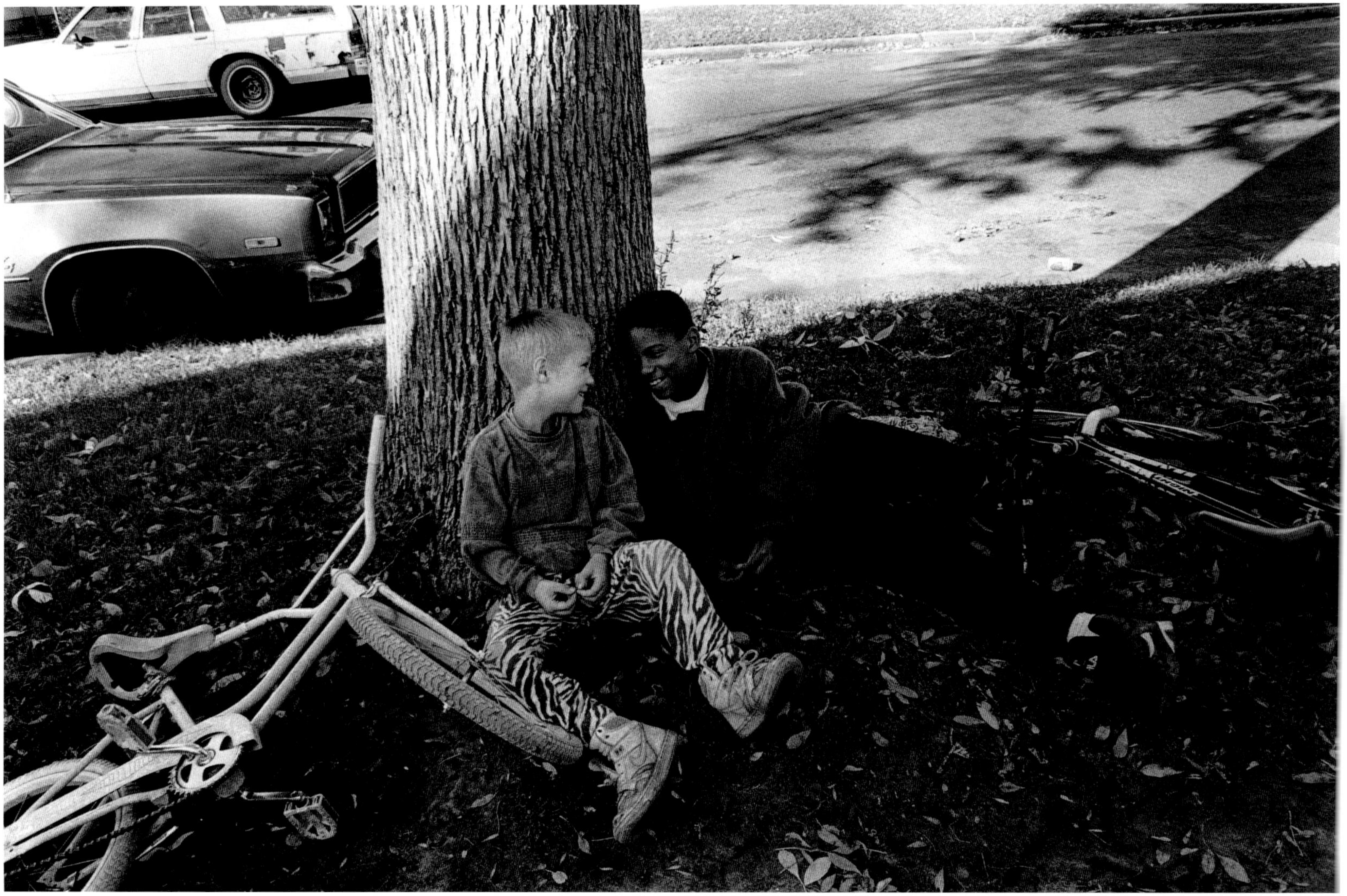

We're best friends. We play on the swing set. We play football. We ride our bikes a lot. We play with other kids, too. But some of them we don't like. Some of them call him honky. They call me nigger. They pick on him a lot. I watch his back so nobody beats him up.

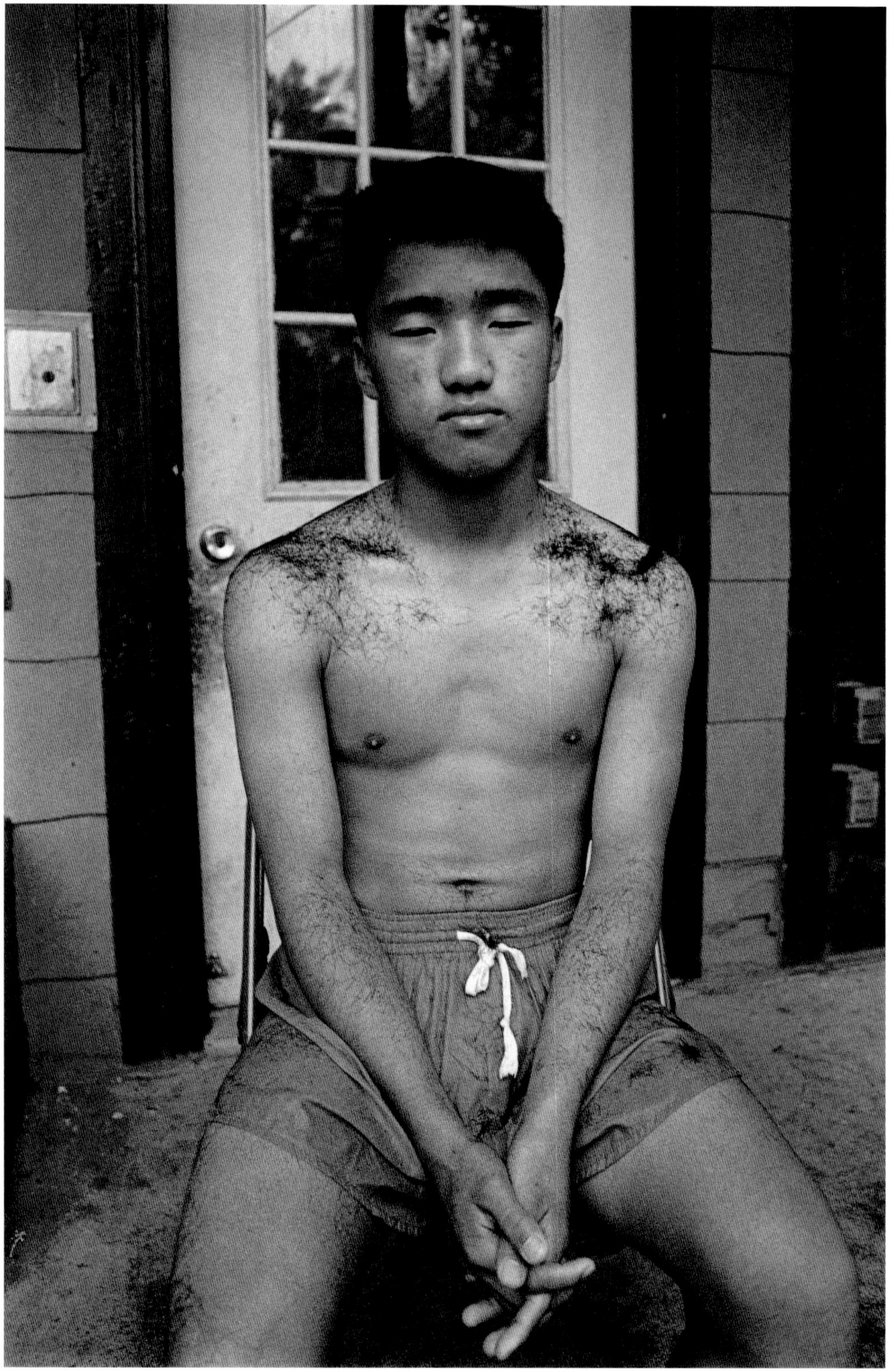

Because the father is in charge of the house, he is the one that does the haircutting. I think short hair is better. It looks better when he goes to school. School is very important. With so many children it's hard for me to support everyone. That's why he should try as best as possible to get a better education.

When he's at school it's good to learn the American culture. But when he's at home he has to learn to be Hmong. I don't know how to be American. I only know how to be Hmong. If he wants to be American, that is okay, as long as he doesn't forget he is Hmong, too.

There's a lot of problems having so many children. Especially when they're only one year apart. My wife and I take shifts to care for them. We try to practice abstinence, but it's hard. It's a Hmong tradition to have many children. In Asia it's beneficial to have many children for labor. But here there's different circumstances. It's financially difficult to have many children here.

I like Frogtown because it's not hilly. It's better for family safety. People won't fall down. Things won't roll down the hill, and there's less chance for accidents. There's too many cars. It's easier to live in a flat place where it snows.

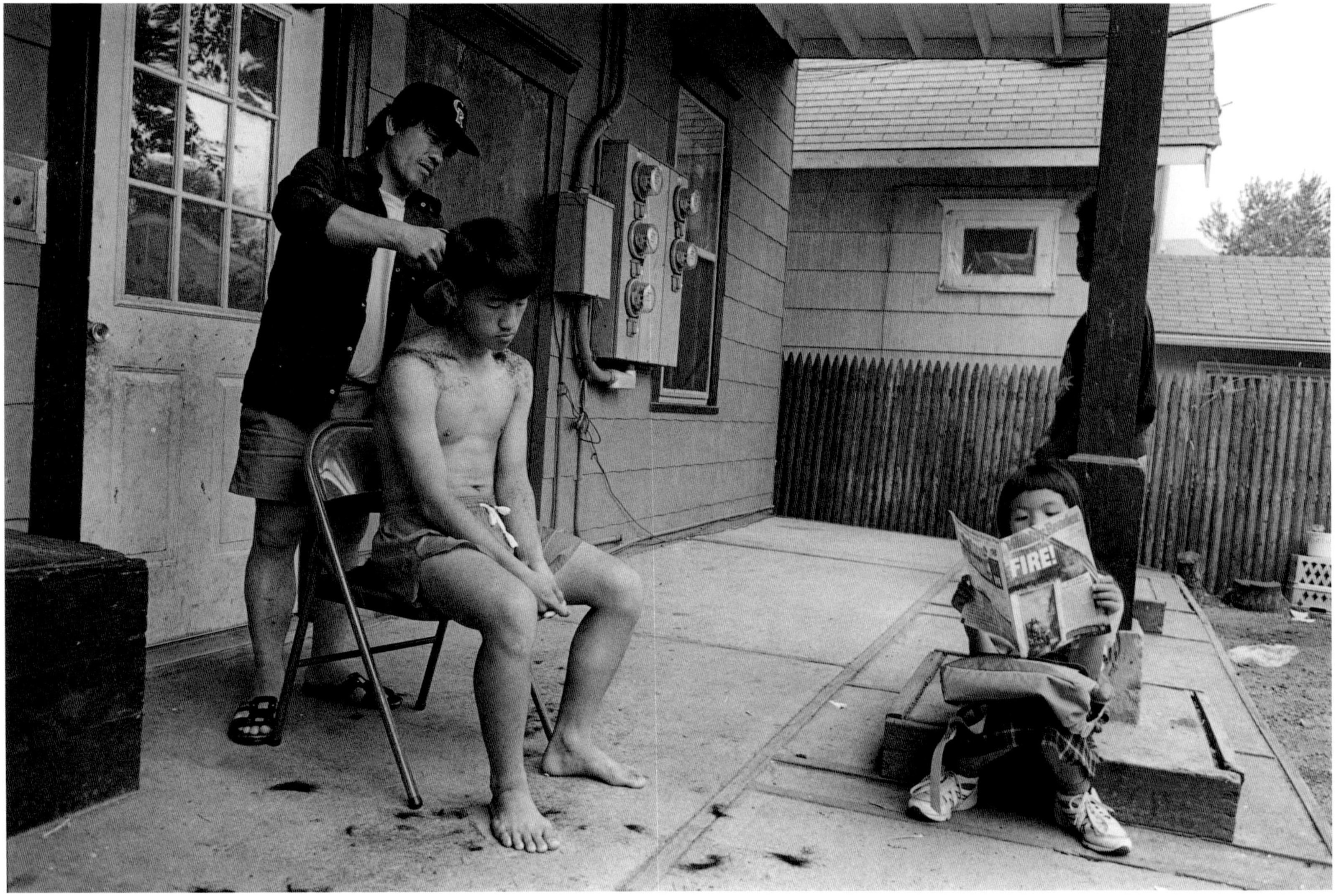
FIRE!

Would you believe I'm thirty-nine? I'm getting a perm for my birthday. My husband is taking me to the Steamboat Inn in Prescott [Wisconsin]. *Then he's taking me to Denny's for a free birthday dinner.*

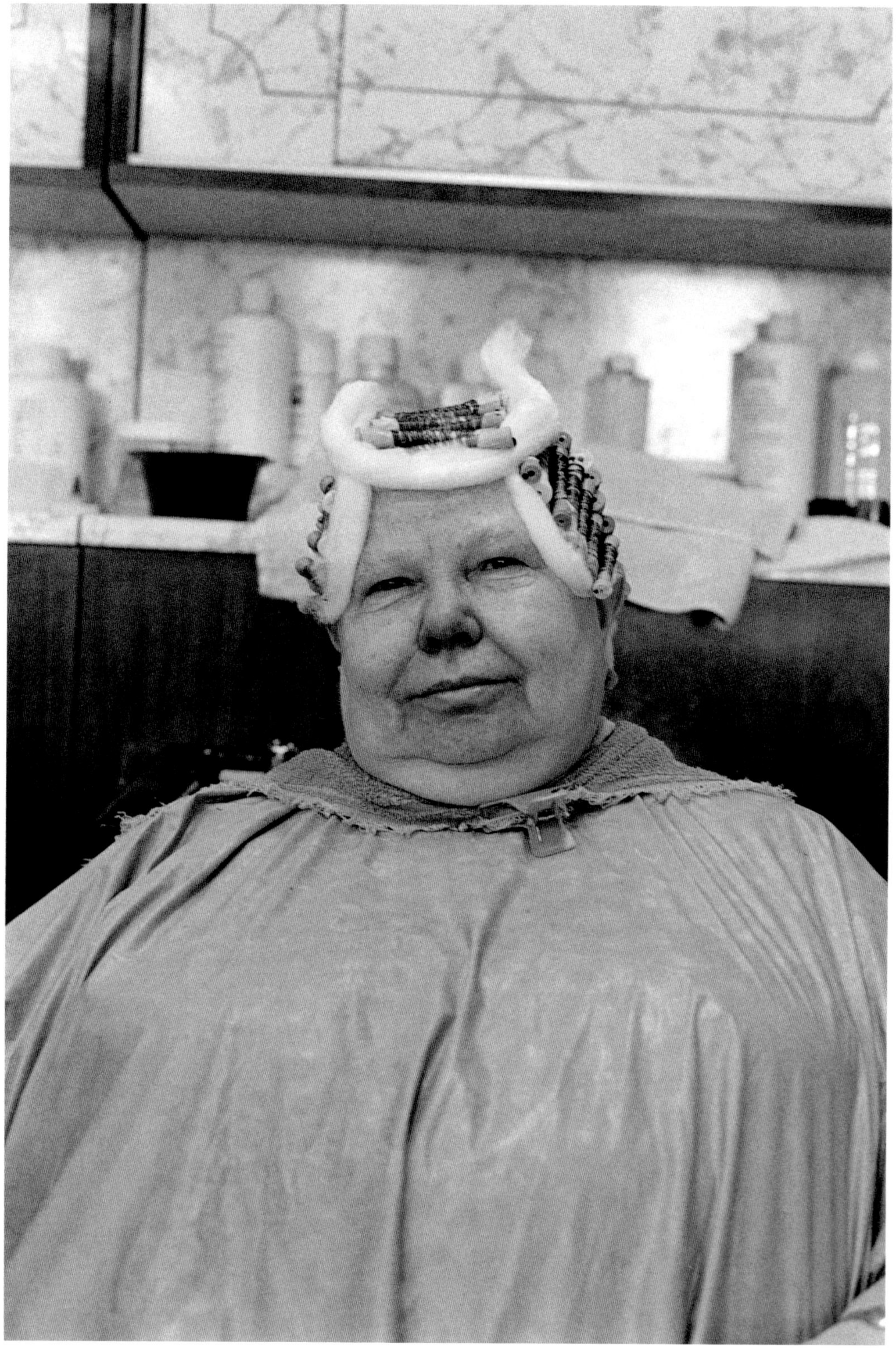

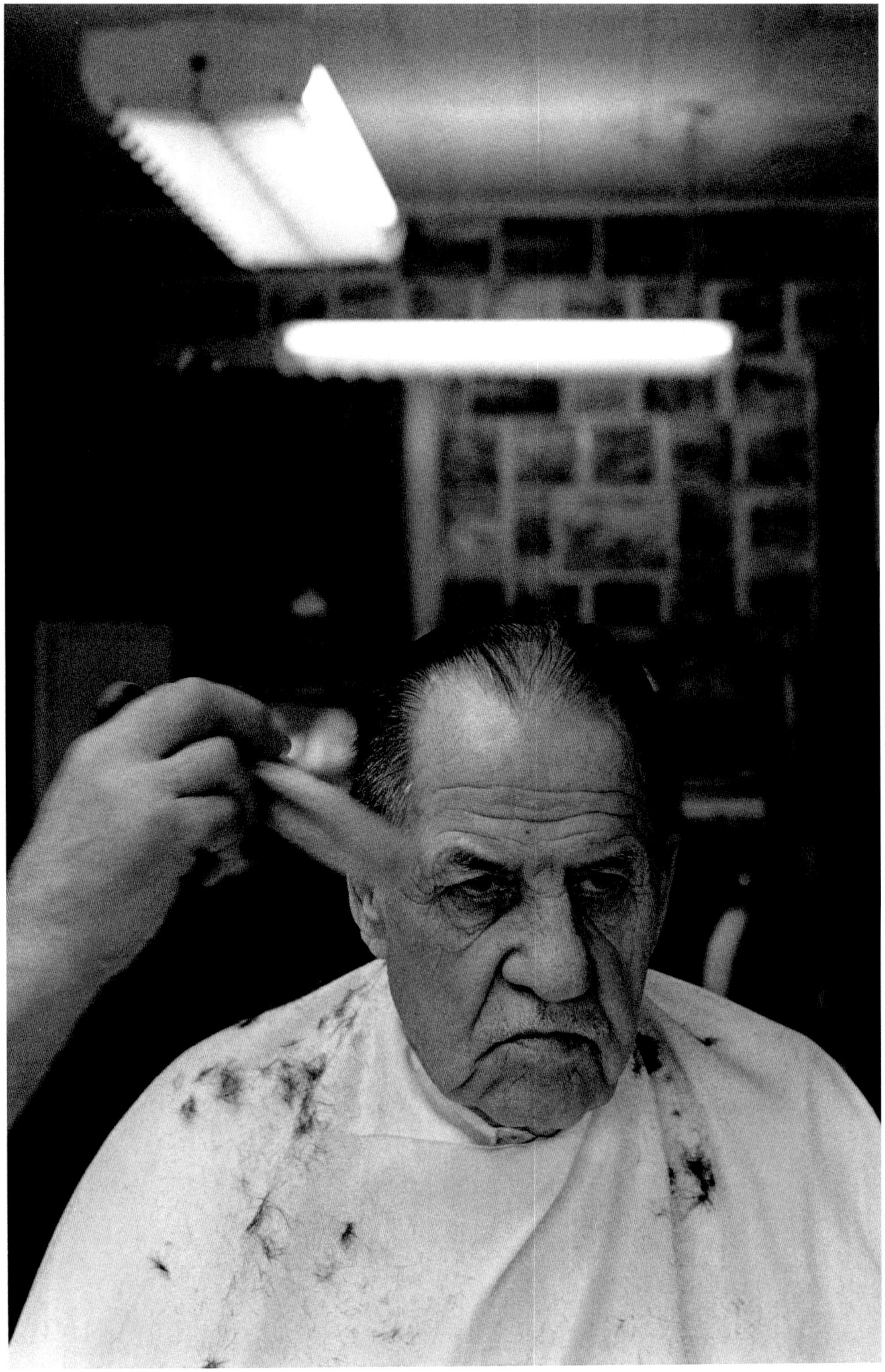

I first started coming here in the 1930s, when I was sixteen. It was called Nick's Barber Shop then. Haircuts were $.35. Now they're $7.50. Still a good buy. Joe here has been cutting my hair since 1950. I've been a good customer. I get it cut every three weeks. If you can stand his BS, you've got it made. That's a lot of BS over forty years. I guess that's why I come here.

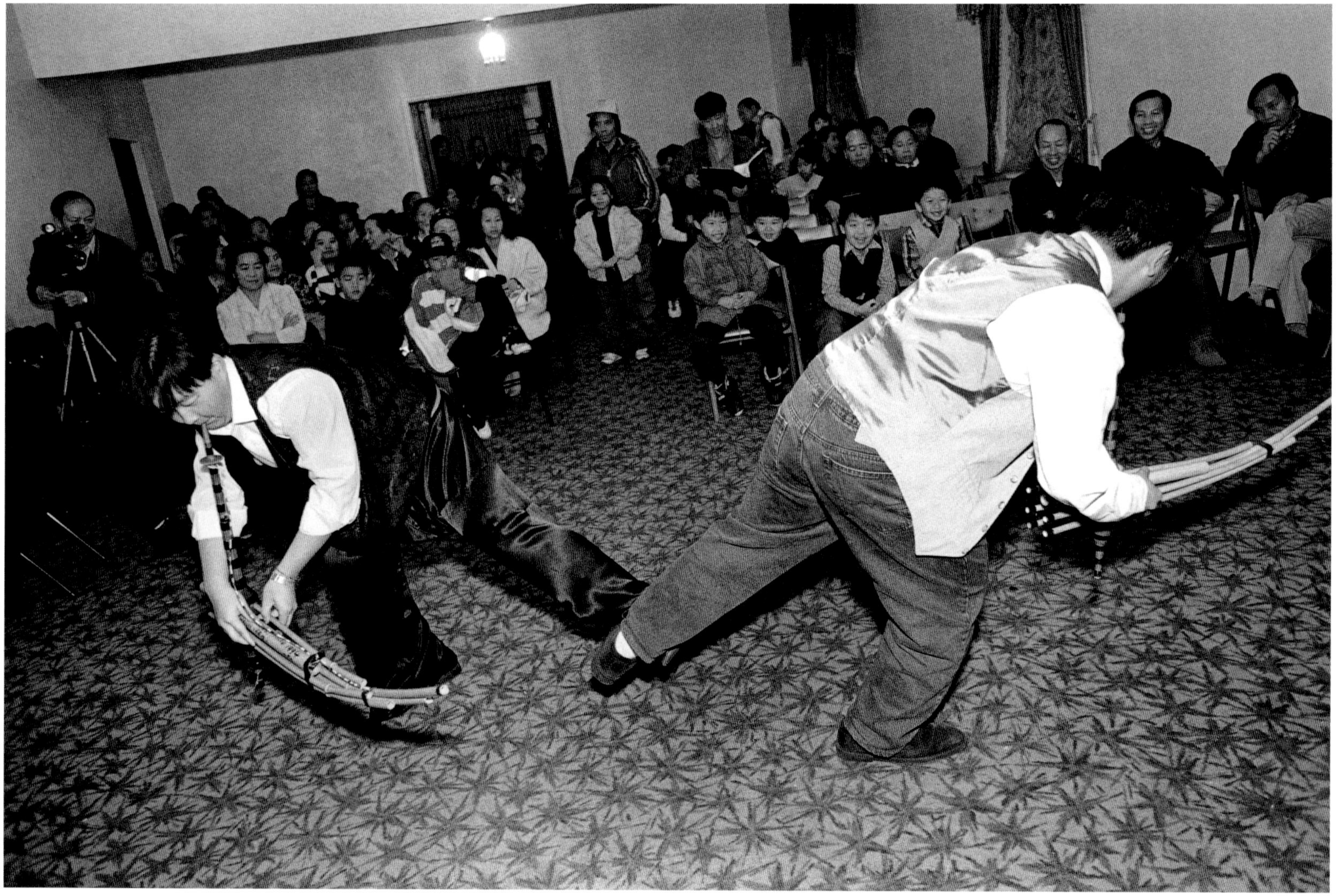

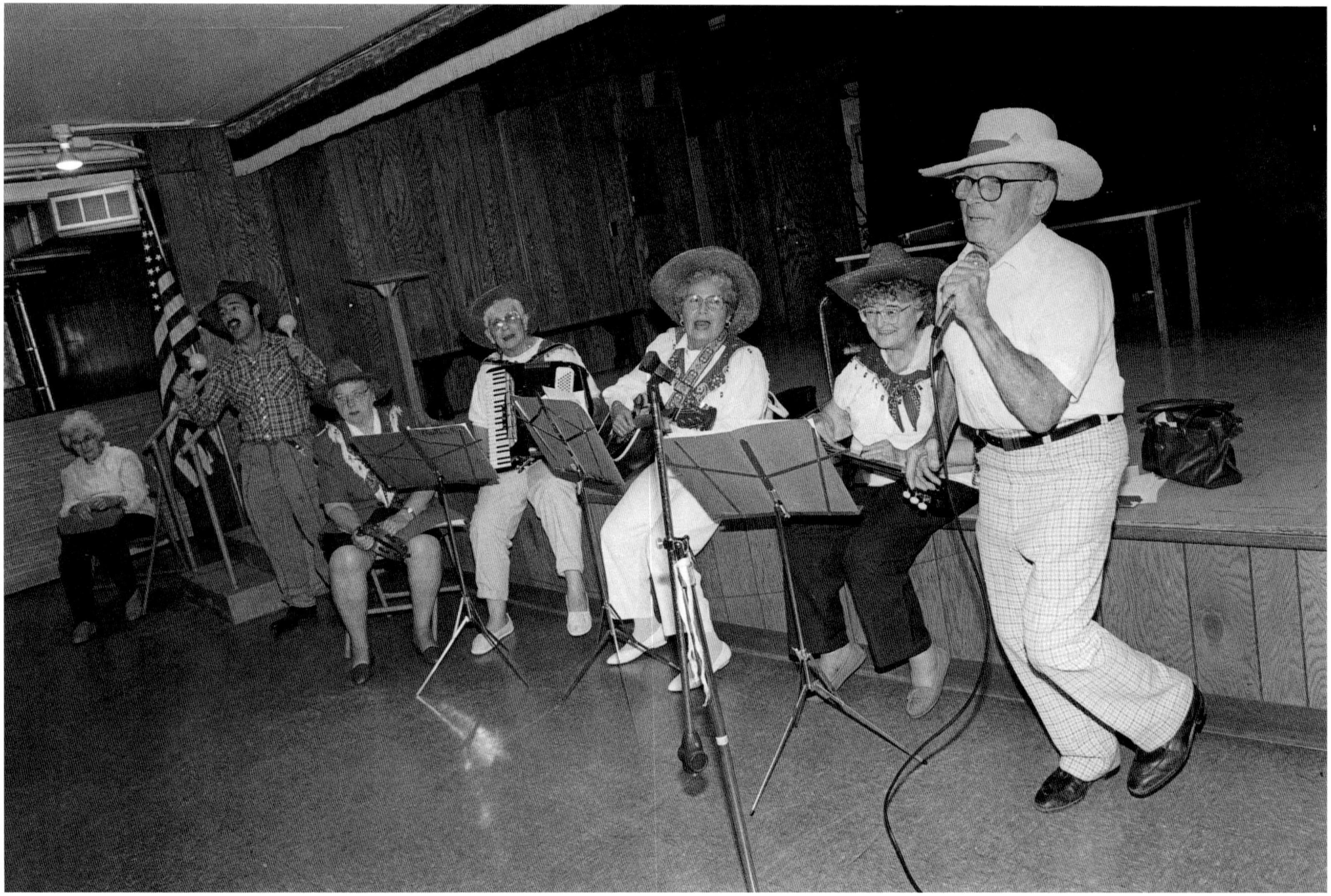

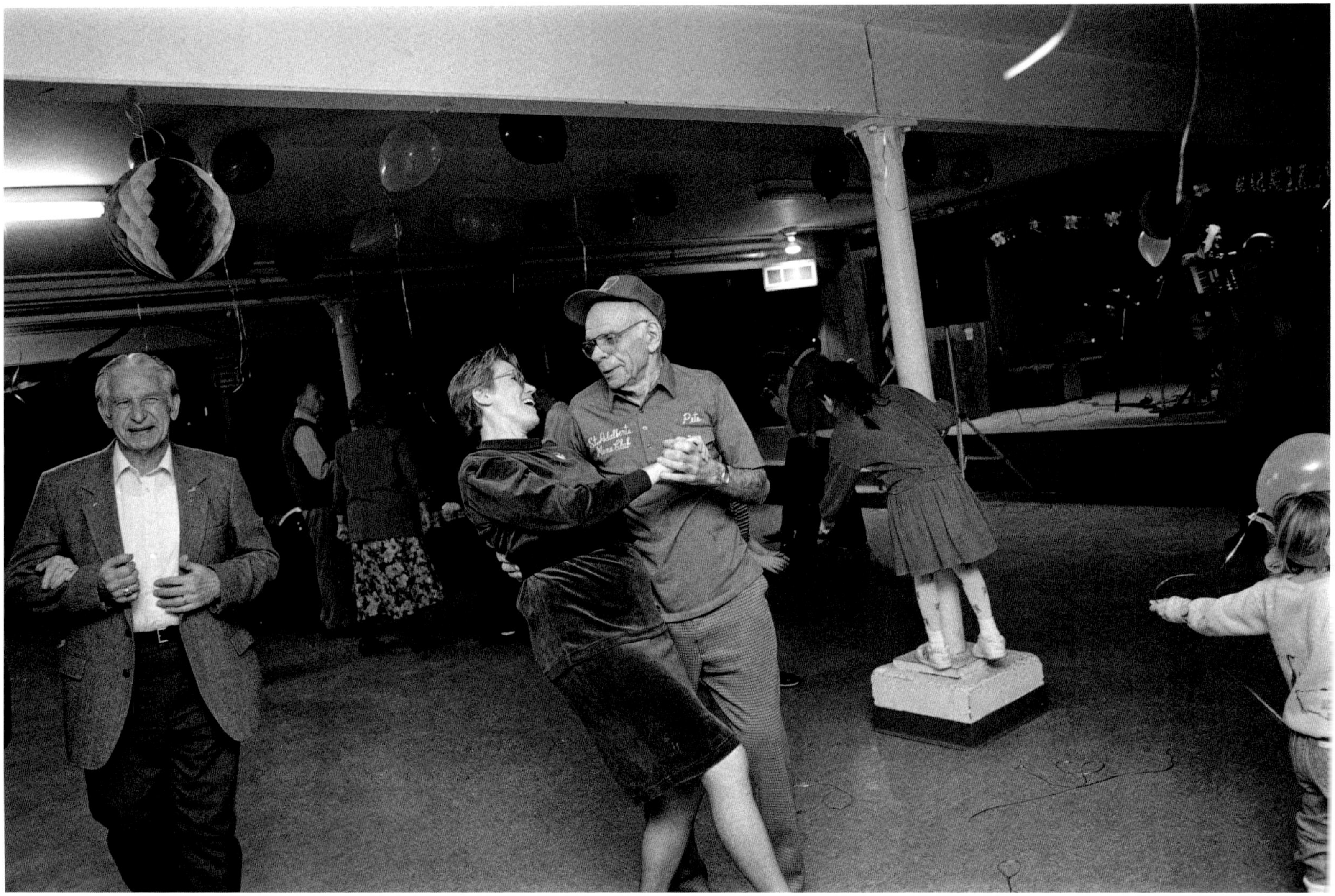

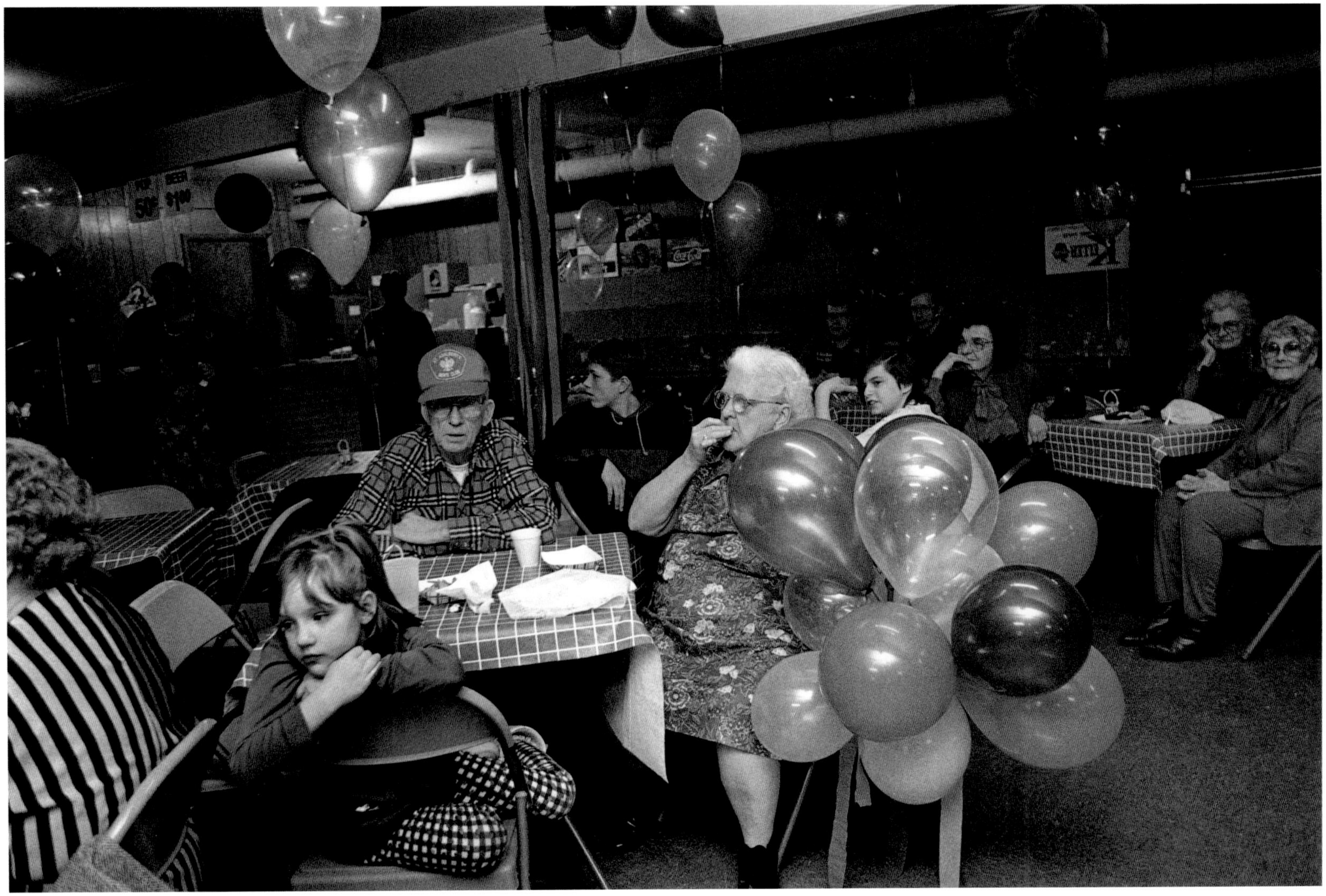

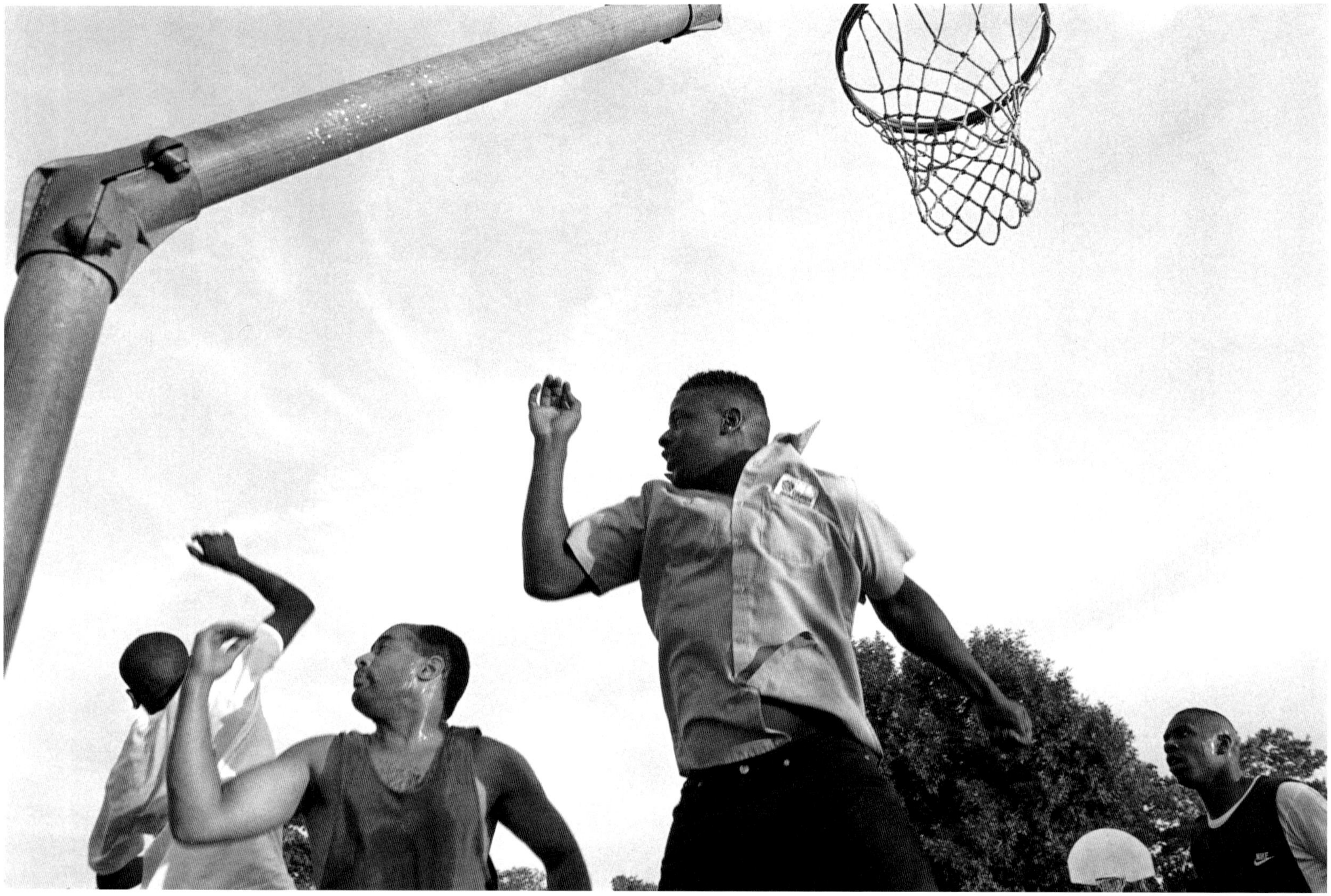

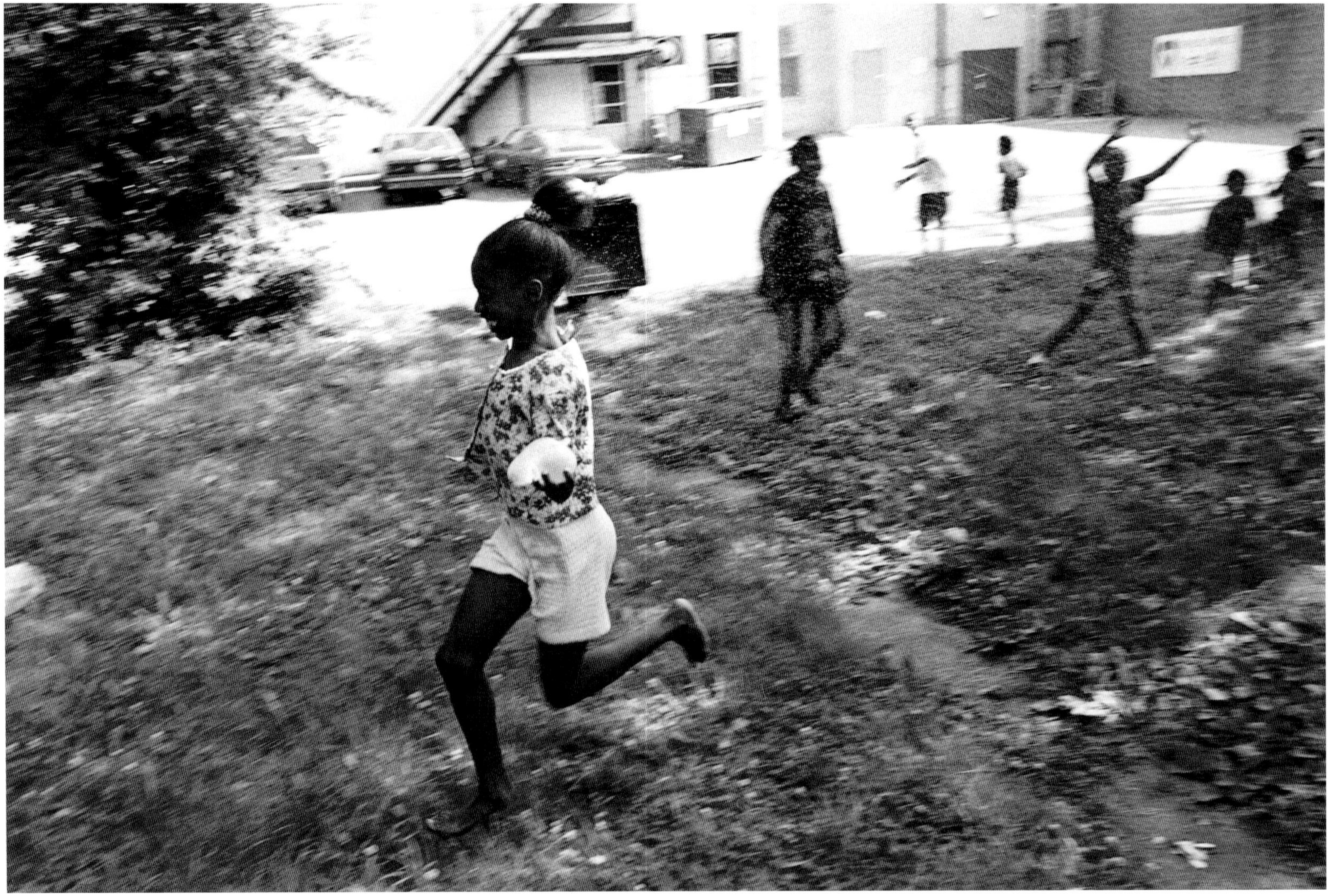

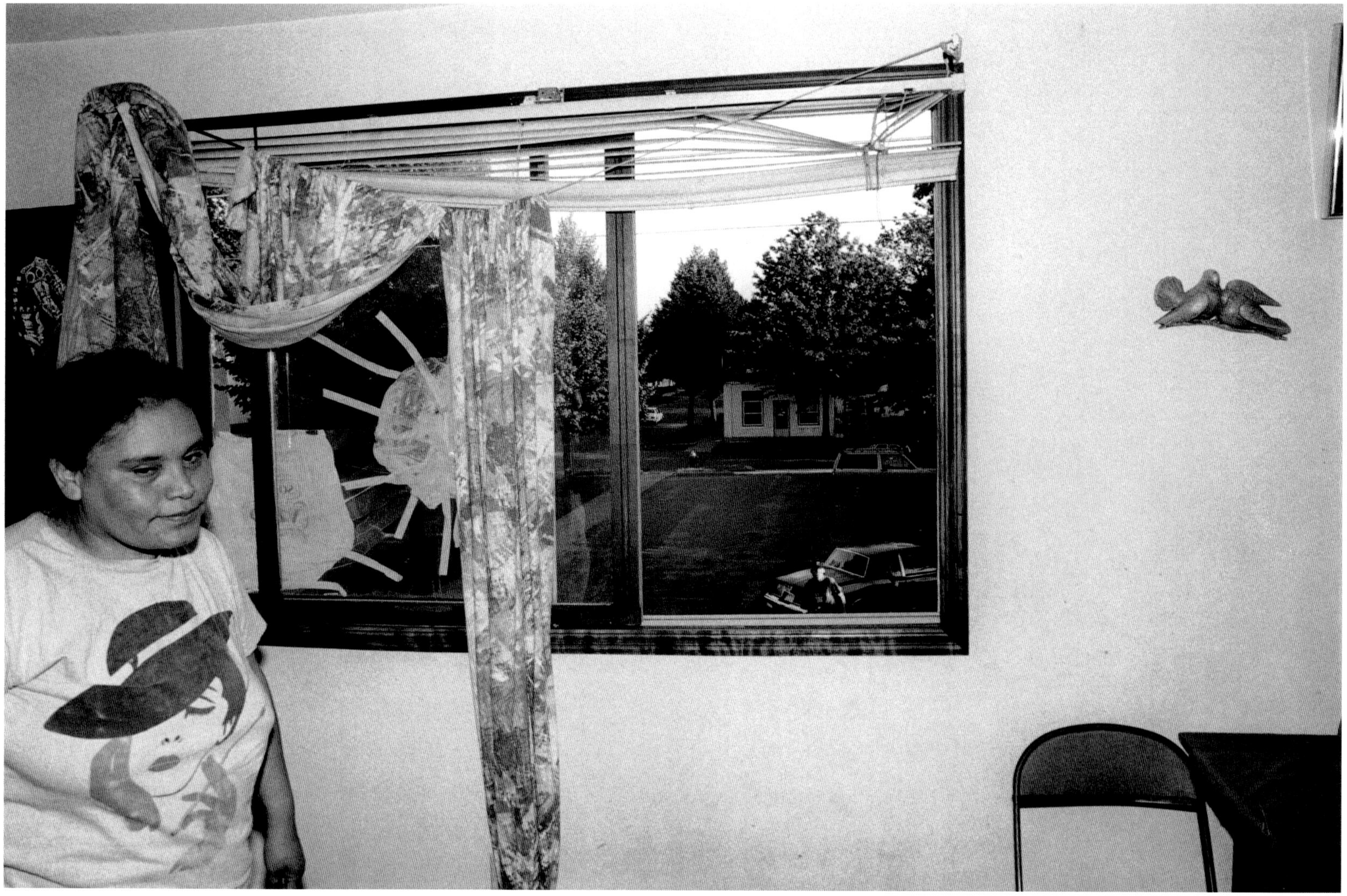

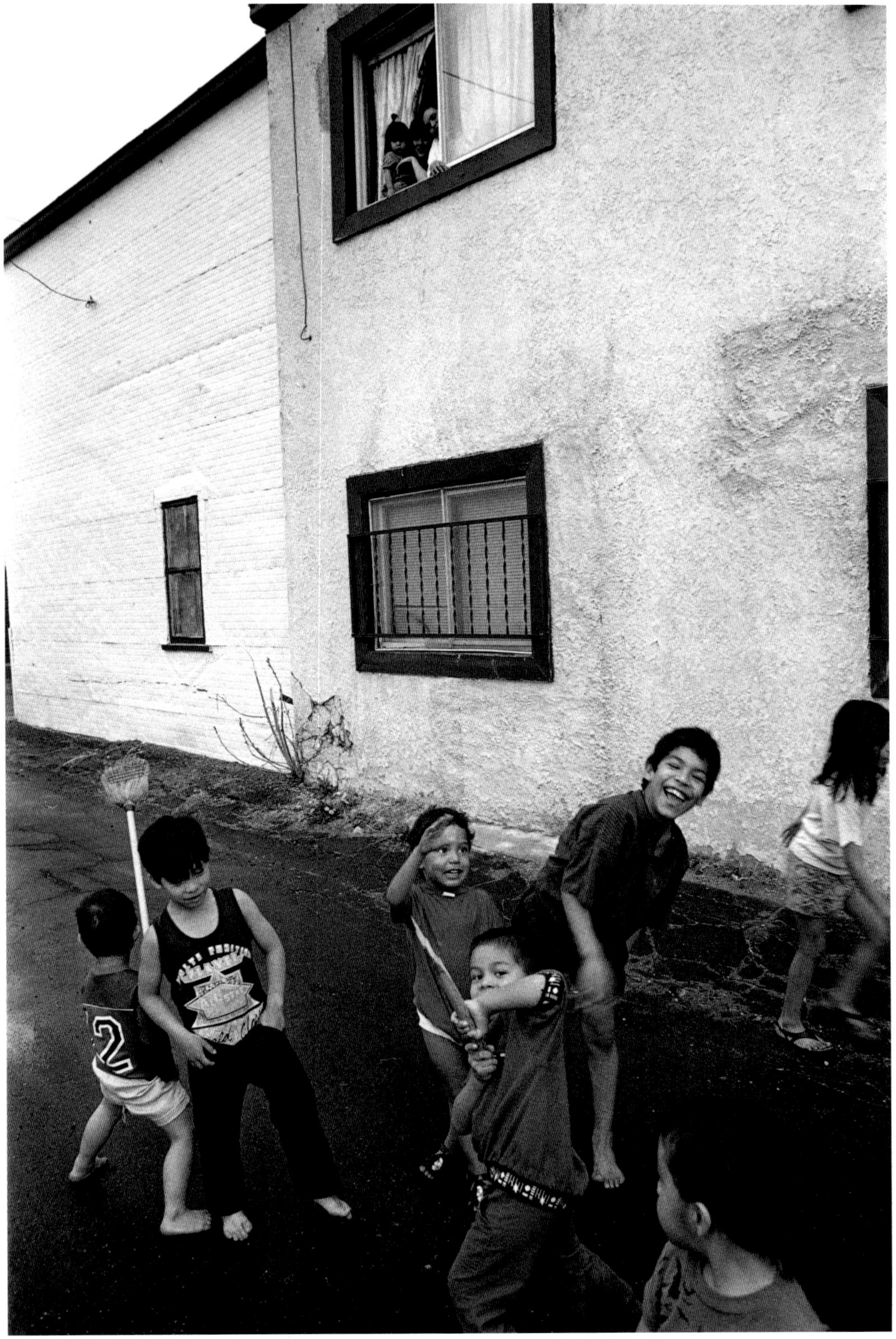

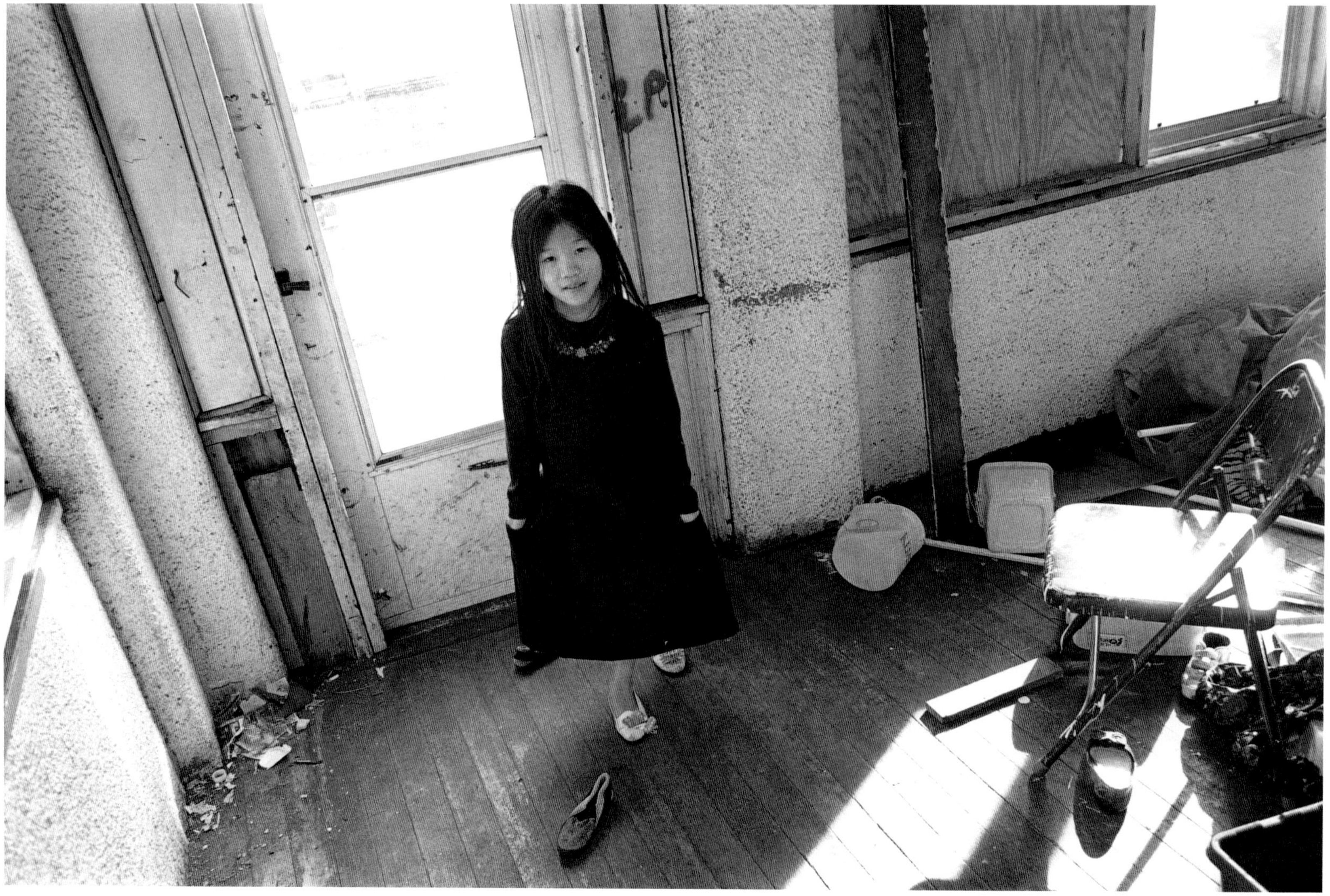

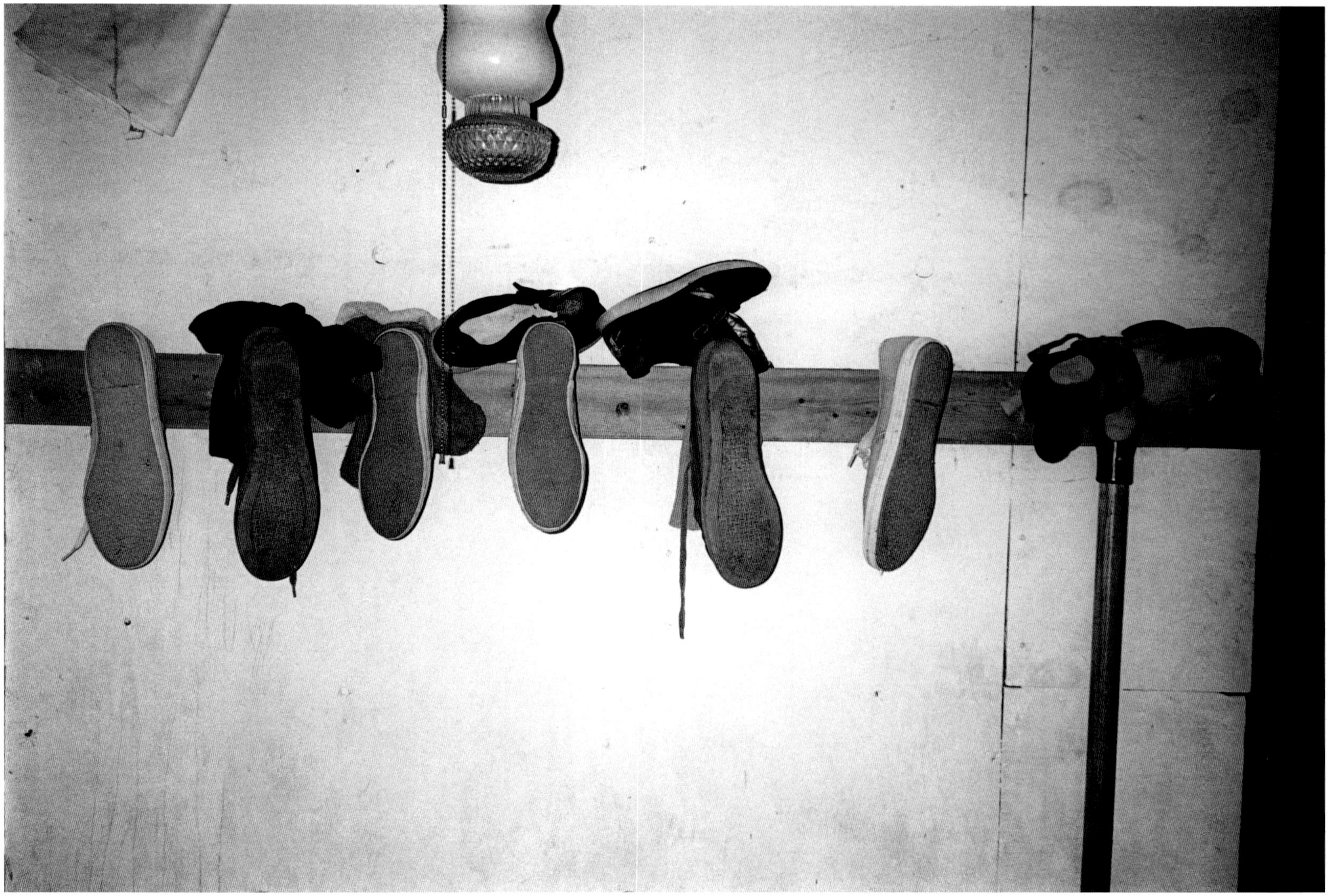

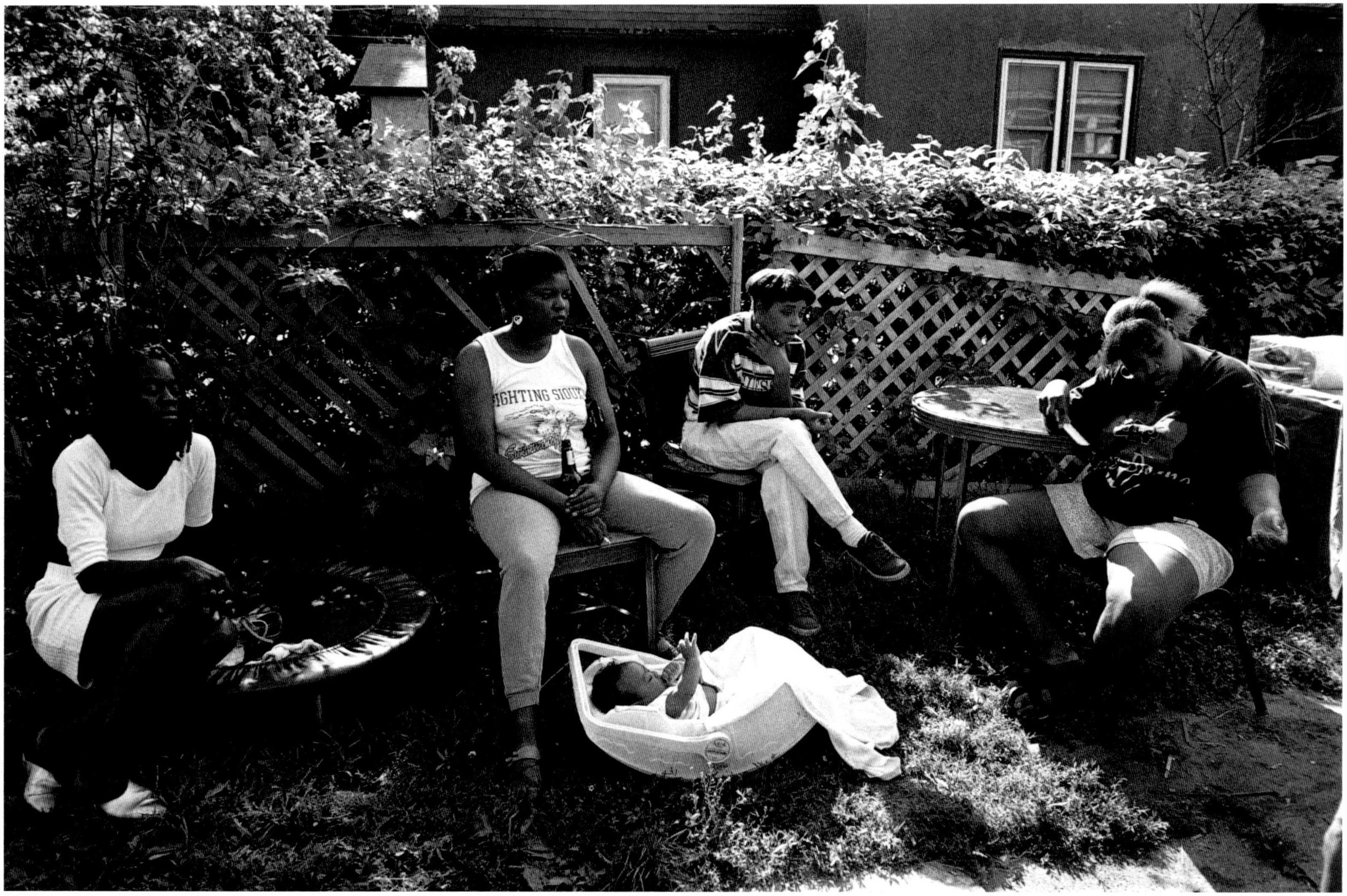

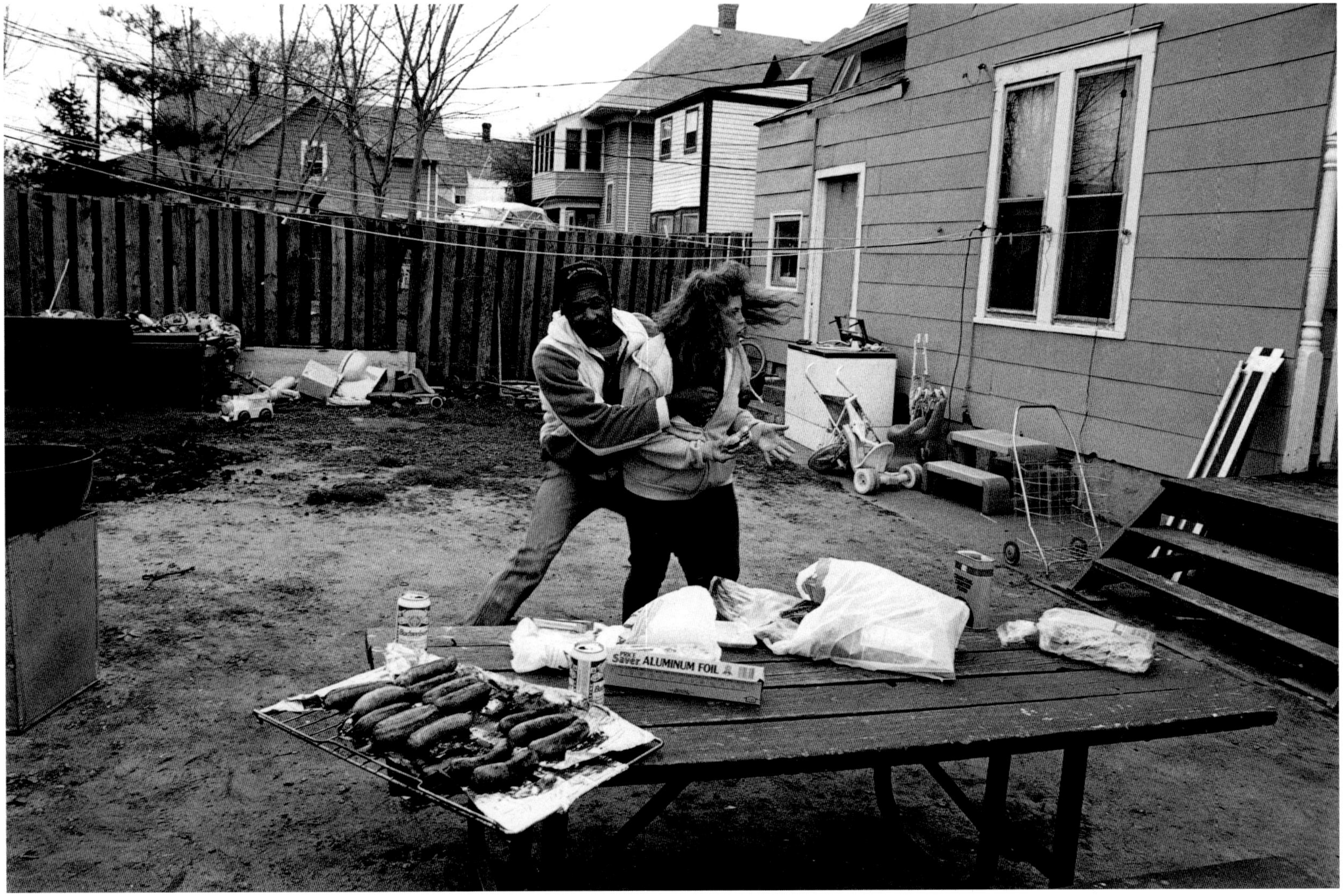
ALUMINUM FOIL

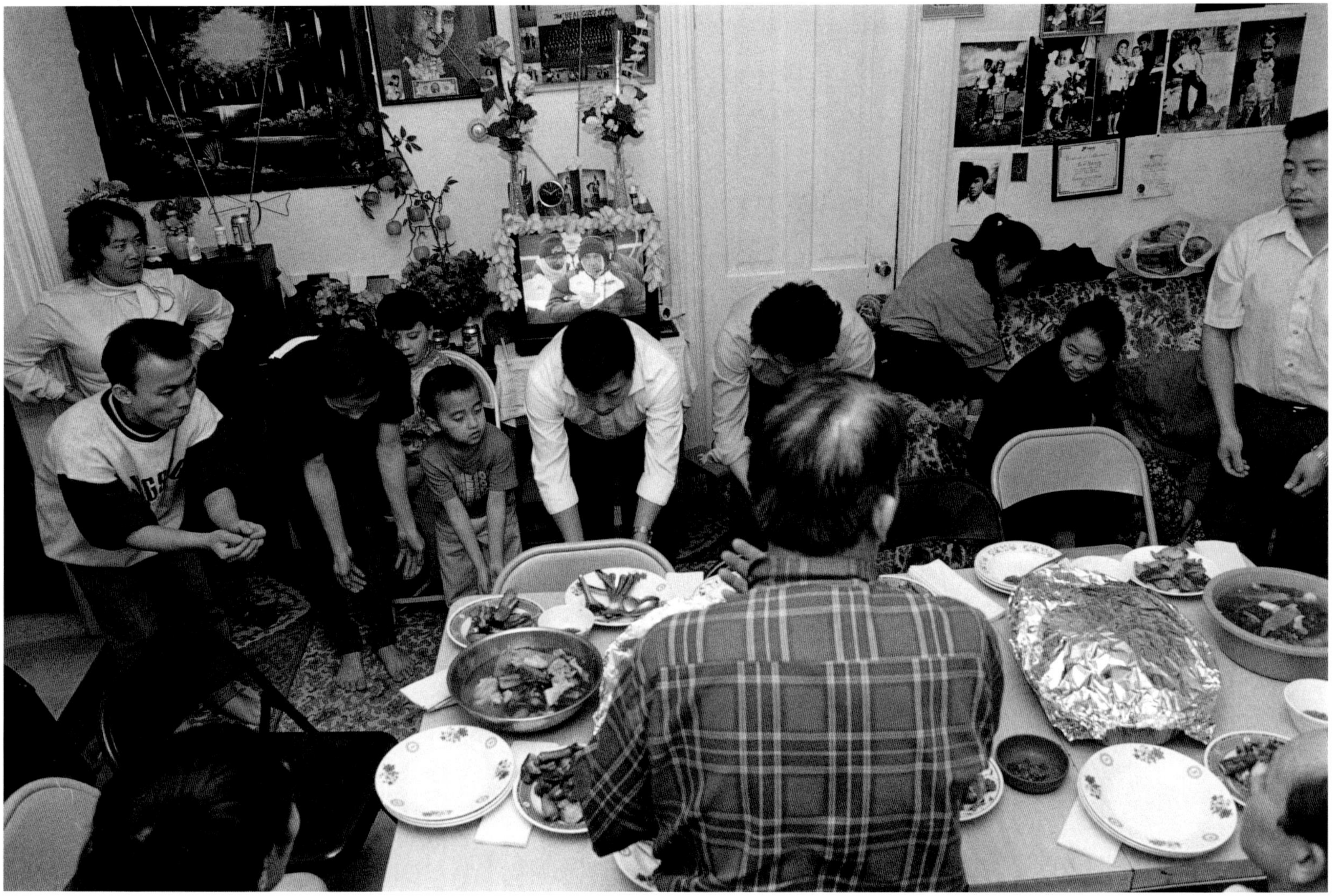

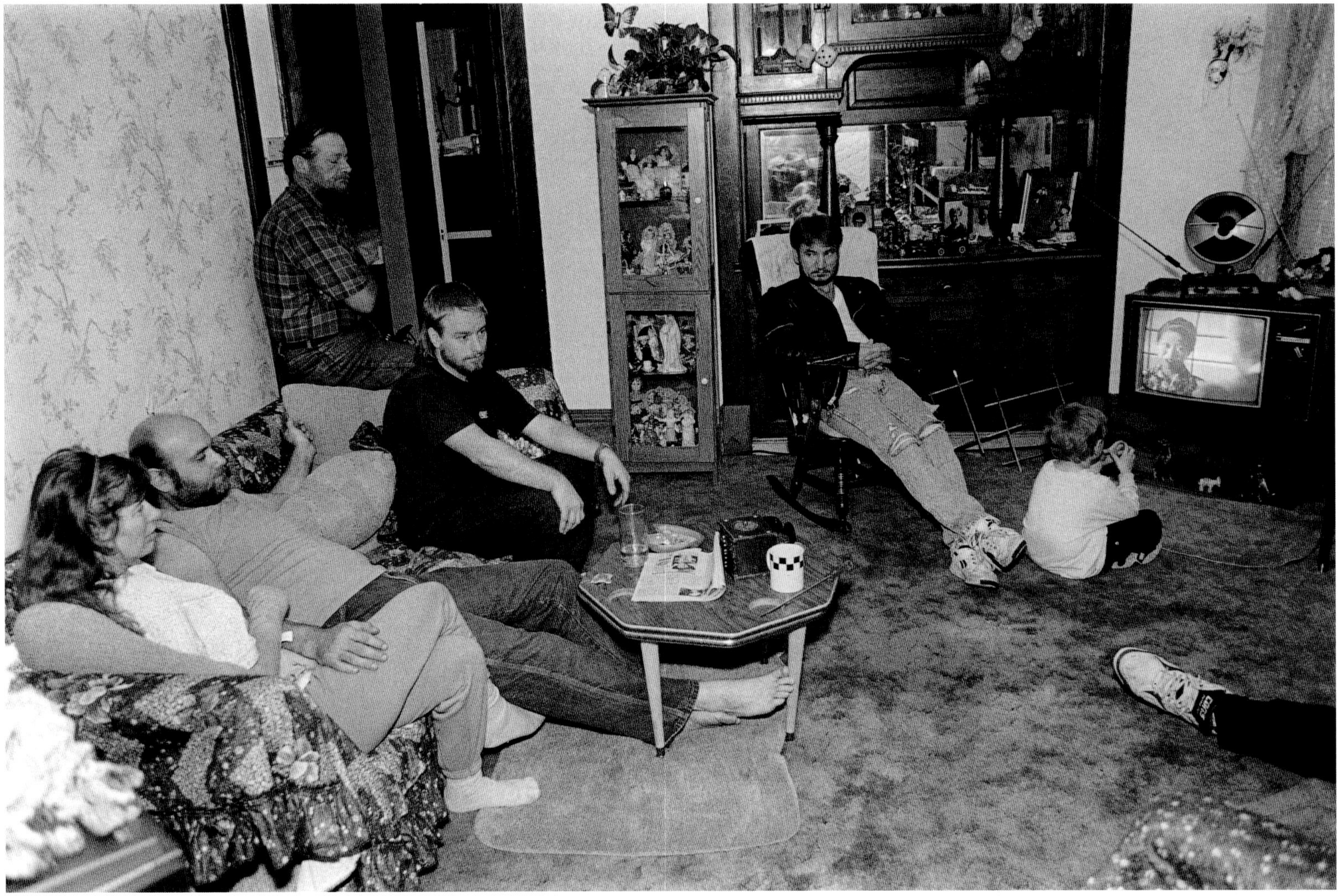

I'm known in this neighborhood as the crazy white man. I've lived on these streets almost twenty-seven years. These three colored guys labeled me that—they were my neighbors—and I just put fresh gravel on my driveway and I had an old car sitting back there and they broke the windows out of it while I was standing there. So I went and got my baseball bat and started cracking knees. They were coming at me with knives and stuff. They got out of the way and said, "I ain't going back to that crazy white man's house." Sometimes there's retaliation. It's probably stupid on both of our parts, but that's the kind of people we deal with every day around here.

But there's a lot of good people in this neighborhood. But you rarely see anybody because nobody really wants to be outside. People don't spend time in their yards like they used to do.

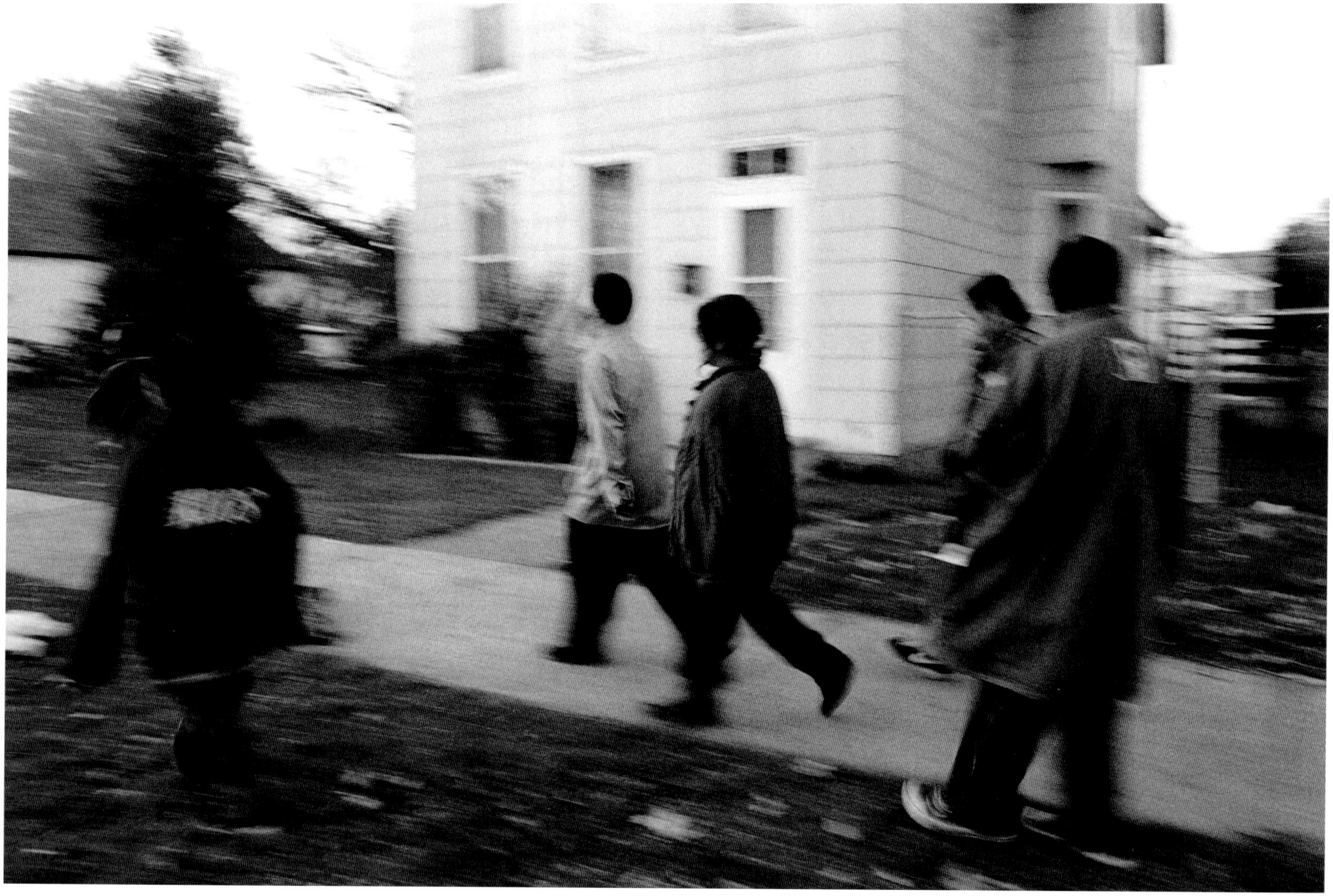

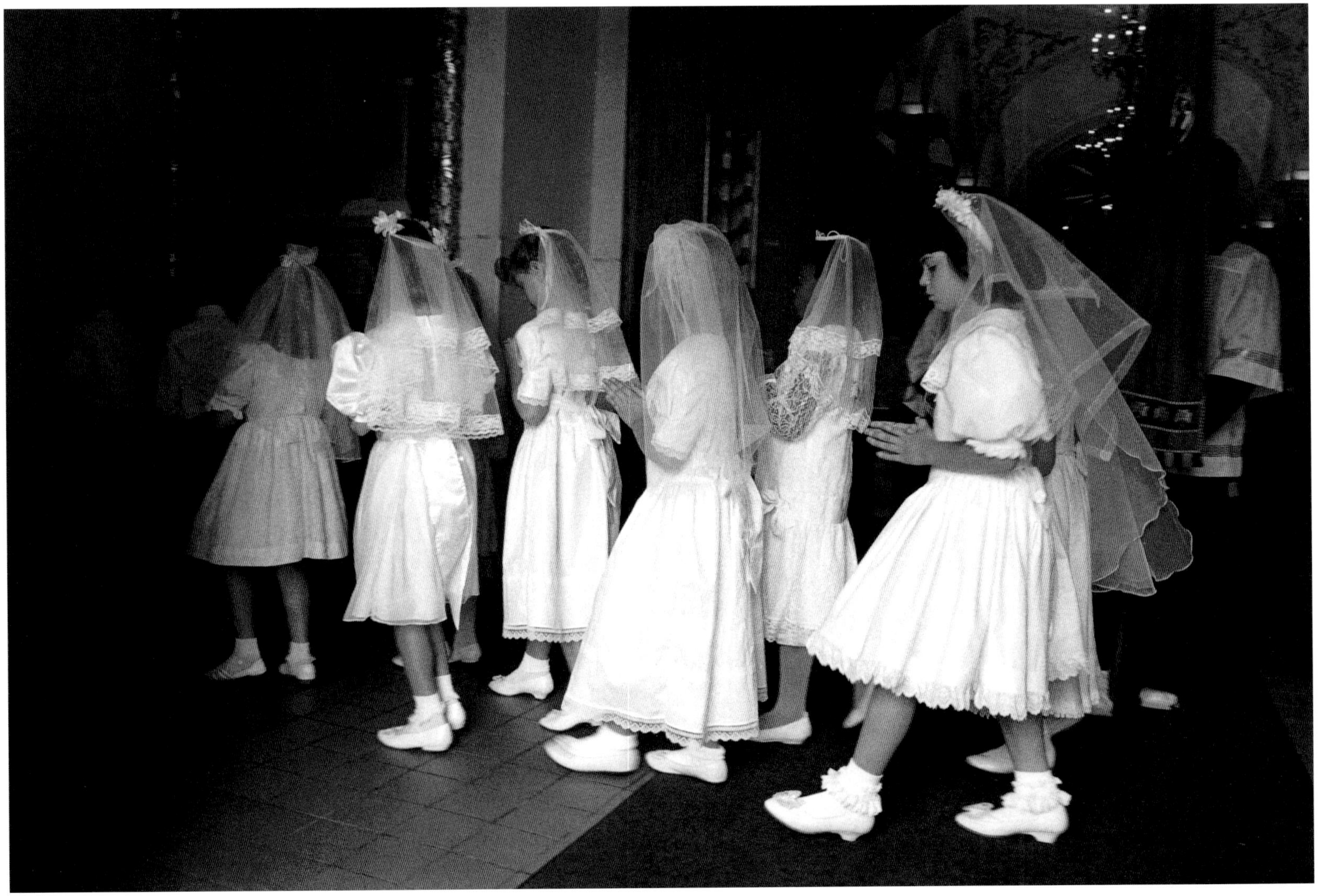

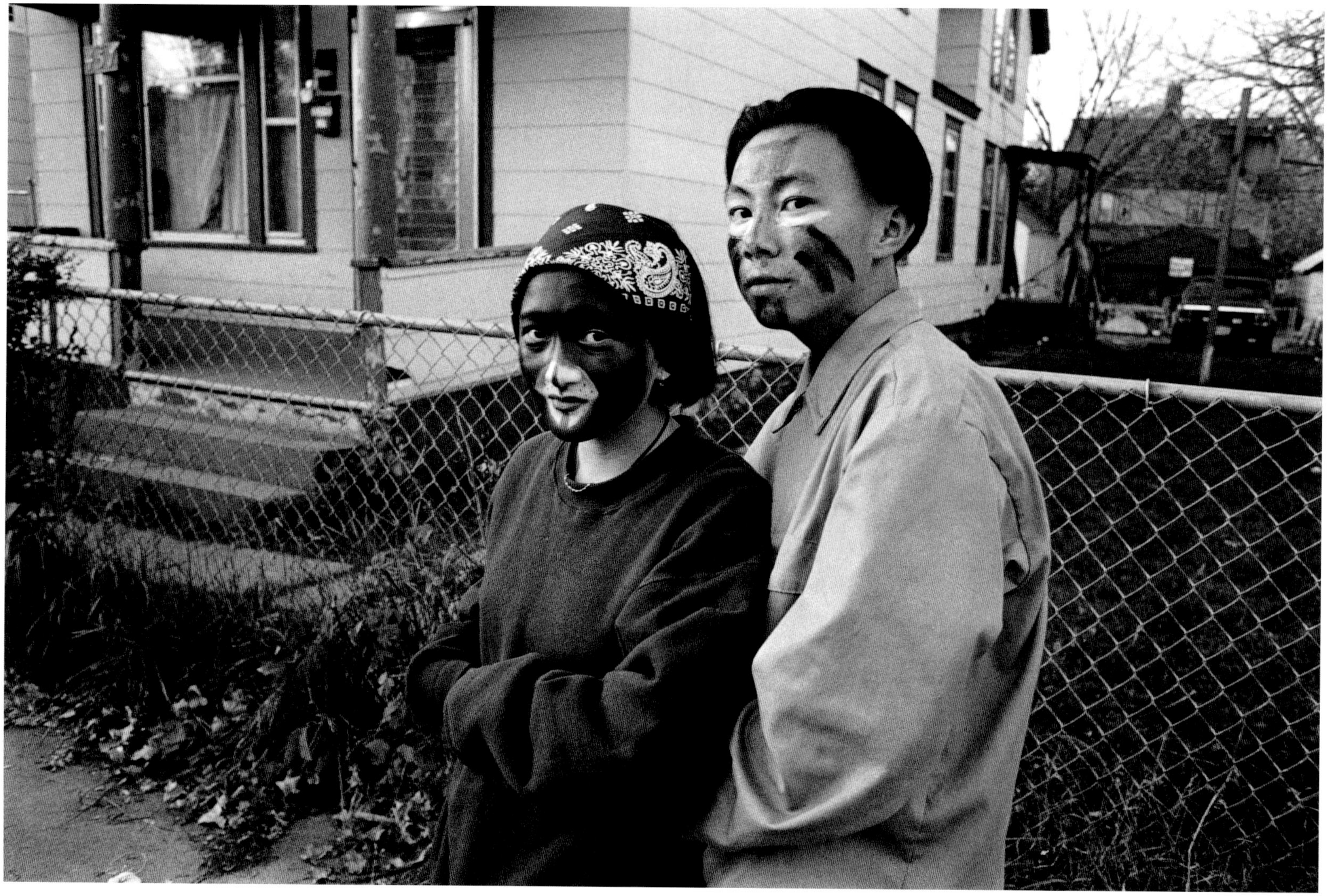

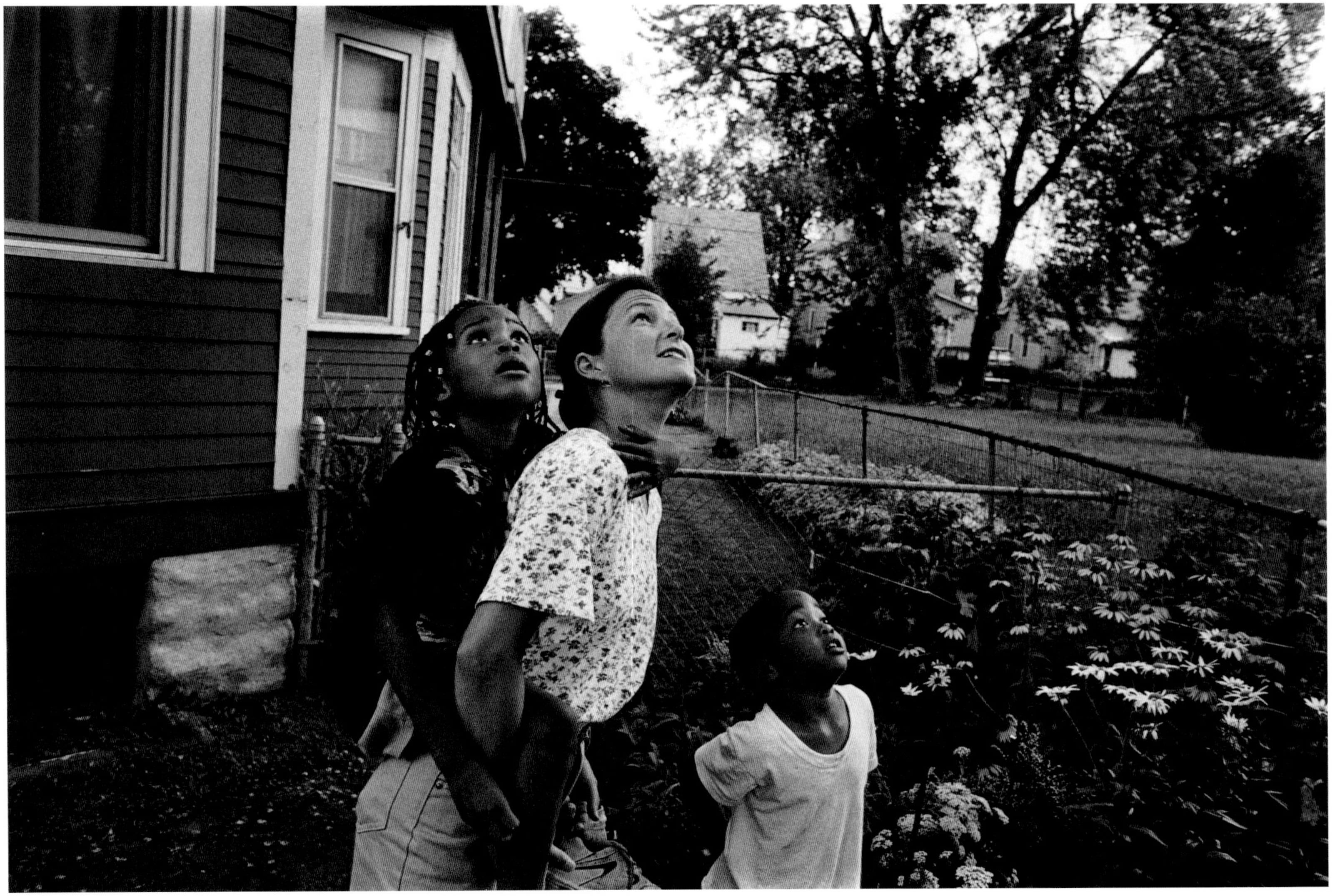

I grew up in the suburbs, and everybody was the same. White, Catholic, Protestant, whatever. A lot of people want to get away from the city. I really think they're insulated from reality. And I don't think I am where I live. I brought some friends over—they were white. And you know, we're surrounded by black people and the little black kids from next door are saying my name and I could just see their attitude. They didn't know how to deal with it. I know that if they were cute little white kids, they would have been laughing and talking. Instead, they didn't say anything. They just looked away. I got the feeling they didn't know how to act around people that were colored differently from them. It really struck me. Was that how I was a couple of years ago?

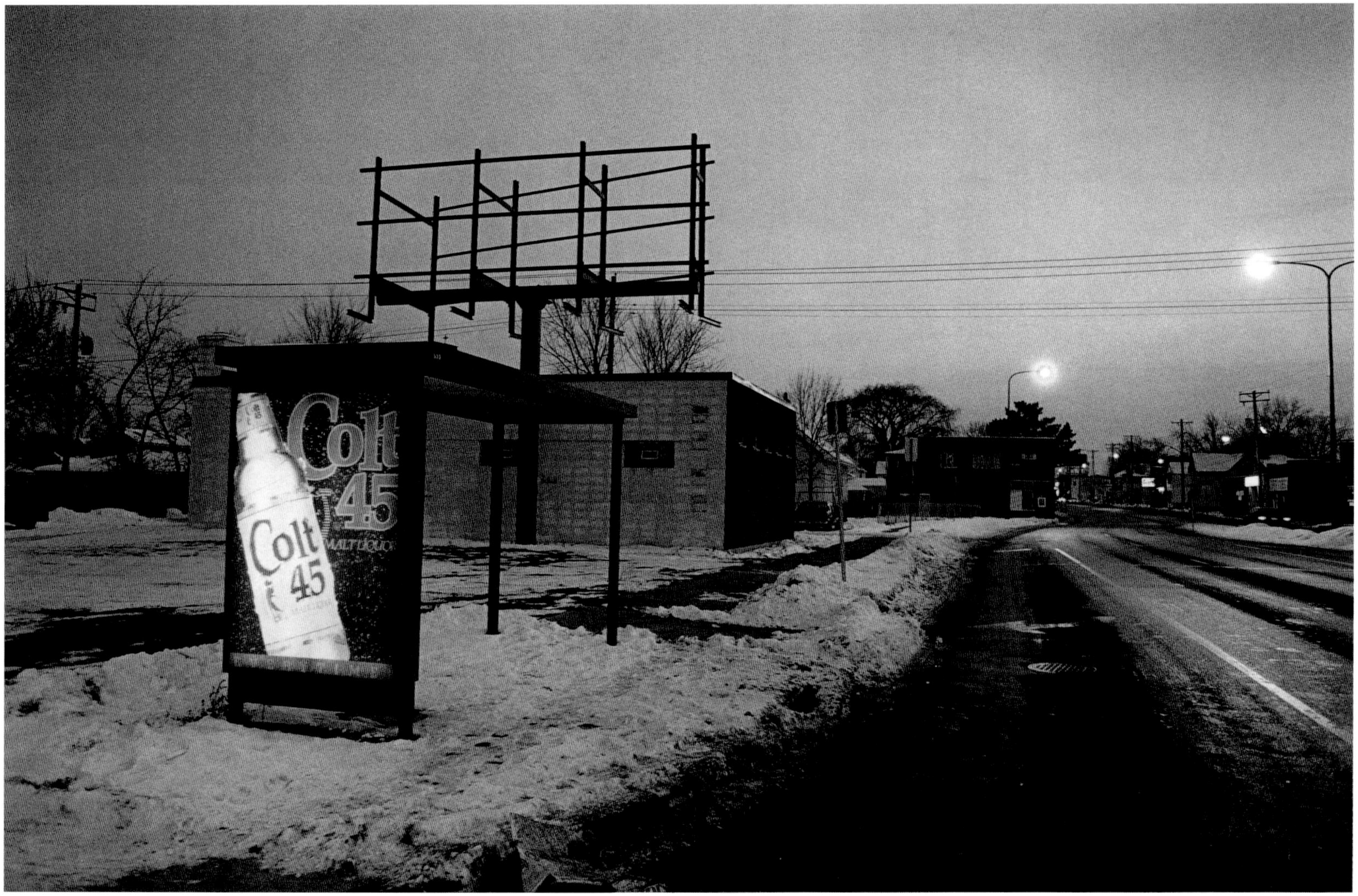
Colt
45
Colt
45
MALT LIQUOR

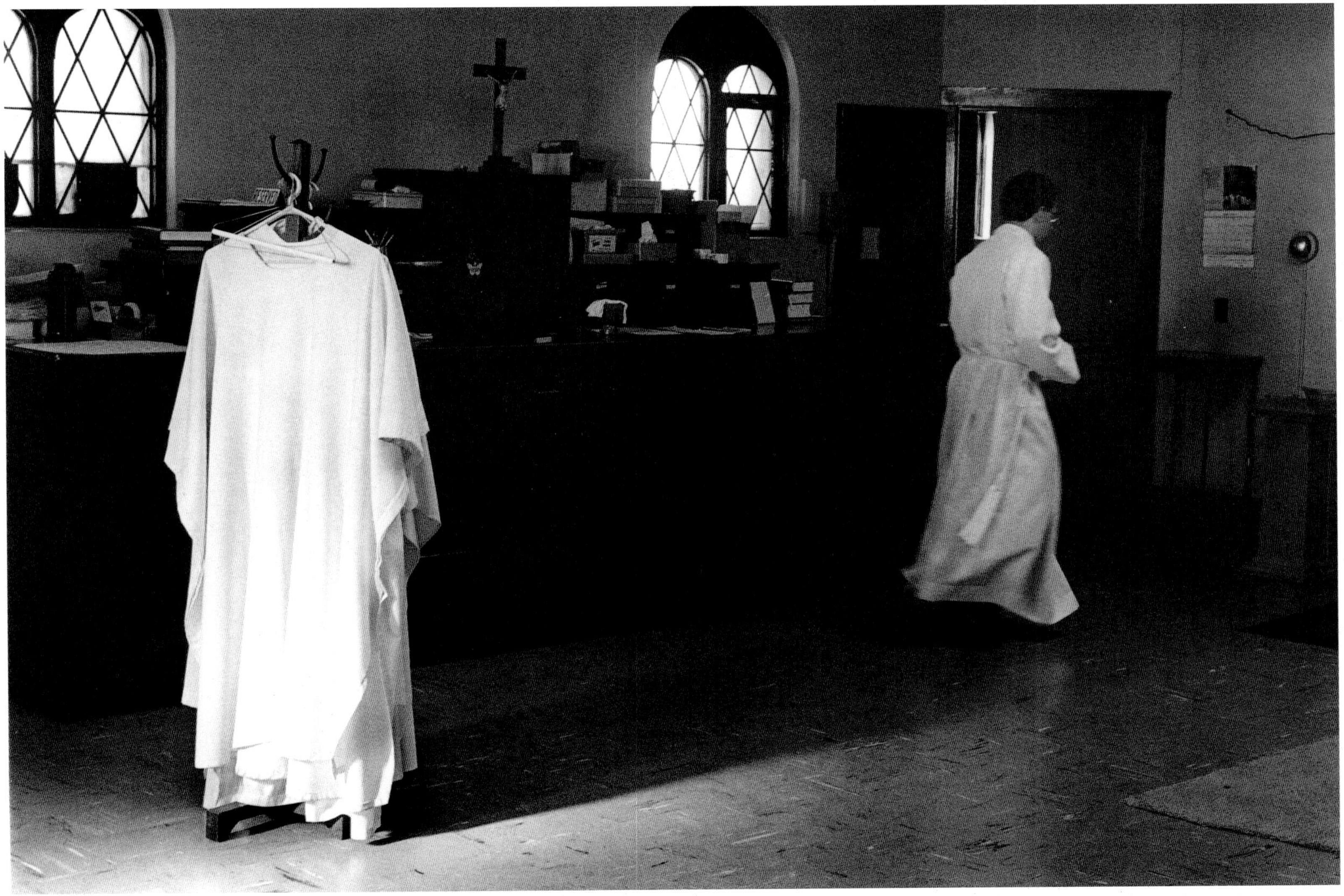

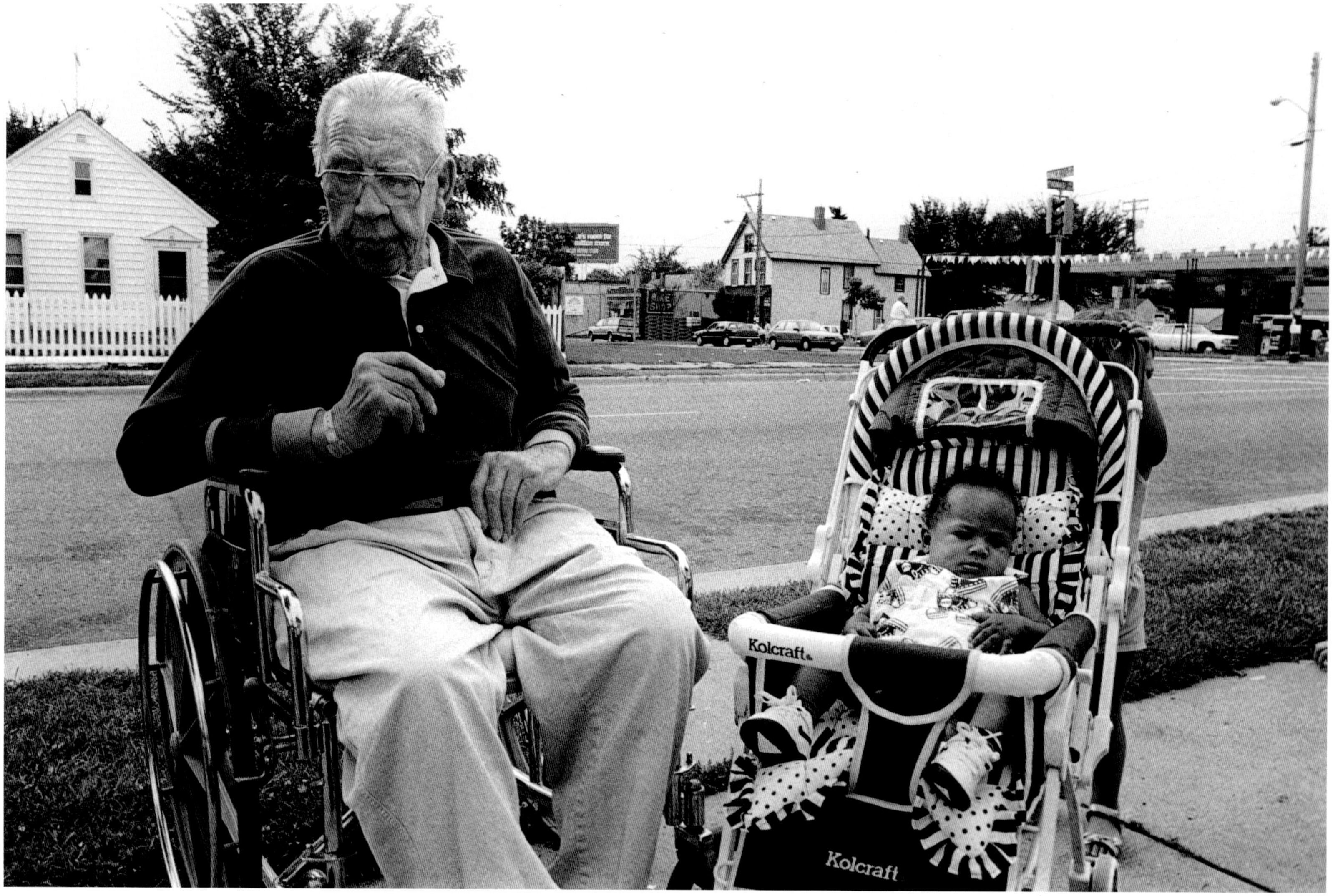
Kolcraft
Kolcraft

Notes on Selected Photographs

Page 9 The woman on the right told me: "We've been living here for over a year. We love the neighborhood. We came from Kankakee, Illinois, and it was getting real bad. A lot of teenagers getting killed and stuff. I wanted to get my kids away from there so I could make something of myself, go to school, and they could make something of themselves. I've got nine in all, six at home. The other ones, believe me, they live close by. My daughter is right across the street.

"I want to go to nursing school to be a Licensed Practical Nurse. But it seems I don't have the, what you call it, gumption. I always figured when my kids got a certain age I was going to do this, I was going to do that. But I think when they get older they require more of your time. They say a mother's work is never done. It's a big sacrifice, and sometimes I wonder what to do."

Page 12 This was taken in August 1993, on the day of the annual Frogtown parade. Coincidentally, the primary phase of St. Paul's mayoral race was in full swing. Most of the candidates were out in force, littering the streets with campaign stickers and turning children into unwitting advertisements.

Page 17 Kevin Kittilson, an attorney who moved to Frogtown in 1978, became fascinated with the neighborhood and immersed himself in its history and folklore.

Page 21 The snakes are Burma pythons owned by Chief—the seated, bearded man with his cap on backward—who is a veterinarian.

Page 22 The boy is standing on the front steps of the Church of St. Agnes, which has the largest congregation of any place of worship in the area and is the tallest structure in Frogtown.

Page 25 These are members of a Twin Cities chapter of the Knights of Columbus, the benevolent and fraternal society of Roman Catholic men. They were serving as honor guards for a procession of the Blessed Sacrament during the observance of the Feast of Corpus Christi at the Church of St. Agnes. The church, which boasts a twenty-two-piece professional orchestra (paid at union scale) and a sixty-five-member choir, has a traditional Sunday service—replete with pageantry—that attracts worshipers from throughout the Twin Cities. Monsignor Richard J. Schuler, the pastor at St. Agnes since 1969, told me, "This used to be a neighborhood church, and people could walk here. But we've lost a lot [of parishioners] over the last twenty years. So now many of our parishioners come from outside the neighborhood."

Page 31 Rock of Ages Missionary Baptist Church

Pages 32 and 33 Father Tim Kernan, the pastor of St. Adalbert's Church, said, "The congregation has changed dramatically in the last decade but especially in the last three years. The parish was founded in 1881 for Polish immigrants. At the height of the parish's history there were about seven hundred fifty large Polish families.

But the Polish population has declined. We still have a lot of people in the congregation with Polish names but only a half dozen who can still speak Polish.

"Now, many of our parishioners are Vietnamese. Four years ago a family came from Vietnam that we sponsored. The father, who served nine years in the prison camps after the war, had a religious experience in the camps. He was a naval commander and knew some English from working with the American troops. He had a fragment of a page from the Bible that he had smuggled into his clothes and kept concealed. He'd pull it out and read it and think about it. It kept him going.

"He went out and rounded up the Vietnamese in the Frogtown area to let them know about St. Adalbert's and that they were welcome here. Soon we had twenty-five families, then forty families. After four years we're up to one hundred Vietnamese families who consider St. Adalbert's their parish home. We have a Vietnamese priest.

"We've struggled with not favoring any group. We also have a contingent of Mexican Americans who come to the parish. We've tried to mold ourselves along the lines of a multicultural parish. It's harder this way, but we'd like to see St. Adalbert's as a sign to Frogtown—with its multiplicity of cultures—that we can live and have a future together."

Pages 34 and 35 According to Key Singvah, a Hmong immigrant who studies at Minneapolis's Augsburg College and is pictured on page 74, Hmong men and women have a tradition of eating separately at celebration gatherings. Whenever a female shaman is present, however, she eats at the head of the table with the men. Men and women often eat together at everyday family meals.

Said Key, "A long time ago people used to think women were inferior. It was not proper for a woman to sit with a man and talk with a man. When people come to visit, the husband has to sit with the man and talk with him, and the wife talks with the women. In the last decade, as Hmong have become adapted to the American culture, we start to think women have the ability to do things as well as men."

Pages 46 and 47 Speaking is the woman, Kenrie Williams, who was editor of the *Frogtown Forum*, a neighborhood newspaper, when this picture was taken in 1993. The paper is no longer in business. A new paper, the *Frogtown Times*, began publishing in 1995.

Page 49 These Hmong men were passing time in the basement of the Hmong Funeral Home while a service was taking place upstairs. Hmong funerals last for three days.

Pages 51 and 52 The curing ceremony lasted over an hour. The shaman, the standing man holding the bowl, performed various ritual actions. These included burning paper (symbolizing money), throwing wooden dowels repeatedly on the floor, and sprinkling water from a bowl—all the while chanting loudly from within a self-induced trance. As all this was happening, people entered and left the cramped room and carried on conversations, sometimes watching the ceremony, sometimes oblivious to it. The atmosphere was circuslike, with the shaman as ringmaster. Every so often, his intonations were punctuated by pig squeals.

Pages 57 and 58 Church of St. Agnes

Pages 59–62 When I first saw Charlie, at a block party, I knew I wanted to photograph him. He stood out because he was wearing this white suit. Moments later, he walked straight up and introduced himself. He spoke in a monotone, his voice childlike. He pulled out a white calling card, which had only his name on it in black type. We set a time during the following week for me to come to his house and take his picture. On that day he answered the door, wearing the same white suit—as I had hoped. He graciously asked me to stay for lunch. It was Campbell's tomato soup, served with plenty of saltine crackers.

Pages 64 and 65 The kheng is a wind instrument that combines six bamboo tubes, each with a thin brass reed, that are set inside a wooden air chamber. The nonprofit Frogtown-based Hmong National Organization, founded in 1982, conducts language and culture classes, mostly for young Hmong; included is a special class to teach kheng-playing. Kee Vang, the organization's program director, told me, "The kheng is our most traditional instrument. It is unique to the Hmong, and it is one of the few things that we have that we can trace back to our roots in China. Hmong all over the world use it for special ceremonies. Because we are a scattered people, the kheng helps unite us."

Page 71 There were several Mexican families living in this house. One father told me, "We have a house in Mexico, but there is no work there. Things are hard there. We want to save some money and go back. But we don't know when that will happen. Family is everything."

One of his sons, then eleven years old, said, "I don't remember much about Mexico. I came to the United States when I was five. But someday I will go back to live because we have a house there. I want to become a doctor and help my people. I don't want to live here. There's too much trouble. Too much gangsters. They broke our window." By the next time I talked to him, several weeks later, he had changed his mind about returning to his homeland: He had since made some friends in the neighborhood.

Page 75 This photograph was taken after the curing ceremony shown on pages 51 and 52. During the six hours I was in the apartment, I was repeatedly offered cans of Mountain Dew to drink. I was later told that in Laos, the Hmong usually serve fruit to welcome guests but that in America now most of them offer soda pop. It is customary to accept a can, whether or not you want it. If you don't intend to drink, it is proper either to set it down for later, put it back in the case so that someone else can have it, or take it home with you.

Page 83 "Like many migratory peoples, [the Hmong] view costume as a special symbol of ethnic identity, as a means to assert common kinship in an otherwise indifferent or adverse environment" (Joanne Cubbs, "Hmong Art: Tradition and Change," in *Hmong Art: Tradition and Change*, exh. cat. [Sheboygan, Wis.: John Michael Kohler Arts Center, 1985], 21). Lou Yang, a child-care coordinator for the Centre for Asians and Pacific Islanders, a nonprofit agency based in Minneapolis, owns four different styles of traditional costumes. Said Lou, "Every Hmong female owns at least one. In Laos, most people had costumes that they wore every day and newer ones that they saved for special occasions. Here in America we only wear them for the New Year or other celebrations. Men also have their own costumes."

Page 84 and 85 There are many "Beware of Dog" signs in Frogtown. The pit bull seems to be the breed of choice. Several people told me that there are organized dogfights on the streets during the summer, late at night. I never witnessed any, although I was rarely in Frogtown late at night. All the dog owners I photographed said they did not condone dogfights.

Page 87 Her chest tattoo read, "Love God."

Pages 92 and 93 Many of the Frogtown Hmong who are now in their fifties and sixties were recruited by the CIA to fight the Vietcong during the Vietnam War. Typical is the story of Youa, who was a guerrilla for twenty years. "I was a good soldier," he told me. "I fought well for the American government. I helped wounded American soldiers like brothers. I saved pilots that were shot down. But when we came to America we weren't treated as well. The government says we should work. As though the work we did as soldiers does not count."

"From 1961 to 1973, thousands of Hmong were involved in a 'secret war,' financed and equipped by the U.S. Central Intelligence Agency. More than 15,000 Hmong soldiers died in the fighting, while a third of the Hmong population left their village fields to become displaced persons dependent on the assistance of the Royal Lao government and the United States Aid for International Development for survival. . . . [The Hmong] helped rescue American pilots whose planes were shot down on bombing raids over northern Laos and North Vietnam. . . . Abandoned and isolated in their mountains, the Hmong became a target of reprisal. . . . The Pathet Lao [Hmong communists aligned with the North Vietnamese] began a policy of genocide. . . . [B]ut more than 100,000 Hmong fled to Thailand over the next fifteen years. . . . The Thai camps of first asylum became a turntable for Hmong dispersal around the world" (Yang Dao, "The Hmong: Enduring Traditions," in *Minority Cultures of Laos: Kammu, Lua', Lahu, Hmong, and Iu-Mien* [Rancho Cordova, Calif.: Southeast Asia Community Resource Center, 1992], 267–70).

According to the Hmong American Partnership, a St. Paul-based nonprofit organization serving the Hmong community, there were twenty-seven thousand Hmong living in Minnesota in 1993—the second-largest concentration of Hmong in the United States after that in southern California.

The first Hmong emigrants arrived in the United States from refugee camps in Thailand in 1976. In the mid-1990s, there were still as many as six thousand Hmong living in these camps. They refused to return to their native Laos, where they feared persecution under a still-repressive regime. Between 1980 and 1990, some twenty thousand Hmong may have been wrongly or forcibly repatriated to Laos. In the spring of 1996 the United Nations announced that all remaining camps would be closed by year's end and that refugees would either have to go back to Laos or resettle in America. It was expected that some three thousand refugees would choose the United States, at least five hundred of whom would go to Minnesota.

Page 94 Rock Temple Church of God in Christ

Page 95 St. Adalbert's Church

Page 98 The basement social hall of St. Adalbert's Church

Page 99 Key Singvah told me, "In the past, people used the blood for food. You didn't want to waste anything, everything was important. Nowadays it isn't as true. But the elders still like the flavor, the taste. After the blood comes out of the animal they always put salt and spices into the blood to keep it alive, so it will stay liquid. Then they will take spoonfuls throughout the day. Most women don't eat the blood. Eating blood is a way to show the women that men are brave enough to kill and to eat blood."

Page 103 This picture was taken at Rock of Ages Missionary Baptist Church, an all-black congregation. About forty people were present each of the several times I attended the regular three-hour Sunday service. The Reverend Theartis V. Williams, who leads the congregation, said: "This my twentieth anniversary of being pastor of this church. We got started in my home before we found this building. I don't believe in black churches or white churches. I believe in God's church. I don't care who you are. If you come in the Rock of Ages, I'll welcome you in. Between the schools, the judicial system, and the churches, they have separated peoples into different ethnic groups. That's wrong. We are all one people. In the seventeenth chapter of Acts, the twenty-sixth verse, God said, "I made all the people that live on all the face of the earth from one blood."

Page 106 Rock Temple Church of God in Christ

Page 111 These girls are writing in their diaries. The two closest to the camera are sisters. The oldest one (on the right) told me, "Our dad told us that we have Cherokee, Chinese, Malaysian and Scottish ancestors. Madagascar, too. I thought we were black. I guess I still think I'm black, but I think it's interesting that we have this different heritage."

The sisters' father later told me, "I talked to a top psychologist, and he told me that the more races you have in you the stronger you are. He said there aren't any pure races. We're all mongrels. I tell people I have five different races in me, and they say, 'You're a Heinz 57.' Like, you know, many varieties. But I feel it makes me richer."

Page 114 This was taken at Rock of Ages Missionary Baptist Church. Sister Katie (on the right) said, "The church I was at before, it didn't seem like there was nothing there for me to do. Just so happened I moved to a place which was right in the rear of this church. Then I met Pastor Williams at a White Castle, and he asked me where do I go to church at, and I told him I don't have a church home. He asked where do I live, and I told him. He said, 'Well then, you live that close to church you've got no problem.' So I started coming here January of '93. Then I started practicing to be an usher. I've been here ever since."

Page 115 I took this photograph at Faith Lutheran Church, which was built in 1914. Nancy Carlson, the church's administrative secretary, told me, "No one ethnic group has ever been in the majority here. Our services have always been in English."

Page 116 St. Adalbert's Church

Page 117 Father Tim Kernan, the pastor of St. Adalbert's Church, said, "The Southeast Asians are the future of Frogtown. Many of them don't read English yet, so they don't know all the bad news about Frogtown. They don't read the headlines. They're willing to buy and fix up houses and make this their home."

Page 118 The triangles are medicinal Band-Aids scented with menthol and camphor. They are good for relieving general ailments such as headaches.

Page 119 This picture was taken on Halloween.

Page 123 Key Singvah said, "My people lived in the mountains. We were farmers. We did things by hand. We didn't have any technologies. When we came to America we went from the 1800s to the twenty-first century. That is not an easy thing to do.

"Most of the elders don't even know how to speak English. They were forced to come here and find jobs, but companies won't hire them. As soldiers they were shot and wounded. Now they are tired and don't want to work. They want to rest. They feel that it's time to retire. But the welfare program tells them that they have to work. So they're frustrated. Many have large families to support, so it's a major problem."

Page 126 Kheng players are vital to Hmong funeral ceremonies. It is believed that the musicians can communicate directly with the spirit of the deceased. As they play they execute many turns, circular moves, and other steps designed to lead the soul through the netherworld and back to earth as well as to mislead evil spirits at important crossroads on the journey.

Pages 127–129 These pictures were shot at a Mardi Gras celebration in the basement social hall of St. Adalbert's Church.

Page 135 I took this photograph outside the apartment of a Hmong family.

Page 138 According to Key Singvah, "One side of the table is the 'higher' side where the elders or more important people sit. This is where the shaman sits. On the south side it can be anybody. They are the ones who bow to the head of the table before the meal begins. Bowing is a way to show respect."

Page 141 Church of St. Agnes

Page 142 This photograph was taken on Halloween.

Page 145 St. Adalbert's Church

Acknowledgments

Many people helped make my work in Frogtown, the exhibition *Frogtown: Portrait of a Neighborhood*, and this book possible.

Photography and interviewing in Frogtown were greatly facilitated by grants from the Minnesota Historical Society's Research Grant program, the University of Minnesota/McKnight Photography Fellowship Program, the Cultural Collaborations Program of the Minnesota State Arts Board, and FORECAST Public Artworks. FORECAST project manager Jack Becker was especially helpful in enabling me to mount the exhibition.

At the Minnesota Historical Society, Deborah Miller supplied vital encouragement in the early phase of the photography and interviewing. Volunteer Maureen DeCamp skillfully transcribed my interviews with Frogtown residents. Jean A. Brookins, Nordis Heyerdahl-Fowler, Alan Ominsky, and Ann Regan of the Minnesota Historical Society Press all were instrumental in shaping this book. Patrick Dooley's skillful design was also vital in this respect. My special gratitude goes to Phil Freshman, whose efforts went far beyond those of an editor.

I am deeply indebted to Owen Ekman for his innumerable contributions as a friend and as an artist. Thanks also go to John Halligan for his unique perspective and to Rich Shelton for his photographic expertise. To Amy Haen, who encouraged and inspired me throughout, I offer heartfelt appreciation.

Thanks are due as well to the Twin Cities journals *City Pages* and *COLORS*, which originally published some of the photographs.

Kevin Kittilson, Frogtown historian, Tony Schmitz, publisher of the *Frogtown Times*, and Kenrie B. Williams, editor of the *Frogtown Forum*, provided valuable assistance at various points along the way.

I must also gratefully acknowledge the support of the Amherst H. Wilder Foundation, Thomas Barry Fine Arts, Patricia M. Blanchard, Mary Todd Rothchild and Daniel Bruggeman, Mary Gallagher and Mark Granlund, Charles Helsell, Mrs. Joe Huie, June Huie, Margaret Humphrey and Joshua E. Seaver, Rebecca Humphrey and Thomas Diederich, Cornelia H. and Kennon V. Rothchild, 3M, the University of St. Thomas, the Walker Art Center, and Cynthia and Hanson Wong.

The donors listed at the front of the book also provided essential support for this publication, which I greatly appreciate. The efforts of the Minnesota Historical Society's development officer, Mark Haidet, and his staff were most helpful in this regard.

Finally, and above all, I thank the hundreds of Frogtowners whom I met and photographed and who are the subjects of this book.

W. Y. H.